Al

AFTER MIDNIGHT

WATCHMEN AFTER *WATCHMEN*

EDITED BY DREW MORTON

FOREWORD BY HENRY JENKINS

AFTERWORD BY SUZANNE SCOTT

UNIVERSITY PRESS OF MISSISSIPPI / JACKSON

The University Press of Mississippi is the scholarly publishing agency of the Mississippi Institutions of Higher Learning: Alcorn State University, Delta State University, Jackson State University, Mississippi State University, Mississippi University for Women, Mississippi Valley State University, University of Mississippi, and University of Southern Mississippi.

www.upress.state.ms.us

The University Press of Mississippi is a member of the Association of University Presses.

Any discriminatory or derogatory language or hate speech regarding race, ethnicity, religion, sex, gender, class, national origin, age, or disability that has been retained or appears in elided form is in no way an endorsement of the use of such language outside a scholarly context.

Portions of chapter 15 appeared in an altered form in "'I am no longer afraid': A Case Study on the Musical Communication of Trauma in Narrative Film and Television," ed. Robin James and Eric Weisbard. Special Issue, *Journal of Popular Music Studies* 33, no. 4 (2021).

First printing 2022
∞

Library of Congress Cataloging-in-Publication Data

Names: Morton, Drew, 1983– editor.
Title: After midnight : Watchmen after Watchmen / edited by Drew Morton.
Description: Jackson : University Press of Mississippi, 2022. | Includes bibliographical references and index.
Identifiers: LCCN 2022026293 (print) | LCCN 2022026294 (ebook) | ISBN 9781496842169 (hardback) | ISBN 9781496842176 (trade paperback) | ISBN 9781496842183 (epub) | ISBN 9781496842190 (epub) | ISBN 9781496842206 (pdf) | ISBN 9781496842213 (pdf)
Subjects: LCSH: Comic books, strips, etc.—Television adaptations—History and criticism. | Comic books, strips, etc.—Film adaptations—History and criticism.
Classification: LCC PN1992.8.T45 A34 2022 (print) | LCC PN1992.8.T45 (ebook) | DDC 741.5/942—dc23/eng/20220805
LC record available at https://lccn.loc.gov/2022026293
LC ebook record available at https://lccn.loc.gov/2022026294

British Library Cataloging-in-Publication Data available

This book is dedicated to the Black lives lost in the 1921 Tulsa Race Massacre and the Black lives ended by the police state in the United States in the 21st century, which the HBO limited series is a reaction to.

To name but a few: Rayshard Brooks, Michael Brown, Philando Castile, Stephon Clark, Manuel Ellis, George Floyd, Eric Garner, Freddie Gray, Andre Hill, Botham Jean, Atatiana Jefferson, Daniel Prude, Tamir Rice, Aura Rosser, Walter Scott, Alton Sterling, Breonna Taylor, and Daunte Wright.

Black lives matter.

CONTENTS

ACKNOWLEDGMENTS

As apparent in the abundance of citations included here, this book would not have been possible without the incredible *Film Quarterly* roundtable put together by Michael Gillespie that included Kristen Warner, Rebecca Wanzo, and Jonathan W. Gray. Quite frankly, reading Kristen and Rebecca's thoughtful posts about the HBO series on a week-to-week basis via my Facebook feed not only made watching the show a richer experience but also provided me with the inspiration to put this volume together. I'd like to thank the four authors for lighting the torch for this book and strongly encourage readers of this book to read it. I hope the chapters included here continue to carry the torch, and I cannot wait to see how the scholarly discussion evolves from here.

I would also like to take a moment to thank a team of friends and colleagues who helped me assemble this wonderful team of contributors: Briana Barner, Chris Becker, John Caldwell, Abigail De Kosnik, Anna Everett, Terri Francis, Frances Gateward, Bambi Haggins, Darnell Hunt, Henry Jenkins, Doug Julien, Denise Mann, Alfred Martin, Tara McPherson, Jason Mittell, Jennifer Porst, Adrien Sebro, Beretta Smith-Shomade, and Greg Smith. One of the biggest challenges in putting this book together was getting beyond my usual methodological sandboxes of comics studies and transmedia studies to recruit some new and unique voices, and I could not have done it without you.

My biggest thanks go to my wonderful roster of contributors. You made editing an anthology seem far easier than I ever anticipated. I appreciated your ability to promptly respond to emails, hit deadlines, and engage with my notes early and often—all in the face of a once-in-a-century pandemic that brought computer screen fatigue, burnout, health problems, and personal tribulations. Not only did you do the job, y'all gave me the greatest gift an editor can hope to receive: an education. It was a joy and an intellectual treat to read each of your chapters; they scratched the same itch that seeing Kristen and Rebecca's Facebook posts did in the fall of 2019. Thank you all.

My thanks to Henry Jenkins and Suzanne Scott for contributing to the book. Your scholarship always inspires me. Thank you to the team at UPM, particularly Craig Gill and Emily Bandy, for helping me shepherd this through a quick and painless process, and to Camille Hale. A particularly big thanks to our peer reviewers, who made the last dash over the finish line on this project the easiest peer review sprint I've ever completed in my fifteen years within the academy.

One final thank you goes to my wife, Nicole Alvarado. Your patience, selflessness, and endless energy for being my biggest cheerleader and partner in solving life's puzzles and problems always push me to be better at everything I do. I'm immensely blessed to have you in my life.

Foreword

ON METAHUMANS AND METATEXTS

HENRY JENKINS

Y'know, superheroes are finished. These days it's all pirates!
—NEWSSTAND DEALER, *WATCHMEN*

The 1986 publication of Alan Moore and Dave Gibbons's *Watchmen* and Frank Miller and Klaus Janson's *The Dark Knight Returns*, alongside the less cited debut of Paul Chadwick's *Concrete*, forced a long overdue reconsideration and critique of the superhero genre.[1] Each, in its own way, asked whether superheroes did more harm than good, whether the masked vigilantism threatened democratic life, whether these characters symbolized a larger search for national identity and purpose. Art Spiegelman's *Maus* sparked further discussions about the cultural status of graphic novels.[2]

The ways *Watchmen* changed our perceptions of superheroes is discussed throughout this book in thoughtful and imaginative ways. That *Watchmen* remains in print and still often surfaces among the best-selling comics titles would probably have surprised its publishers at the time, though DC understood that something important was taking place here, at least enough to strip away the usual sea monkeys advertisements to free space at the back of the book for additional story content.

In 1993, Scott McCloud's *Understanding Comics* made the case that comics were a medium, not a genre, and could tell a wider range of stories than the market currently allowed.[3] So why not pirates? Moore and Gibbons asked readers to contemplate what comics might look like in a world where superheroes had not smothered the development of every other genre in the late 1950s and early 1960s.

Throughout, a young Black boy reads *Tales of the Black Freighter*, a comic he mocks for its refusal to wrap up its story in a single issue (a criticism some fans leveled against *Watchmen*). *Black Freighter*'s dark, desperate tone captures the moral malaise running through American society as the apocalypse inevitably approaches—it's already too late for warnings! Soon, text and images from the comic overlay the real-world events, providing pointed commentary. We might situate *Black Freighter* as one text among many alongside the advertisements, billboards, corporate logos, and graffiti that draw our attention. But *Watchmen* #5 includes an excerpt from *Treasure Island Treasury of Comics*, which places *Black Freighter* in an alternative history of American comics:

> The close of the 1950s saw E.C.'s line of Pirate titles dominating the marketplace from a near unassailable position. The brief surge of anti-comic book sentiment in the mid-fifties, while it could conceivable have damaged E.C. as a company, had instead come to nothing and left them stronger as a result. With the government of the day coming down squarely on the side of comic books in an effort to protect the image of certain comic book inspired agents in their employ, it was as if the comic industry had suddenly been given the blessing of Uncle Sam himself—or at least J. Edgar Hoover. (n.p.)

EC comics, fans argued, were—and had always been—for discerning adults with their brutal plots, their critical stance towards mainstream culture, and the lurid and expressionistic artwork. Gibbons drew *Black Freighter* as a pastiche of the visual styles associated with EC artists, such as Johnny Craig, Bernard Krigstein, John Severin, Al Williamson, and others. *Treasure Island Treasury of Comics* also mimics the writing style of these comics advocates—appraising individual writers and artists, contrasting different titles, identifying golden ages and fallow periods articulating the strengths of particular runs. In an inside joke, Joe Orlando, who was then serving as DC's primary editor in charge of special projects, was described as the first artist involved with *Black Freighter*, recruited by longtime DC editor Julius Schwartz. Orlando had been an EC artist and a story editor for Warren Publishing's *Creepy*. Moore plays with his own reputation for writing overly detailed scripts (and for his shaman-like persona) in the portrayal of writer Max Shea, whose career includes a descent into pornography, some time in a mental institution, and publishing some critically acclaimed novels. This detailed account of the emergence of pirate comics suggests that the dominance of superheroes was not an inevitability.

These glimpses into an alternative pirate-centric comics culture are consistent with what Jim Collins wrote at the time about *Watchmen*'s "narration by amalgamation"—the building up of the story world through bits and fragments of other texts, especially pastiches of various forms of publishing at the end of each issue.[4] Often contemptuously described as "filler stories," such back-of-the-book content was a long tradition in American comics, but here, the excerpts from Hollis Mason's *Under the Hood* (his best-selling memoir), the police and psychiatric files on Walter Kovacs, a *Playboy*-style interview with Sally Jupiter, and memos from Veidt's marketing department, among other content, add depth to the world-building. *Watchmen* gained its literary reputation less by evoking other literary works than from acknowledging other media practices.

These segments transform *Watchmen* from a graphic novel to a multimodal text. They situate the characters within a highly mediated culture, much as Miller and Janson use representations of television discussion programs, say, to disrupt and comment on the events in *Dark Knight* and *Concrete* fills its frames with Concrete action figures, candy, Happy Meals, and other mass culture. Collins writes, "The hyperconsciousness of contemporary popular narratives depends upon a simple realisation on the part of both the producer and the audience that popular culture has a history; early texts do not simply disappear or become kitsch, but persist in their original forms as well as diverse reactivations that continue to be a source of fascination for audiences, providing pleasures in the present and forming a fundamental part of culture memory."[5] Collins's account situates these graphic novels within larger conversations across the arts about postmodernism. Rather than seeing these quotations and pastiches as marking the implosion of meaning, Collins recognized them as encoded references to broader histories and popular memories that could be endlessly mined by those with the literacy and expertise to know how to read them. The image of the raft in *Black Freighter*, stitched together from bits and pieces of the bodies of his dead crewmates, offers a morbid metaphor for the postmodern text, showing how fragments can be put to new purposes and yet still carry memory traces of their prior life.

Writing a 2015 postscript, Collins describes how the "exuberant intertextuality" he had discovered in *Watchmen*, manifested in contemporary paratextual and transmedia practices, became "ubiquitous" over the next two decades.[6] Zack Snyder struggled with how to incorporate these other representational practices into his *Watchmen* film, seeing *Under the Hood* and *Black Freighter*, at least, as central to his conception, but his sprawling, overly faithful rendition left no room for this content. An animated *Black Freighter* and an *Under the Hood* mockumentary were released together on a separate DVD and were ultimately reintegrated into yet another Snyder cut. This "filler" content also inspired some key elements in Damon Lindelof's television series, such as the Oscar Micheaux pastiche, the all-black *Oklahoma!*, and the Henry "Skip" Gates hologram, each tapping Afro-centric archives. One could argue that cowboys were to the Lindlof version as pirates were to Moore and Gibbons's original. *American Hero Story* expands *Under the Hood*'s backstory and Pirate Jenny (Jessica Camacho), a member of the Tulsa police, is a shoutout to "Pirate Jenny's Song" from *Threepenny Opera*, which gave the Black Freighter its name. The television series, as much as the original graphic novel, participates in Collins's "narration through agglomeration," mapping the storyworld through bits and fragments of its media practices. And if we look elsewhere on contemporary television, the advertising and sitcom pastiches in *WandaVision* or the pseudo-news segments that flesh out the alternative history in *For All Mankind* come to mind, this legacy also influences many other media properties.

After Midnight unpacks these various intertexts, discussing how these alternative *Watchmen* open more diverse possibilities within genre storytelling as their producers tap other histories and popular memories, addressing the current moment of reckoning with America's racial politics. *Watchmen after Watchmen* suggests that newer extensions treat *Watchmen* itself as the raw material assumed by subsequent readers and producers. Here, we see a continuation of Collins's fascination with "exuberant intertextuality," as this book's contributors dig deeper into the texts, paratexts, and metatexts that constitute *Watchmen* as a transmedia phenomenon. This remixing of earlier works requires attention to innovation within formulas rather than invention, on generativity rather than originality. The urgency of the television series, in particular, suggests our culture is not done with *Watchmen*.

NOTES

1. Alan Moore and Dave Gibbons, *Watchmen* (New York: DC, 1986); Frank Miller and Klaus Janson, *The Dark Knight Returns* (New York: DC, 1986); Paul Chadwick, *Concrete: The Complete Short Stories* (Milwaukee, OR: Dark Horse, 1996).
2. Art Spiegelman, *Maus: A Survivor's Tale* (New York: Pantheon, 1986).
3. Scott McCloud, *Understanding Comics* (Seattle: Tundra, 1993).
4. Jim Collins, "Batman: The Movie, Narrative—the Hyperconscious," in Roberta Pearson, William Uricchio, and Will Brooker, eds., *Many More Lives of the Batman* (London: BFI, 2015), 163.
5. Collins, 159.
6. Collins, 167.

Part One

ADAPTATION, REMEDIATION, AND TRANSMEDIA

As expressed by Alan Moore and Dave Gibbons's not-too-subtle themes of interrogating superhero psychology and the ethics of power inherent in the conception of superheroes (the "Who watches the Watchmen?" thematic heartbeat of the series), *Watchmen* provides readers with a roster of complex and imperfect superheroes. To name but a few, the team includes the fascist Rorschach, whose binary view of morality and inability to compromise seems capable of rendering judgment on everyone but himself, and Silk Spectre, whose childhood traumas and fraught relationship with her mother have left her emotionally trapped. The comic not only subverts the fairly glowing psychological sketches of superheroes offered up by DC and Marvel from the 1940s to the 1980s, but it does so in the narrative arc as well: the heroes "fail" to thwart a major disaster and instead must accept a devil's bargain with the book's antagonist, their own colleague Ozymandias.

Moreover, as Henry Jenkins describes in his foreword, the book goes even further to deconstruct the medium itself by building in meta-reflections on comic books via the *Tales of the Black Freighter* parallel story and the use of back-matter material that challenges the medium specificity of comics—juxtaposed panels arranged in deliberate sequence, to borrow from Scott McCloud—by introducing case files, scientific monographs, newspaper clippings, and fake autobiographies rich with narrative information. In summary, *Watchmen*'s claim to fame lies in its postmodern critique of the superhero story, both in content and in form.

Both *Watchmen* sequels—the DC maxiseries *Doomsday Clock* (2017–2019) helmed by Geoff Johns, Gary Frank, and Brad Anderson and the HBO limited television series *Watchmen* (2019) created by Damon Lindelof—continue these thematic and formal tropes, making the methodological lens of adaptation, remediation, and transmedia storytelling an obvious starting point for analysis. The six chapters published here pick up those various threads, beginning with Jayson Quearry's consideration of how the *Watchmen* paratexts illustrate a larger strategy at DC Comics to provoke readers to take a "deep dive" into the newly expanded universe. Dru Jeffries, on the other hand, analyzes how specific moments in film history are utilized by *Doomsday Clock* (film noir) and *Watchmen* (the works of Oscar Micheaux) to complicate their interpretations of the superhero mythos. In chapter 3, Chris Yogerst and Mark C. E. Peterson place the protagonist of the HBO series, Angela Abar, in dialogue with the work of Joseph Campbell to describe what superhero mythology has become when confronted with the "harder surfaces" of economic and social relations. Next, Laura E. Felschow considers how the HBO series was positioned by the conglomerate and creator as a paradoxical "original" "remix" that is still canon, muddying its status to the original series and begging the question "Who is this television show for?" In chapter 5, Zachary J. A. Rondinelli approaches a similar question by analyzing the "Peteypedia" transmedia extension of the television show as a way to discuss how paratextual transactions can collaborate with readers in a back-and-forth process of meaning making between the original text and its adaptation in order to both renegotiate past experiences with and create new knowledges about the larger *Watchmen* universe. Finally, Alisia Grace Chase considers how the television show's adaptation of costuming, the "image garment," can be contrasted with that of Zack Snyder's film adaptation (2009).

Chapter 1

"NOTHING EVER ENDS"

How *Watchmen* Paratexts Became Part of DC Comics's "Deep Dive" Strategy[1]

JAYSON QUEARRY

Like a Rorschach blot, the question of who deserves culpability for instigating the decades-long feud between Alan Moore and DC Comics can be interpreted differently depending on how someone looks at it. To some, it may appear DC wrote contracts to help them perpetually retain the rights to the Watchmen characters; to others, *Watchmen* was treated no differently than any other work-for-hire creation in superhero comics. Whatever the case, DC has long been in a stalemate situation with *Watchmen*, not wanting to taint its hallowed reputation by associating it with the larger DC Universe (hereon DCU), but equally looking to incorporate it into the industrial strategies that maintain and market such a universe to readers.

Moore has indicated that contractual discussions about the twelve-issue miniseries initially favored the creators: "We were told that *Watchmen* was going to be a title that we owned and that we would determine the destinies of."[2] Had that promise come to fruition, it would have been uncommon in an industry that typically requires creators to forfeit ownership rights. With *Watchmen*, Moore claims DC stipulated "that when the work *went out of print*, then the rights to it would revert" to the creators.[3] What Moore and co-creator Dave Gibbons were unable to anticipate was the growing demand for trade paperbacks (TPBs) over the next three decades and the resounding critical and financial success of *Watchmen*.[4] Both of those developments stopped DC from taking *Watchmen* out of print in one form or another, advertently retaining them the copyright.

From Moore's perspective, that result was a calculated manipulation, a belief that led to him severing all ties with DC. From DC's perspective, as voiced by the current chief creative officer of the company, Jim Lee, "This is not a situation where we have taken things from Alan. He signed an agreement and yet he said 'I didn't read the contract.' I can't force him to read his contract."[5] A harsh response for sure, but one Moore should have anticipated from his previous dealings with DC. Originally, he wanted to use characters from Charlton Comics (which had recently been purchased by DC) for *Watchmen* but "was unable to secure permission . . . [because] he wanted not only to use them but to render them unusable for future projects," a mandate that should have foreshadowed DC's overall intellectual property (IP) strategy for Moore.[6]

Superhero comics publishers have long operated off of a business model that prioritizes the creation, acquisition, and retention of an extensive library of IPs. I contend that DC (and Marvel) Comics prioritizes such a practice as a means of encouraging a deep-dive mentality in their readers. By owning thousands of IPs, publishers can create hyperlinked connections between them which make the universe appear vast and complex while also pointing readers towards properties they were previously unaware of. While Bart Beaty has claimed that "the ever-increasing complexification of superhero storytelling . . . has narrowed the audience to only the most committed readers," there can be no denying that each company has—for better or ill—pursued these practices for decades.[7] The resurgence of the superhero genre in the late fifties and early sixties set the tempo for the industry appealing to these types of adamant readers. Fanzines like *Xero* and *Alter Ego* overseen by longtime readers (soon to be professionals), like Roy Thomas and Gary Friedrich, indicated a readership who loved digging into the minutiae of superhero comics. Likewise, Phil Seuling's organization of the first comics conventions, starting in 1968, made the industry aware of interest in collecting and scouring over older issues. DC would appeal to that communal spirit with the incorporation of letters columns in 1958 as a means of creating "a new type of proximity . . . between readers and publishers."[8] In courting these groups, both major publishers began favoring dense, interconnected narrative continuity across their titles.[9] Even if comics sales have decreased overall compared to earlier periods, the exploratory desire inherent in the deep dive has existed as a selling point for a devoted subset of readers so long within the industry that neither company appears able to give it up.

Ever since the original comics miniseries finished, *Watchmen* has always posed a problem for the publisher in that regard; it owns the IP, but the story itself has a pretty definitive ending. Unlike its other IPs, *Watchmen* does not avail itself to continued, serialized publication. Whereas nearly every other DC-owned IP can be used to redirect audiences to another related IP in an (ideally) endless chain of successive purchases, *Watchmen* stands alone. At least it *did*. Over the last eight years, DC Comics has aggressively exploited its copyright ownership in order to expand the Watchmen brand across numerous paratextual releases. Even though Moore envisioned the original *Watchmen* as a form of intertextual commentary on the history of the superhero genre, engaging with other IP through allusion and homage, the miniseries itself has long existed as a singular text. The assortment of prequels known as *Before Watchmen* and the official crossover-event-cum-sequel, *Doomsday Clock*, changed that, initiating a web of hyperlinked connections that bridge the *Watchmen* IPs with those of the DCU.[10] Whereas *Watchmen* has always seemed to be an exception to the rule, DC capitalizing on its copyright ownership to link the IP to its larger library confirms an industrial commitment to the "deep-dive" strategy, hoping that fans will get caught in a chain of connections that never end.

EXTENDED GUTTERS—THE DEEP DIVE AS HYPERLINKED NETWORK

Those who have a history with reading superhero comics understand how tantalizing it can be to explore their history. For anyone who has never or inconsistently read superhero comics, other genres and media have likely provided a similar experience: franchises that have led to lengthy online searches, a seeking out and devouring of paratexts, or getting lost in speculative conversations. While there may be comparable instances in other media, superhero comics are explicitly designed to encourage and perpetuate research, piquing the reader's curiosity in hopes that they will engage in an exploration of the larger narrative universe. This is why I have chosen the term deep dive—a common parlance for an engrossing, thorough examination of a subject—to describe what this industrial strategy produces in the reader.

Upon picking up a superhero comic for the first time, the reader may be intrigued to follow the serialized narrative of that series—to see how a story will continue in the coming issues—but there will also be allusions to information not resolved within that series alone. In other media, information introduced in the course of a narrative usually impacts the outcome of that narrative. Superhero comics regularly introduce information that has no relevancy to the plot of an issue but does within the larger narrative universe. Someone interested in superhero comics will be intrigued by references to conflicts, deaths, relationships, backstories, and so on that are mentioned but not directly contextualized. They will not only be curious enough to figure out what and who these things are independently, but they will also partially be guided by an industrial design that suggests where to look and what to look at next. Like clicking through a series of webpages, there will always be another hyperlink to send audiences down a never-ending research rabbit hole.

By owning a deep catalog of superhero IP, comics companies avoid rights barriers that keep other media conglomerates from combining properties. In turn, that allows publishers the ability to freely include any IP from their catalog alongside another, making it far easier to link disparate titles together. On one hand, that permeability allows the fictional universes overseen by these companies to appear organically interrelated, with the effects of one title's narrative impacting other series. On the other, publishers hope that sort of narrative continuity will entice readers to expand their purchasing habits in order to keep apprised of the overall serialized story. Once comic conventions and the direct market began to appear in the seventies, the ability to locate back issues and dive further into a library of titles became more of a possibility than ever before.[11] Of course, that density of narrative material paired with the comics subculture's history of projecting an exclusionary attitude has resulted in potential readers shying away from superhero comics as well. Publishers have consistently worked to balance a wealth of "deep dive-able" narrative continuity with user-friendly numbering and jumping-on points. Online resources—now eclipsing the physical archives of conventions and direct market stores as the most accessible research tool—have the potential to dull some of those barriers, further encouraging investment by way of availability, anonymity, and plentitude.

As the industry develops links between all of the titles they are publishing and have ever published, a webbed connectivity begins to take shape, resembling the hyperlinked design of the world wide web. Superhero publishers have relied on editor's notes (explicit footnoting of other titles), crossovers, team-ups, cameos, references within dialog, and an omission of information as means to introduce readers to new IPs or continuity as well as elicit curiosity about the larger narrative universe. Andrew J. Friedenthal has contended that retroactive continuity, or retconning,[12] within superhero comics acts as another means of linking various titles together; "the editable hyperlink, rather than the stable footnote, has become the de facto source of information in America today," in part because "it reached its present form as a result of the complicated workings of superhero comic book continuity."[13] In this way, superhero comics resemble a hyperlinked network, one that has industrially been constructed to send readers on a deep dive into the publication history of these companies.

That system, though used to great effect in superhero comics, does not originate there. A lengthy history of early forms of hyperlinking within reference texts predates the strategy Marvel and DC would become so efficient at utilizing. Michael Zimmer charts the earliest form of the hyperlink back to the "*renvois*, a system of cross-references featured prominently in the *Encyclopédie*,"[14] which "was published by Denis Diderot and Jean le Rond d'Alembert in France, beginning in 1751."[15] Closely resembling the webbed structure practiced by superhero comics, the *renvois* was a cross-referencing system that connected one concept within the *Encyclopédie* to another elsewhere in the volume. Zimmer stresses that Diderot and d'Alembert's underlying purpose for devising the *renvois* cross-referencing system was so that readers could "organize and navigate information following their own intuitive means, based not on imposed hierarchies or alphabetization but on their own habits of thinking: *following leads, making connections, building trails of thought*."[16] The self-motivated researching emphasized within the latter quotation reflects what superhero publishers have learned to encourage over time. By pointing readers backwards, sideways, and forwards to a vast publishing catalog of titles, these companies have created a semistructured system of connections that both purposefully directs readers towards particular titles and leaves enough room for the reader to dive in whichever direction they wish.

Of course, that unidirectional structure does not precisely replicate what an online hyperlink has the ability to do. Alexander Halavais points out:

> Although hyperlinks may perform the functions of a scholarly reference, they often function in ways that references cannot. . . . For example, because electronic documents are more easily updated, it is possible to have two documents with hyperlinks pointing to each other, something that generally does not occur in printed literature. . . . Unlike a traditional citation . . . hyperlinks allow for the instant "jump" to other texts.[17]

Within superhero comics, these abilities are restricted but similarly navigable. For instance, *Doomsday Clock* #12 includes a page where the retired superhero Johnny Thunder remembers he had previously bonded with the genie he once wielded as a power source. This moment is a direct reference to an event that happened in Geoff Johns's written *JSA* #37. Even though the *Doomsday Clock* issue provides no editor's note or explicit footnote to that back issue, by omitting an explanation for when or why Thunder and the genie merged, an onus is put on the reader to search for an answer; some will, some will not, but the reference exists to create curiosity. As Halavais suggests, within comics there can be no immediate "jump" back to *JSA* #37, which requires the reader to search out answers online, from friends, at a local comic shop (LCS), or elsewhere.[18] Assuming the reader does finally land upon *JSA* #37 in some form (a physical copy, a digital file, in a TPB, as a blurb on a wiki), that issue, unlike a programmable hyperlink, will not point back to *Doomsday Clock* #12. But it will point back to other issues and storylines, perpetuating the deep dive.

That example is only one of many within issue 12. A single comic will regularly include far more than one hyperlinking reference to a different paratext, which is where the reader's personalized pathway comes into effect. Within superhero comics, the means of hyperlinking between paratexts can take multiple forms, not only an uncontextualized reference like the previous example. Steven J. DeRose has assigned descriptors to the multiple ways hyperlinks can be programmed to redirect a user, many of which are applicable to their equivalent within comics. The latter example could be referred to as an intensional link, because it—counter to an extensional link—points back to a singular destination (in this case *JSA* #37).[19] Another form of intensional links that gets used by publishers are "*vocative* [links] . . . [which] invoke a particular document *by name*."[20] For instance, had the panel included an editor's note that read "See *JSA* #37," the research time would decrease as the reader would only have to track down that issue online or at an LCS. Of course, some benefit exists in DC or other companies refraining from the explicitness of a vocative link as the research a reader has to conduct to uncover an answer could potentially lead him or her to discover other paratexts. A similar intention lies behind what DeRose refers to as "a *taxonomic link* . . . [which] leads to multiple target locations, but does not impose an order on them"; a sort of shotgun spray of titles for readers to dive into. [21] An appearance or cameo by any superhero can take this form, as most superhero IPs have hundreds, if not thousands, of issues featuring them for readers to seek out.

In terms of *Watchmen*, these types of hyperlinks only existed within the enclosed miniseries, which posed a problem for DC's deep-dive strategy. After the *Watchmen* collection hit number 1 on the trade paperback sales charts in 2008 and 2009 (around the release of Zack Snyder's film adaptation),[22] DC began to, as Lee puts it, "reach out to the new readers and see if we can convert them into long time readers."[23] The subtext there being that the company needed to provide somewhere to go so that readers did not stop at *Watchmen*. Absent Moore's blessing, DC stopped short of producing direct sequels for fear that backlash from critics and fans would hamper sales. Because of the contract Moore and Gibbons originally signed, however, that apprehension could only last so long. In June 2012, an assortment of prequels (eight individual miniseries and a one-shot) jointly dubbed *Before Watchmen*

(*BW*), became the first official additions to the continuity of the *Watchmen* storyworld. Though *BW* did receive backlash from certain fans, the first four releases ended up earning the fifth, sixth, seventh, and eighth slots on the highest single-issue units ordered charts, respectively.[24] That same month, the *Watchmen* collection also became the third highest ordered[25] TPB, in contrast to its eighty-seventh position[26] a month prior, indicating a renewed interest alongside *BW*'s publication. The strategy appeared to have worked.

DOOMSDAY CLOCK—HYPERLINKING THE WATCHMEN WITH DC

Having tested how audiences would respond to additional Watchmen material with *BW*, DC seems to have found the relatively accepting response evidence enough to push forward with similar endeavors. The choice to start with a line of miniseries restricted to the Watchmen storyworld before pushing further by incorporating them into the mainline DCU seems calculated to ease *Watchmen* into the deep-dive design. The first direct moves in this direction came with the release of *DC Rebirth* #1 in May 2016, an oversized special issue that not only set out to retcon continuity established during The New 52 era of DC Comics, but begin the process of crossing over *Watchmen* with the superheroes of the DCU. [27] In the issue, writer Johns and various artists (including Gary Frank, who would go on to draw all of *Doomsday Clock*) allude to the presence of Watchmen characters in the DCU by way of quotes from the original miniseries, panels featuring Dr. Manhattan's recognizable blue glow, and a scene where Batman discovers the Comedian's smiley-face button—basically the logo of *Watchmen*—in the Batcave. Following a tantalizing Tweet by Johns on January 1, 2017, and a short crossover called "The Button" in *The Flash* and *Batman* comics, an interview between Johns and Aaron Sagers served as an official announcement for *Doomsday Clock*.[28] A month later, a *Variety* article ran with the headline "Damon Lindelof to Develop 'Watchmen' for HBO," a corporate synchronization of press releases that suggests a coordinated effort on the company's part to expand Watchmen on multiple fronts, allowing these transmedia paratexts to flow into one another.[29]

Throughout *Doomsday Clock*, Johns and Frank layer in imagery of moths being lured to flames, an (un)aware acknowledgment that the allure of profits was too great for DC to resist, but equally a metaphor for the irresistible pull the company wants their hyperlinked universe to have on readers. Ideal for any series encouraging deep-dive behavior, *Doomsday Clock* points in multiple directions, depending on the reader's particular entry point. If the reader comes to the miniseries with only prior knowledge of DC superheroes and little to no familiarity with *Watchmen*, then a selection of intentional links direct them back to particular issues of that miniseries. Issue 3, for instance, details the backstory of Reggie Long, the new Rorschach. Portions of the issue flashback to Reggie's childhood, depicting his perspective on events detailed in *Watchmen* #6, primarily, Reggie's father, psychiatrist Malcolm Long, and his growing obsession with his patient, the original Rorschach, Walter Kovacs. Specifically, page 5 of *Doomsday Clock* #4 features two panels of Reggie's mother standing in a doorway as her husband works at his desk, direct inversions of those shown on page 13 of *Watchmen* #6. By omitting further information about Malcolm's story, while emphasizing *Doomsday Clock*'s sequel status, these moments direct readers back to the original comics as a means of gaining a fuller picture. Relatedly, in the same issue of *Doomsday Clock*, Reggie's flashbacks involve a minor character from *Watchmen*, Byron Lewis aka Mothman. Lewis's inclusion both picks up threads from the original *Watchmen*—which readers can follow backwards—and utilizes a character featured in *BW: Minutemen*, creating hyperlinks between all major Watchmen comic paratexts.

If the reader has read *Watchmen* but has never ventured further into DC Comics, then the inclusion of characters such as Superman, Batman, Wonder Woman, Firestorm, Lex Luthor, Saturn Girl, and Black Adam act as taxonomic links to countless issues featuring them. While the latter characters appear throughout the miniseries, issue 9 purposefully includes a four-page sequence of wordless panels showing various teams of characters from all corners of the DCU traveling to confront Dr. Manhattan. Without any context—no introductory blurbs are provided—these pages rely on one of superhero comics' basic strengths, the intriguing iconicity of costumed heroes, to turn these images into taxonomic links, making unfamiliar readers search out answers if they want to discover who these characters are. Within that same issue, one page shows Green Lantern Guy Gardner threatening Dr. Manhattan by listing off (and manifesting holograms of) past supervillains the heroes have defeated. Gardner's dialog and the images of the Anti-Monitor, Doomsday, and Superboy-Prime allude to specific event series from DC history, such as *Crisis on Infinite Earths*, the "Death of Superman" storyline, and *Infinite Crisis*. These references act as intensional links that potentially lead the reader back to those storylines.

Approaching the conclusion, Johns uses Dr. Manhattan's meddling with the continuity of the DCU as both a thematic representation of the deep dive and an actualization of it. The powers of Dr. Manhattan—the ability to simultaneously exist in the past, present, and future—have always been an allegory for the way readers take in a comics page; our eye can see all panels on a page at once—the past and future of the narrative. Over the course of *Doomsday Clock*, Dr. Manhattan becomes an embodiment of the deep dive, able to hyperlink between time periods and alternate realities within the DC Multiverse, just as readers are able to apprehend the bigger picture of the universe by jumping from issue to issue. This makes the miniseries not only a sequel to *Watchmen* and the fulfillment of DC's plan to include the Watchmen storyworld into the deep-dive design of the mainline universe, but also a symbolic discussion of that strategy's importance to superhero comics.

Beyond simply linking *Doomsday Clock* to past DC comics, Johns goes a step further and utilizes Manhattan's symbolic potential to peak into the hypothetical future of the DCU within this final issue. In having the character narrate potential future events—a new addition to the multiverse called Earth-5G and a "Secret Crisis" that hints at a Marvel/DC crossover—Johns provides the potential for future authors to create links from *Doomsday Clock* to forthcoming events.[30] While these foreshadowed events may not happen exactly as Johns/Manhattan has described them here—plenty of editorial and industrial roadblocks could stop them from ever coming to fruition—the links are there, ready for an enterprising writer (maybe even Johns himself) to complete the opposite end of the link.

Given that Johns has incorporated these deep-dive hyperlinks to previous and (possible) future comics into *Doomsday Clock* (not to mention other series he's written), the reasonable question to ask is: If the strategy is continually used, does it actually produce the intended results? Gauging that becomes quite difficult, considering that the strategy conceivably links readers backwards to any number of titles from a variety of years published in numerous formats. A few extra sales of a TPB for one of the crossover events referenced by Guy Gardner in *Doomsday Clock* #9, for instance, may not be a success by other creative industry standards, nor would it likely make a blip on the top TPB sales charts. Given the serialized release schedule of superhero comics, there is also no consistent jumping off point for the deep dive; readers may pursue a link in the middle of reading a series, after it has concluded, or a couple months later, excluding the possibility of a singular pattern across the consumer base. Likewise, in the Internet era, the number of readers who search out information on a wiki or online database rather than purchase a physical or digital edition becomes nearly impossible to track.

Recognizing the randomness inherent to the directionality of the deep dive, the goal of the strategy seems less oriented towards generating sharp spikes in sales and more the nurturing of long-term investment. Any volume sold or wiki article read incrementally increases the potential for deeper investment in the continuity and history of a narrative universe. Asking whether there is any sales data that indicates whether that strategy works or not may be somewhat of a moot point, in the end. The most telling answer may simply be that the industry does keep utilizing the strategy. Either they are seeing the results they want, or they have relied on the system so long that they are fearful of diverging too far from it. No matter the reason, DC continues to include hyperlinked references between the titles they publish, providing an opportunity for a reader's curiosity to lead them deeper and deeper down into the universe.

CONCLUSION

During the writing of this chapter, DC began publishing a twelve-issue *Rorschach* miniseries. Written by Tom King and illustrated by Jorge Fornés, the miniseries acts as yet another sequel to *Watchmen*. Additionally, a miniseries entitled *Flash Forward* saw Wally West's Flash become imbued with Dr. Manhattan's powers, around the same time as a Bat-Manhattan appeared in the Batman-centric event crossover *Dark Knights: Death Metal*. All of this proves that the floodgates are open, and DC is aggressively pursuing any and all methods of further incorporating the Watchmen characters into the larger DCU. By doing so, the company has effectively removed any aura of prestige around these characters in favor of turning them into the same serialized icons that power the "deep dive-able" quality of superhero comics.

Since the seventies, Marvel and DC have made "freelancers sign a form acknowledging their status of work-for-hire contractors," always as a means to fully control an expansive library of IPs.[31] These publishers have utilized that control to construct vast universes, held together by hyperlinking continuity that readers can endlessly dive into. *Watchmen* has always been a conundrum in that regard as "the very notion of a complete story runs counter to the[ir] business model."[32] After testing the waters with *BW*, *Doomsday Clock* became the company's means of finally linking the Watchmen brand to their mainline universe, making sure that, for readers, "nothing ever ends."

NOTES

1. I would like to thank Dr. Ethan Tussey for convincing me to present on this topic during a departmental colloquium, as that presentation inspired this chapter. Likewise, Dr. Greg Smith's notes and insight on an early draft were, as always, essential to shaping the final product.

2. Kurt Amacker, "Interview with Alan Moore," *Seraphemera*, accessed April 30, 2020, http://www.seraphemera.org/seraphemera_books/AlanMoore_Page1.html.

3. Amacker (emphasis added).

4. TPBs are commonly reprints of single-issue comics bound together in a softcover volume, sometimes incorrectly referred to as graphic novels.

5. Tommy Cook, "DC Comics Co-Publishers Dan DiDio and Jim Lee Talk *Before* Watchmen at the Los Angeles Times Festival of Books," *Collider.com*, published April 22, 2012, https://collider.com/dan-didio-jim-lee-before-watchmen-interview/.

6. Andrew Hoberek, *Considering Watchmen: Poetics, Property, Politics* (New Brunswick, NJ: Rutgers University Press, 2014), 92.

7. Bart Beaty, "Superhero Fan Service: Audience Strategies in the Contemporary Interlinked Hollywood Blockbuster," *The Information Society* 32, no. 5 (2016): 319.

8. Jean-Paul Gabilliet, *Of Comics and Men: A Cultural History of American Comic Books*, translated by Bart Beaty and Nick Nguyen (Jackson: University of Mississippi Press, 2009), e-book.

9. David Hyman, *Revision and the Superhero Genre* (Cham, Switzerland: Palgrave Macmillan, 2017), 16. Hyman states that "to understand superhero continuity, one must recognize that many superhero narratives are doubly inscribed. On one level, they are individual stories bound by the textual conditions of their transmission. However, each individual story is also part of vast and ongoing intertextual continuums that serve as the fictional 'realities' in which they take place." My understanding of continuity within this chapter follows Hyman.

10. The clever selection of *Doomsday Clock* as a title even gestures at the intended merger of the Watchmen and DC Universes, as the phrase is famously associated with the original *Watchmen* comics while also abbreviating down to the company's initials.

11. Any issue older than the most recent release is often referred to as a back issue.

12. Retconning entails updating, altering, or erasing information that was previously canonical.

13. Andrew J. Friedenthal, *Retcon Game: Retroactive Continuity and the Hyperlinking of America* (Jackson: University Press of Mississippi, 2017), 8–9.

14. Michael Zimmer, "Renvois of the Past, Present and Future: Hyperlinks and the Structuring of Knowledge from the Encyclopédie to Web 2.0," *New Media & Society* 11, no. 1–2 (2009): 96.

15. Zimmer, 102.

16. Zimmer, 107 (emphasis mine).

17. Alexander Halavais, "The Hyperlink as Organizing Principle," in *The Hyperlinked Society: Questioning Connections in the Digital Age*, ed. Joseph Turow and Lokman Tsui (Ann Arbor: University of Michigan Press, 2008), 42.

18. Subscription-based digital archives for each company's back catalogs (Marvel Unlimited and DC Universe) have increased the ability to pair reading recommendations with issues. I have to wonder when or if either company will start embedding literal hyperlinks into their digital comics.

19. Steven J. DeRose, "Expanding the Notion of Links," in *Proceedings of the Second Annual ACM Conference on Hypertext* (November 1989), 254.

20. DeRose, 254 (emphasis original).

21. DeRose, 253 (emphasis original).

22. John Jackson Miller, "Top Comics by Year," *Comichron.com*, accessed July 11, 2020, https://www.comichron.com/vitalstatistics/topcomicsbyyear.html.

23. Cook.

24. John Jackson Miller, "June 2012 Comic Book Sales to Comics Shops," *Comichron .com*, accessed July 11, 2020, www.comichron.com/monthlycomicssales/2012/2012-06.html.

25. John Jackson Miller, "June 2012 Graphic Novel Sales to Comics Shops," *Comichron .com*, accessed July 11, 2020, www.comichron.com/monthlycomicssales/2012/2012-06.html #graphicnovels.

26. John Jackson Miller, "May 2012 Graphic Novel Sales to Comics Shops," *Comichron .com*, accessed October 19, 2020, www.comichron.com/monthlycomicssales/2012/2012-05 .html#graphicnovels.

27. The New 52, which was an initiative launched by DC in the summer of 2011, rebooted a majority of the company's continuity with the release of fifty-two titles, all starting at issue 1.

28. Aaron Sagers, "Exclusive: DC Comics' Geoff Johns Reveals Teaser, Details on *Watchmen*/ Rebirth Title *Doomsday Clock*," *Syfy.com*, published May 14, 2017, https://www.syfy.com/syfywire/ exclusive-dc-comics-geoff-johns-reveals-teaser-details-on-watchmenrebirth-title-doomsday.

29. Debra Birnbaum, "Damon Lindelof to Develop 'Watchmen' for HBO," *Variety.com*, published June 20, 2017, https://variety.com/2017/tv/news/damon-lindelof-the-watchmen -hbo-1202473414/.

30. Prior to Warner Entertainment being bought out by AT&T, DC had plans to enact an initiative called 5G (for Fifth Generation) that would have seen younger characters take over the mantles of Superman, Batman, and Wonder Woman, while their alter egos aged realistically. That project has since been transformed into a two-month event entitled *Future State*, published in the first quarter of 2021.

31. Gabilliet, e-book.

32. Hoberek, 88.

Chapter 2

FLICKERS OF BLACK AND WHITE

Cinema and Genre in *Watchmen* and *Doomsday Clock*

DRU JEFFRIES

I move to reshape this universe so that I might see how it forms around Superman.
I change the past to challenge the future.

—DR. MANHATTAN, *DOOMSDAY CLOCK* #10

Much of the scholarship devoted to Alan Moore and Dave Gibbons's *Watchmen* has framed the landmark superhero comic in relation to literature.[1] In the present-day franchise, however, it is not literature but rather the cinematic medium that haunts *Watchmen*. Though Moore and Gibbons's miniseries makes few direct references to cinematic works, seemingly presenting "an Earth in which movies have little presence," cinema occupies a central role in both of its contemporary sequels.[2] As the embodiment of revisionism in the superhero genre *par excellence*, cinema's markedly increased presence in these sequels—namely, HBO's nine-episode television miniseries *Watchmen* (2019) and DC Comics's twelve-issue comic book crossover event *Doomsday Clock* (November 2017–December 2019)—might be understood as an appropriate and necessary acknowledgment of cinema's predominant role in sustaining the superhero genre in contemporary culture. While the popularity of superhero comic books peaked during World War II, postmillennial Hollywood has renewed and expanded the genre for global mass audiences, effectively reorienting superhero stories as a primarily cinematic phenomenon in the mind of the average consumer. More than merely reflecting cinema's importance to the genre in the present, however, *Watchmen*'s sequels both juxtapose serialized superhero narratives against specific moments in film history in an attempt to excavate what a superhero comic might refer to as the genre's origin story. The relationships these sequels posit between cinema and the superhero genre are crucial to understanding their distinct articulations of the superhero's cultural meaning, either emphasizing (in the case of *Watchmen*) or sublimating (in *Doomsday Clock*) the genre's foundational associations with white supremacy.

This chapter will analyze and compare the diegetic and symbolic roles of cinema as a motif across both HBO's *Watchmen* and DC's *Doomsday Clock*. Most obviously, *Watchmen* and *Doomsday Clock* each deploys a fictional cinematic metatext—that is, a film that exists within the diegetic world and functions as a critical commentary on the primary narrative action—that performs much of this symbolic work. In *Watchmen*, we have a fictional 1921 silent feature, *Trust in the Law!*, directed by pioneering independent African American novelist/filmmaker Oscar Micheaux;[3] in *Doomsday Clock*, scenes from a fictional 1954 film noir directed by Jacques Tourneur, *The Adjournment*, are interspersed throughout the narrative, echoing the role played by the *Tales from the Black Freighter* comic in the original *Watchmen* comics. These metatextual appeals to actual filmmakers and specific moments in American (film) history encourage us to understand the emergence and development of superhero comics in relation to Hollywood filmmaking and its historical contexts—namely, the resurgence of the Ku Klux Klan in response to D. W. Griffith's *The Birth of a Nation* (1915), and the racialized anxiety embodied by the postwar noir cycle, respectively. In addition to these cinematic metatexts, both sequels also use the character of Superman—often held up as the first true comic book superhero—as a metonym for the genre he inaugurated. In both cases, the representation of Superman in relation to the aforementioned cinematic metatexts reveals each narrative's overarching vision of the superhero genre: whereas *Watchmen* recontextualizes Superman (and thereby the genre *in toto*) as a whitewashed appropriation of Black struggle in a white supremacist nation, *Doomsday Clock* ultimately attempts to hold Superman up as an uncomplicated embodiment of hope, renouncing the cynicism of Moore and Gibbons's original miniseries in order to insist upon the continued centrality of pure (read: white) heroism in the superhero genre.

SECRET ORIGIN: WHITE SUPREMACY, SILENT CINEMA, AND THE SUPERHERO

In most accounts of the superhero genre's emergence, *Action Comics* #1 (1938)—Superman's inaugural appearance—is given pride of place as "the Big Bang of the Golden Age of Comics, the start point for superhero histories."[4] As novelist Michael Chabon elaborates, "There were costumed crime-fighters before Superman (the Phantom, Zorro), but only as there were pop quartets before the Beatles. Superman invented and exhausted his genre in a single bound."[5] Despite being described in his first appearance as a "champion of the oppressed," Superman's closest antecedent is arguably found not in the pulp adventures or dime novels cited by Chabon but rather in Griffith's *Birth of a Nation* and its source novel, Thomas Dixon Jr.'s *The Clansman* (1905). As Chris Gavaler describes in "The Ku Klux Klan and the Birth of the Superhero," these fictionalized representations of Klansmen inaugurate many of the genre tropes that would later come to be seen as hallmarks of the superhero, including the adoption of a secret identity; a commitment to enacting "justice" and a "pro-social mission" through unlawful, often violent means (i.e., vigilantism); and a distinctive costume with an iconic emblem on its chest.[6] As a product of two Jewish-American creators in the late 1930s, Superman inarguably represented a more progressive vision of American culture than the Klan, but the ideological schism between them only serves to conceal, rather than negate, their fundamental similarities. Even though "Siegel and Shuster turned Superman's stated mission against the Klan," Gavaler writes, "the formula of a disguised hero disregarding laws and using violence to enforce his own moral judgements still embeds fundamental Klan values. Content cannot erase form, and the more overt the anti-Klan politics of a superhero the greater the contradiction in his actions."[7]

Ian Gordon understands Superman as "a product by which we consume virtue," a cultural barometer of what is considered virtuous at any particular moment.[8] In this light, Superman reveals that even if overt white supremacy had fallen out of favor in polite society by 1938, light skin nevertheless remained an implicit prerequisite for American virtue. Despite being an alien from the planet Krypton, Superman easily passes as human, male, American, and white—the same four conditions that allowed the Klan to wield moral (if not legal) authority over Black Americans and other minorities in preceding decades.[9] As Sean Guynes and Martin Lund summarize, "The source of racial injustice in the field of superhero comics lies in the very fact that the superhero, as a generic figure and in many, if not most, of its specific manifestations, is a white male ideological formation nested in and supporting the discourses of power on which American society trades."[10] Superman's whiteness, then, should be considered a kind of superpower in itself, the baseline condition that facilitates the seemingly paradoxical reconciliation of extralegal force and a prosocial mission.[11] The superhero may have a more inclusive social agenda than the Klan, but he can never represent a radical challenge to white supremacy so long as his moral authority relies upon white privilege. This tension between the supposed moral goodness of the superhero and this debt to white supremacists, however, is rarely acknowledged—including in revisionist works like Moore and Gibbons's *Watchmen*, which casts a critical eye upon superhero psychology more in terms of sexual "deviancy" (e.g., homosexuality, kink) than white supremacy. (There are no nonwhite superheroes in their *Watchmen*.)[12]

In this context, the most striking intervention of HBO's *Watchmen* may be its willingness to recognize and interrogate its genre's origins, to perform the radical critique that a white Superman never could. It operationalizes this critique first, and most clearly, through its aforementioned cinematic metatext, *Trust in the Law!*, which raises the specter of the superhero genre's urtext, *Birth of a Nation*. Though *Trust in the Law!* is a fictional film, placing it along the timeline of Oscar Micheaux's actual career suggests it can be treated as a spiritual sequel to his 1920 film, *The Symbol of the Unconquered*. Significantly, *Symbol* was Micheaux's response to the KKK's (proto-)superheroic depiction in *Birth of a Nation*, boldly flipping that film's racialized good/evil hierarchy on its head. As Micheaux scholar Ronald J. Green describes, the film's climax "is the obverse of the denouement of *The Birth of a Nation* in which the Klan rescues the 'good' guys, and gals, from the blacks."[13] Though this sequence is missing from the film's only known extant print, Mark Reid has suggested that "the 'colored man with bricks' who defeats the Klan in *Symbol* can be considered a superhero."[14] The fact that this—arguably the first Black "superhero," if only loosely—is lost to history is both tragic and, perhaps, not coincidental. Was *this scene* in particular simply lost by chance, or was it deliberately removed from circulating prints as an act of censorship? The disappearance (or erasure) of the "colored man with bricks" (as the intertitles, quoting a contemporaneous film review, describe him) might be considered analogous to the historical whitewashing of Hooded Justice—and with him, the Black origins of "costumed adventuring"—in the world of *Watchmen*.

Trust in the Law! introduces an alternative Black cinematic hero in the form of historical figure Bass Reeves (1838–1910), a deputy US marshal. Unlike *Birth of a Nation*, however, *Trust* stops short of representing its protagonist as a superhero. Whereas Griffith's Klan "[oversteps] lawful processes to combat perceived menaces for the supposed good of society,"[15] *Trust*'s masked figure is a deputized agent of the state, explicitly denounces mob justice, and urges citizens (and impressionable viewers like the young boy, William, in the audience) to "trust in the law." Backpedaling from *Symbol*'s representation of restorative violence against racist whites, *Trust* nevertheless embodies Micheaux's vision of Black uplift by demonstrating the importance of trusting, rather than rejecting, the rule of law—something white Americans, as represented by Griffith's Klan, are not obliged to do. As

Green summarizes, "Micheaux and many African Americans welcomed the American rules, including those of capitalism, for the same reason those rules had attracted immigrants to America—those rules were supposed to give immigrants a chance to have a middle-class life."[16] They also put Black Americans at the mercy of whites willing to bend or break those rules.

Micheaux's fantasy of equal opportunity and treatment under American law is immediately and sharply undercut in *Watchmen*, however, as the screening of *Trust* is violently interrupted by the Black Wall Street massacre, a literal explosion of true American carnage—fueled in part by white resentment for Black citizens having achieved a measure of self-sufficiency under capitalism—just outside the theater.[17] Like a scene out of Griffith's film, whites in and out of Klan robes descend upon the Greenwood district of Tulsa, Oklahoma, aided by "local police officers and national guardsmen siding with whites in a battle against African American residents."[18] Young William's parents sweep up the boy and, in a unsubtle nod to Superman's Kryptonian parents, place him in a vehicle that will spirit him away from the annihilation of their world. William will later rechristen himself William Reeves in honor of his cinematic hero, a surname that also resonates with George Reeves, the actor who played Superman in TV's *Adventures of Superman* (ABC, 1952–1958).[19] In 1938, it is an encounter with the newly published *Action Comics* #1 that inspires Reeves to counter the Klan's—now known as Cyclops—"pro-social mission" with his own countermission by becoming a vigilante himself, Hooded Justice.

The chronology of these events—Tulsa, 1921; Superman, 1938—suggests, however, that Reeves is less a Black appropriation of Superman than Superman is a whitewashed appropriation of Black struggle against white supremacy. By presenting the origins of its world's first nonfictional superhero, Hooded Justice, as both a variation on Superman's origin and the product of a cinematic lineage stretching back to *Birth of a Nation*, *Watchmen* points directly at the superhero's obligatory whiteness, drawing out the chain of associations between the emergent genre, Griffith's Klan, and Black struggle. In so doing, *Watchmen* insists upon the instability and fundamental ambivalence of the superhero; rooted in white supremacy, the genre may repudiate its own origins but can never fully transcend them. As Gavaler writes, "The surface agenda of the superhero is malleable and evolves with social contexts, but his modus operandi is the formula's unacknowledged constant. Hoods and capes change colour, but it is always a fist clenched inside the glove."[20] From here, we'll turn to film noir and its role in negotiating the racial politics of the superhero in both *Watchmen* and *Doomsday Clock*.

SUBLIMATED BLACKNESS: FILM NOIR, *THE ADJOURNMENT*, AND "THIS EXTRAORDINARY BEING"

Watchmen's sixth episode, "This Extraordinary Being," details the origins of Hooded Justice while elaborating on cinema's complicity with white supremacy. Most overtly, it does so by making cinema a central part of Cyclops's racist plot.[21] In this episode, white supremacists hijack film screenings in Black neighborhoods with mesmeric messages intended to provoke explosions of violence, effectively turning innocent Black filmgoers into the animalistic subhumans they are depicted as in *Birth of a Nation*. The message here seems clear: that media representations have real-world effects, and that those produced by Hollywood—from *Birth of a Nation* to the seemingly more innocuous film being screened in the scene, *The Secret Life of Walter Mitty* (Norman Z. McLeod, 1947)—reinforce hegemonic whiteness and anti-Black racism.[22] As the acceptability of overt white supremacy has declined in American culture, its ideology has not been displaced but rather naturalized and normalized through popular media. A perfect example of covert white supremacy in Hollywood cinema can be found in the postwar film noir cycle, which is explicitly incorporated into *Doomsday Clock* and stylistically integrated into "This Extraordinary Being." We'll start with the former.

Beginning in the second issue and recurring throughout the series thereafter, *Doomsday Clock*'s fictional noir metatext, *The Adjournment*, functions analogously to *Tales from the Black Freighter* in the original series, turning *Watchmen*'s innovative metatextual density into a replicable narrative formula. Moore and Gibbons's fictional pirate comic performs a running commentary on *Watchmen*'s main narrative action while also contributing to its world-building: *Black Freighter*'s "story provides an obvious analog not only for Veidt's plan to sacrifice millions in order to end the Cold War but also for all the moral compromises in the putative pursuit of good that Rorschach, Manhattan, and the other characters make throughout the book," while also demonstrating that the popularity of crime and horror comics extended well past the 1950s in *Watchmen*'s alternate 1980s, such that pirate stories specifically come to fill the space occupied by superheroes in our culture.[23] *The Adjournment*'s conventional noir narrative is used similarly throughout *Doomsday Clock* to parallel or comment upon specific character and story beats using an alternative generic register. As such, *The Adjournment* performs the same narrative function as *Black Freighter* while, like *Trust in the Law!*, juxtaposing the superhero genre against actual Hollywood history—in this case, the postwar noir cycle.[24] It's the latter that interests me here.

Film noir has been widely understood as an aesthetic embodiment of American malaise and anxiety in the aftermath of World War II. While these films rarely dealt explicitly with race—and when they did, they were arguably more inclusive "than dominant US social practices of the time would have required"[25]—some scholars have theorized that the anxieties they do represent, and the dark aesthetic used to represent them, are "always and everywhere about race."[26] As Eric Lott summarizes in his article "The Whiteness of Film Noir," the cycle addressed white anxieties over race, and Blackness in particular,

> not by presenting it outright but by taking the social energy associated with its social threat and subsuming it into the untoward aspects of white selves. The "dark" energy of many of these films is villainized precisely through the associations with race that generated some of that energy in the first place. Film noir is in this sense a sort of whiteface dream-work of social anxieties with explicitly racial sources, condensed on film into the criminal undertakings of abjected whites.[27]

The displacement of white criminality onto the dark, shadowy, "black" figures of noir "absolves whites of the responsibility for evil and moral ambiguity," keeping such responsibility safely associated with the racialized Other.[28] In this light, noir may be considered as complementary to the superhero genre as described earlier: whereas the superhero redeems the white vigilante in terms of modern virtue, noir draws an association between blackness/Blackness and criminality that depicts white transgression as a "fall from (g)race."[29] In both cases, whiteness retains its sheen despite being on the wrong side of the law, while Blackness is erased, criminalized, or both.

Like *Trust in the Law!*, the evocation of noir in *Doomsday Clock* also indirectly alludes back to the superhero genre's prehistory, presenting an alternative narrative of its emergence that points not to the Klansman as its relevant predecessor but rather to the white detective of pulp fiction. In *Doomsday Clock*, this influence is extended to postwar noir cinema. In the third issue, a television news report describing the emergence of superheroes on the world stage on one channel is interrupted by a broadcast of *The Adjournment* on another. The grammatically seamless connection between the two sentences represented in these juxtaposed panels implicitly credits film noir for playing a crucial part in the production of superheroes: a superpowered individual "was recruited by the ***mysterious unnamed head*** of the [Department of Metahuman Affairs] and exposed to [. . .] the 1954 classic, starring ***Carver Colman*** in his ***final role*** as private investigator ***Nathaniel***

Dusk*.**"[30] *Doomsday Clock* thus urges readers to draw a line of causality from postwar noir's representation of "the 'dark' side of the white Western self" to the increasingly dysfunctional (white) superhero inaugurated in comics like *Watchmen*.[31] Earlier on the same page, the fictional actor Colman is described as a sexual "deviant," while later in the same issue, a character in *The Adjournment* tells Dusk, "I can see the ***noose around your neck from here," both of which associate Colman/Dusk with *Watchmen*'s Hooded Justice (whose identity remains unknown in the comics, though he is presumed white and of German descent).[32]

"This Extraordinary Being" is to *The Adjournment* as *Symbol of the Unconquered* is to *Birth of a Nation*. While *Doomsday Clock* juxtaposes its superhero story against a perfectly conventional and formulaic noir, complete with hard-boiled narration, chiaroscuro lighting, and a duplicitous femme fatale, "This Extraordinary Being" follows in the tradition of Black neonoir, rejecting classical noir's sublimation of racial anxieties and lack of diverse representation while redeploying its aesthetics to articulate "such black-centered issues as rage against whites, criminality, and community."[33] If traditional noir took the energy associated with white anxieties over race in America and sublimated it into corrupted representations of whiteness—"a collective white reappropriation of the very fear they instil in the black population, the very violence they inflict on its members," per Julian Murphet[34]—in this episode Reeves takes the much more salient threat of white supremacy and channels its own energy against it. Combining the iconography and tactics of the Klan—the pointed hood, the lynching noose, the illegal violence—with the virtuous whiteness of Superman, Hooded Justice combats the former and subverts the latter. Whereas in traditional Hollywood cinema luminous white skin was symbolic of purity and enlightenment,[35] such that the darkening of the white figure (via lighting) in noir evinced moral transgression, here it is identified as part of the mask that must be put on in order to enact righteous violence within American society. If the white-centric superhero genre rests upon a contradiction between form (adapted from the Klan) and content (Superman as "champion of the oppressed"), as described earlier, Hooded Justice's racial masquerade emphasizes—indeed, makes a mockery of—the compulsory whiteness that Superman shares with the Klan, making the connection between them near-explicit.[36] As Dan Flory writes, Black filmmakers working within and updating the noir paradigm present "ways of knowing about American society that are highly critical of it, yet that also promise to make insights into the dissolution of its unconscious white supremacism easier to formulate."[37] In contrast to the classical noir of *The Adjournment*, this episode's affinity with Black neonoir thus offers itself as a perfect vehicle to continue and extend the critique began in the first episode. In the final section, we'll turn to a broader comparison between *Doomsday Clock* and *Watchmen*.

CONCLUSION: RETCONS AND REPARATIONS

In addition to their interest in cinema and film noir in particular, both of *Watchmen*'s parallel sequels are organized around a common narrative conceit: the retcon. Referring to a new narrative that retroactively modifies the facts, or at least our understanding, of a previous text, retcons have become the lifeblood of long-running superhero serials, allowing companies to relegate problematic or unpopular stories to "alternate" realities or even "reboot" their entire line of comics to start over with a clean narrative slate.[38] DC Comics in particular has long relied upon this strategy to manage its "convoluted and labyrinthine narrative history," always trying to strike a delicate balance between maintaining devoted readers (to whom this labyrinthine narrative history remains important) while also providing easy points of entry for new readers (to whom the labyrinthine narrative history is intimidating).[39] Beginning with *Crisis on Infinite Earths* (1985–1986), DC's approach has been to justify occasional narrative resets through cataclysmic in-universe events, whose ultimate purpose is to erase and reset what has come before, resulting in "*tabula rasa* (a 'blank slate'), onto which a brave new world can be etched."[40]

As of this writing, at least, *Doomsday Clock* is DC's most recent attempt to perform this kind of metadiegetic management. Beginning seven years after the events of the original *Watchmen*, the narrative begins with Ozymandias and a new Rorschach leaving *Watchmen*'s self-contained narrative universe for the main DC universe in search of Dr. Manhattan. From the company's perspective, the narrative's purpose is at least twofold: one, to integrate Moore and Gibbons's standalone *Watchmen* into DC's ongoing continuity, thereby creating future opportunities to exploit the lucrative comics franchise in ongoing publications; and two, to diegetically rationalize the company's most recent narrative reboot, *DC Rebirth*, by collecting all its previous reboots under a single narrative umbrella. In short, *Doomsday Clock* retcons the company's already-retcon-riddled publishing history, reconciling its many competing timelines and parallel Earths by revealing Dr. Manhattan as the invisible hand behind these previous retcons.[41] (Since comic book readers tend to hate reboots, this makes Dr. Manhattan the villain of the story.) Inconsistencies between Superman's origins as represented in *Action Comics*

#1 and *The Man of Steel* #1 (1986) are thus newly understood as the consequences of Dr. Manhattan—who, as Jared Gardner points out, "sees time like a comic reader"[42]—putting theoretical physicist Bryce DeWitt's "many worlds interpretation" to the test by intervening in Superman's history.[43] Manhattan follows "Superman's trail of influence" across DC's history, discovering that changes to his life "affect not only ***this*** world, but ***every world*** in the ***multiverse***."[44] Eventually, he finds that his manipulations are resisted by "an innate hope that fights back to the surface,"[45] which we can understand as DC's current vision of the superhero genre. As *Doomsday Clock* author Geoff Johns put it, "DC Comics, like in the DNA , is all about hope and inspiration, so we needed to get back to that."[46] *Doomsday Clock* thus posits a complex, ever-evolving narrative universe whose center of gravity throughout innumerable revisions and relaunches is inexorably Superman and the values he represents—in other words, it presents a vision of the superhero genre that is centered around the power of whiteness to impart a sense of hope and moral clarity to the world. But if *Doomsday Clock* ultimately wants us to understand the superhero genre as a beacon of hope, this chapter has shown that it is, at best, an exclusionary hope based on a selective reading of the genre's history.

HBO's *Watchmen* also deploys the retcon, but with the opposite aim. While I have described the series as a sequel throughout this chapter, the episodes discussed herein function equally as a transmedia prequel to the original comics, revealing Hooded Justice's identity and expanding his backstory in a way that prompts viewers to understand Moore and Gibbons's work in a different way—namely, for what they omit from their critique of the superhero genre and the ongoing violence of that omission. HBO's *Watchmen* does effectively what Dr. Manhattan claims to do in *Doomsday Clock*, as quoted in the epigraph at the beginning of this chapter: it changes its predecessor's diegetic past in order to challenge its genre's future. *Watchmen* represents a reckoning with the genre's past, a clear-eyed assessment of the superhero's long-implicit association with white supremacy and, perhaps, a step towards a new vision of the genre that takes this knowledge into account.

We might understand *Watchmen*'s stance towards the superhero genre through another concept that is central to the series: reparations. Referred to within the diegesis as "Redfordations," reparations represent an effort not to erase or forget past injustices, but rather to reckon with them directly and attempt an appropriate corrective in the present.[47] With respect to the superhero genre, *Watchmen* reaches into the past and acknowledges its historical entanglement with white supremacist ideology. But it doesn't stop there—from this acknowledgment, the series proceeds to retcon the genre's origins, at least within its own storyworld, by revealing the first "costumed adventurer"—its Superman figure—to be Black. Similarly, while Adrian Veidt interprets Dr. Manhattan's adoption of Cal Abar's Black body as an inappropriate act of racial appropriation, this too might instead be considered in terms of reparations—that is, as an attempt to correct the historical whitewashing of the superhero figure by transferring power from Jon Osterman (like Superman, a descendant of Jews) to a Black American. What effect this reckoning will have on superhero stories to come, however, remains to be seen.

NOTES

1. See, for instance, Sara Van Ness, *Watchmen as Literature: A Critical Study of the Graphic Novel* (Jefferson, NC: McFarland & Company Inc., 2010), and Andrew Hoberek, *Considering Watchmen: Poetics, Property, Politics* (New Brunswick: Rutgers University Press, 2014).

2. Dana Polan, "*Watchmen* from the Point of View of Cinema and Media Study," *Cinema Journal* 56, no. 2 (Winter 2017): 148.

3. Micheaux is not identified as the film's director within the series itself, but rather in the show's supplementary web materials, known as "Peteypedia." For more on Peteypedia's paraextual function, see Zachary Rondinelli's chapter in this volume.

4. Chris Gavaler, *On the Origin of Superheroes* (Iowa City: University of Iowa Press, 2015), 13.

5. Quoted in Gavaler, 5.

6. Chris Gavaler, "The Ku Klux Klan and the Birth of the Superhero," *Journal of Graphic Novels and Comics* 4, no. 2 (2013): 201–2. Gavaler also draws a compelling parallel between the representation of the Klan's origins and Batman's, the latter of which "repeats not only Griffith's structure—hero alone, chance inspiration, first image of costumed persona—but also the 'superstitious' rationalization for the disguise. Griffith's scene dramatizes the first costume origin story, one duplicated in later iconic superhero texts" (202).

7. Gavaler, 203.

8. Ian Gordon, *Superman: The Persistence of an American Icon* (New Brunswick: Rutgers University Press, 2017), 17.

9. Passing as white is a recurring theme in Micheaux's films as well. See Charlene Regester, "The Misreading and Rereading of African American Filmmaker Oscar Micheaux," *Film History* 7, no. 4 (Winter 1995): 431.

10. Sean Guynes and Martin Lund, "Not to Interpret, But to Abolish," in *Unstable Masks: Whiteness and American Superhero Comics*, ed. Sean Guynes and Martin Lund (Columbus: Ohio State University Press, 2020), 3.

11. This is perhaps why Hal Blythe and Charlie Sweet defined the superhero, in part, as "an adult, white male who holds a white collar job in his secret identity" and "'morally superior,' so, as previously discussed, when he acts outside of the law 'no reader thinks of the illegality'" (quoted in Gavaler, "The Ku Klux Klan," 201). In the American context, whiteness is a necessary precondition for operating outside of the law with impunity.

12. That said, an excerpt from the fictional right-wing newspaper *New Frontiersman* featured at the end of *Watchmen* #8 (1987) directly compares superheroes to the KKK: "*Nova Express* makes many sneering references to costumed heroes as direct descendants of the Ku Klux Klan, but might I point out that despite what some might view as their later excesses, the Klan originally came into being because decent people had perfectly reasonable fears for the safety of their persons and belongings when forced into proximity with people from a culture far less morally advanced" (30).

13. Ronald J. Green, *With a Crooked Stick: The Films of Oscar Micheaux* (Bloomington: Indiana University Press, 2004), 59.

14. Mark Reid, "Pioneer Black Filmmaker: The Achievement of Oscar Micheaux," *Black Film Review* 4, no. 2 (Spring 1988): 6.

15. Gavaler, 193.

16. Green, 4.

17. Chris M. Messer, "The Tulsa Race Riot of 1921: Toward an Integrative Theory of Collective Violence," *Journal of Social History* 44, no. 4 (Summer 2011): 1227–28.

18. Messer, 1217. While the KKK was effectively defunct as an organization by the time *Birth of a Nation* was released in 1915, the film's release and subsequent popularity was strategically used to spark renewed interest in the Klan, such that by 1921 they were again thriving across the nation. See Maxim Simcovitch, "The Impact of Griffith's *Birth of a Nation* on the Modern Ku Klux Klan," *Journal of Popular Film* 1, no. 1 (1972): 45–54.

19. Several other characters' names resonate with Superman's transmedia history, including Cal (phonetically identical to the first syllable of Superman's Kryptonian name, Kal-El); the Clark family (recalling Superman's civilian identity Clark Kent), from whose farmland we see a rocket land (recalling Superman's arrival on Earth) in episode 5, and whose baby is named Lois Clark, recalling Clark Kent and his love interest Lois Lane; and, more loosely, Angela Abar (named for the blaxploitation film *Abar: The First Black Superman* [Frank Packard, 1977]).

20. Gavaler.

21. The singular eye of the Cyclops also resembles the lens of a film projector.

22. Given *Watchmen*'s attention to detail, it's likely that the selection of *The Secret Life of Walter Mitty* has further resonances. Most obviously, it can be read as an oblique reference to another Walter with a secret life (Kovacs, AKA Rorschach). The film's protagonist works as a writer for a pulp magazine, reinforcing the accepted historical connection between the superhero genre and pulp magazines. The film's structure as a series of loosely connected fantasy sequences, each inspired by pulp fiction, within an overarching narrative frame echoes the episode's sprawling narrative structure. Last, the film timestamps the scene's action to approximately September 1947, which helps situate the viewer historically.

23. Hoberek, *Considering Watchmen*, Kindle loc. 1336.

24. *The Adjournment* is based on a minor DC comic from 1984, *Nathaniel Dusk: Private Investigator* and its 1985 sequel, *Nathaniel Dusk: Private Investigator II*.

25. Dan Flory, "Ethnicity and Race in Film Noir," in *A Companion to Film Noir*, ed. Andrew Spicer and Helen Hanson (Chichester: Blackwell Publishing Ltd., 2013), 402.

26. Kelly Oliver and Benigno Trigo, *Noir Anxiety* (Minneapolis: University of Minnesota Press, 2003), 4.

27. Eric Lott, "The Whiteness of Film Noir," *American Literary History* 9 (1997): 551.

28. Oliver and Trigo, 4.

29. Lott, 548.

30. *Doomsday Clock* #3, 13.

31. Lott, 543.

32. *Doomsday Clock* #3, 24.

33. William Covey, "The Genre Don't Know Where It Came From: African-American Neo-Noir Since the 1960s," *Journal of Film and Video* 55, no. 2/3 (Summer/Fall 2003): 61.

34. Julian Murphet, "Film Noir and the Racial Unconscious," *Screen* 39 no. 1 (Spring 1998): 31.

35. Lott, 548.

36. Racial ambiguity is a central concern of both Micheaux's filmography (often framed in terms of "passing") and film noir. See J. Ronald Green, *Straight Lick: The Cinema of Oscar Micheaux* (Bloomington: Indiana University Press, 2000), 183–92, and Oliver and Trigo, *Noir Anxiety*, 1–26, respectively.

37. Dan Flory, "Black on White: *Film Noir* and the Epistemology of Race in Recent African American Cinema," *Journal of Social Philosophy* 31, no. 1 (Spring 2000): 82.

38. While "retcon" is not synonymous with "reboot," retcons are often used to create in-story justifications for reboots. See William Proctor, "Reboots and Retroactive Continuity," in *The Routledge Companion to Imaginary Worlds*, ed. Mark J. P. Wolf (London: Routledge, 2017), 230–33.

39. Proctor, 226.

40. Proctor. The fact that this strategy actually multiplies, rather than reduces, the complexity of the resulting storyworld(s) seems to inevitably lead to future reboots.

41. For more on *Doomsday Clock*, see Jayson Quearry's contribution to this volume.

42. Jared Gardner, *Projections: Comics and the History of Twenty-First Century Storytelling* (Stanford: Stanford University Press, 2012), Kindle loc. 3799.

43. *Doomsday Clock* #10, 14.

44. *Doomsday Clock* #10, 19.

45. *Doomsday Clock* #10, 25.

46. Quoted in Proctor, "Reboots," 224.

47. The portmanteau "Redfordations" combines reparations with the Hollywood actor-cum-president, implicitly linking reparations with cinema.

Chapter 3

TRUST IN THE JOURNEY

HBO's *Watchmen* and Superhero Mythology

MARK C. E. PETERSON AND CHRIS YOGERST

When Alan Moore and Dave Gibbons's *Watchmen* series dropped in the 1980s, it served as a bombshell that changed the way we not only view comics, but also how we interpret and engage in superheroes. The graphic novel's ability to draw on real history (Vietnam, Richard Nixon, nuclear warfare) in an alternate reality forces the reader to consider the motivations, ideology, and intentions of heroes in our own world. Heroes are complicated, some of them stray from their noble origin—if they have one—while others may have misplaced intentions. Others, fortunately, stay close to their heroic journey.

HBO's *Watchmen* miniseries showrunner Damon Lindelof "hopes that his series will connect the past with the present and be as timely as Moore's 1986 comic series was during its time."[1] The series serves to revise our sense of heroism in how it relates to our larger social and political climate. A revisionist narrative "strives to *see* again, so as to *esteem* and *estimate* differently, so as to aim correctively."[2] For all the assumptions that superheroes are simplistic, these characters offer a great deal of insight into modern mythology. As Richard Reynolds observes, "The superhero narrative was the first (and arguably, so far, the only) new myth to express the expansion of human action and identity in the post-industrial age."[3] As the genre evolved, superhero characters became increasingly complicated, layered, and relatable. Reynolds continues, "It is remarkable that such an enduring myth of the information age—the superhero—should have been created so early in the postindustrial era."[4] Superheroes have enjoyed increased exposure beyond the comic book medium for decades, simultaneously expanding their reach and depth.

Like previous iterations of the *Watchmen* universe, the HBO series provides a deeply relevant and relatable tale. Eisner award-winning writer and television producer Jeph Loeb argues that "the moral stories we tell are very much biblical in nature, in the sense that there are consequences to the characters' actions."[5] While defining the superhero genre, Richard Reynolds explains how "at least some of the superheroes will be earthbound gods in their level of powers."[6] Regarding HBO's *Watchmen*, Angela/Sister Night operates as a prime example of the potential reach and depth of superheroes. Like many of the heroes and villains in the *Watchmen* mythos, Angela may not have super-human powers. Angela's power, at least for most of the series, resides in her determination to protect her family, discover truths, and fight crime. As Jennifer Stuller observes, superheroes are "strong-willed, committed, resilient, and skilled" and become super by surpassing the limits of the human body and mind.[7] Angela fits these criteria on many levels. Her career fighting crime was successful as a police officer, though her move away from the field after Seventh Kavalry assailants broke into her home on Christmas showcases her commitment to her family.

Angela suits the superhero narrative because she possesses what Peter Coogan sees as three essential components of every superhero: mission, power, identity. For Coogan, mission means "to fight evil and protect the innocent; this fight is universal, prosocial, and selfless."[8] Angela selflessly leaves the force to protect her family, but her move to suit up as Sister Night and continue to fight evil is equally selfless. She refuses the call and goes back to her family before ultimately answering the call from a new angle. Power consists of "all those abilities and qualities that raise a person's performance above that of ordinary people."[9] For Angela, this means her physical and mental strength. Her brilliant ability to use her intellect to best her opponent's rivals that of Batman. A superhero's identity "is composed of two elements: the code name and the costume."[10] Angela has Sister Night and her hooded cape. The hood is a clear nod to her father's past, though she doesn't realize it at first.

Further, her resilience led her to pick up the mask as Sister Night when another call to action came her way. Under the cover of a mask, Angela will be better suited to go after criminals like the Seventh Kavalry, a mob made up of Rorschach wannabes who executed an orchestrated attack on law enforcement on Christmas Eve night. With her real identity secret, her home remains safe from any retaliation against Sister Night. Stuller continues by arguing the unique features of female superheroes in the form of collaboration, love, and mentorship. Rejecting the "lone wolf" attribute characteristic of many male superheroes, Angela worked with both the police force as an officer and the masks as Sister Night. The altruism comes through with her dedication to family throughout her transformation between crime fighting roles.

In discussing the female hero's journey, Sandra J. Lindow observes, "Women, like men, attain heroism through the pursuit of truth."[11] Part of Angela was always searching for a lost part of herself or, perhaps, this forgotten piece of her family's past. Discussing heroines in modern mythological popular culture, Lindow continues, "the protagonists of these tales are all traumatized by encounters with embodiments of evil."[12] Angela is of course traumatized by the home invasion, but she prevails as any intelligent female hero would: with intelligence, creativity, courage, and alliance. As Lindow claims, "rugged individualism is out; networking is in."[13] Angela, and the *Watchmen* universe as a whole, show that heroism must be an altruistic team sport, otherwise it runs the risk of individuals losing sight of serving the common good.

JOSEPH CAMPBELL AND THE MONOMYTH

One of the best tools for finding meaning in the trajectory of a heroic narrative is the classic "hero's journey" established in Joseph Campbell's *Hero with a Thousand Faces*. Campbell's sense of world mythology offers a template we can use to test, and then analyze, what it means to be a superhero.

We don't wish to make any claims for Campbell's mythic archetype beyond its usefulness as a heuristic prism, one that throws narrative structures into sharper relief. In the case of Lindelof's *Watchmen* series, Angela (Regina King) and her "mask" (Sister Night) serves as an excellent example of Campbell's hero's journey in the way her narrative creates meaning and relatability. The characters surrounding Angela/Sister Night offer counterexamples of failed journeys which, nonetheless, provide their own opportunities for relatability.

That kind of relatability, as Campbell accounts for it, is found in the axioms on which he grounds his interpretation of mythology in general: that myths are relational narratives rather than explanatory discourses (that is, their function it to put us into relation with the world rather than explain the world) and that Jungian psychology provides a kind of model for what makes any experience, mediated by narrative, relatable to individuals—that these stories, in other words, relate us to experiences common to all human beings. Campbell's approach, despite a few temporal and methodological wrinkles, provides a compelling point of departure for thinking through the great stories of our various cultures, whether identified as myth or not. In the current case, HBO's *Watchmen*, we can situate these modern-day superheroes within Campbell's social-psychological reading of mythological function.[14]

One more nagging detail needs to be addressed before we consider how the HBO *Watchmen* series embodies or reiterates the mythological template Campbell provides: Campbell's use of gender. *Hero with a Thousand Faces* was written in 1948 and embodies the gender paradigms of that era: most tellingly, the question of whether women can be heroic at all. Campbell identifies the hero, as historically depicted in the mainstream of Western mythologies, as male. That is an accurate, historically dependent, depiction, but if we want to make use of his monomyth in an age when these oppressive paradigms are finally beginning to loosen and fade, we must factor out this historicism. Fortunately, it is not difficult to recast the hero's journey in ways that accommodate nonbinary interpretations of gender and, as we'll see, such an adjustment seems to improve the heuristic insight Campbell's treatment provides.

In other words, the obvious challenges to Campbell's work, his dependence on Jung and a gendered 1948-era treatment of "heroes," are not terminal to this approach. You can find places throughout his work where he attempts to shake loose from his own paradigmatic assumptions about gender. For example, Campbell notes, "The hero is the man or woman who has been able to battle past his [or her] personal and local historical limitations to the generally valid, normally human forms."[15] Angela's connection to Campbell's journey will show how its applicability is not shackled to the shortcomings of the era in which it was written.

One of the most useful features of Campbell's monomyth, taken as a heuristic device, is that it can help us recognize plot trajectories within larger, epic narratives that might otherwise have gone unnoticed. These navigational guidelines are difficult to discern directly from the episodes as presented: HBO's *Watchmen* is told in fragmented flash-backs, flash-forwards, and flash-sideways, as if embodying Dr. Manhattan's atemporal worldview—one that seems, to those of us stuck in three dimensions, to be fractured and fractal. Angela's journey, as it unfolds in the episodes, recurses these same fracture lines. However, if we sort out her journey into a normal, three-dimensional, space/time chronology, her path from childhood forward displays the characteristics of Campbell's monomyth. Once we do that, the waypoints, the doors through which she passes on her journey, easily display Campbell's notion of the hero's journey without having to use a shoehorn.

It is of course possible to force any storyline, or piece of a storyline, into Joseph Campbell's mythological scaffolding—but trying on an interpretive scaffolding is a lot like trying on shoes. The shoe box might indicate your exact size, but you still have to try them on, and walk around in them, before you can be sure. The following use of Campbell's monomyth to interpret the plot trajectory of Angela-as-Hero is exactly that kind of walkabout. We begin therefore not where the series begins, during the race riots in Tulsa, but where Angela begins, in Vietnam.

SEPARATION AND DEPARTURE

The hero's journey, according to Campbell, follows the broad outline of separation, initiation, and return with some optional facets within each of these three overarching moments. Separation begins with a call to adventure that can take a number of different forms: some heroes are reluctant, some heroes are thrown into the adventure without being asked, and some heroes refuse to go. Angela's moment of separation, like Luke Skywalker's, was not willing. As a child in Vietnam, she saw her parents killed in a bombing. Thrown into an orphanage, she is catapulted on to the trail, and trial, of her life without the opportunity to refuse.

SUPERNATURAL AID

As the hero embarks on their journey, one of the early stages is the appearance of supernatural aid. This is famously illustrated by the appearance of Obi-Wan Kenobi in the original Star Wars trilogy. Lucas had read Campbell rather deeply and mapped his characters explicitly into Campbell's monomyth.

And here's the first example where reestablishing the chronology of Angela's life makes us consider the role played by different characters. It would be easy to start digging around in the fractal discontinuity of the episodes-as-aired to find an example of an Obi-Wan who comes to Angela's aid—but that begins to require a shoehorn. Tracked chronologically, however, we can observe that magical assistance arrives in Vietnam to rescue her from her orphanage in the person of her grandmother, who, as supernatural assistance often does, explains to her her origins: *where she is from*—Tulsa. Her grandmother delivers the first hint that Angela belongs somewhere and that the world is bigger than the four walls of her orphanage. Once again, the parallels to Luke Skywalker seem clear and interesting. Angela and Luke both come from desert planets.

While Angela's grandmother reveals to her her origins, supernatural aid also appears in the form of a kind police officer who literally hands young Angela her future vocation, the route along which her life toward herohood will be directed: as a police officer. She hands Angela her badge. With her destiny, the compass to her future career now literally in her hands, she crosses the first threshold out of her orphaned life and begins her journey in earnest. The recognition that the path is before us, and that we must follow it, is a crossing of the first threshold. We might even suggest that the Wicked

Orphanage Nanny constitutes this first threshold guardian, overcome by the appearance of Angela's grandmother. The kind police officer, to add extra resonance to the sacrifices often required to overcome threshold guardians, provides a blood sacrifice of her parents' murderer.

BELLY OF THE WHALE

Campbell's next stage, belly of the whale, is the darkest plunge of despair before engaging in the significant portion of her mission as a hero. It is tempting to suggest that this moment is captured by Angela sitting in the orphanage, painting endless Dr. Manhattan dolls (reminiscent of Pinocchio, a marionette himself, who spent time in the belly of a whale on his journey to become a real boy). And there is a gigantic alternative staring us in the face, in both the graphic novel and the HBO series: the giant squid teleported into New York by Ozymandias in order to bring about world peace. As the darkest point in human history, squid or whale, this seems to qualify.

But for Angela we can stick with Campbell's diagnostics and point toward Angela climbing out of the grave site at the sheriff's funeral, and not only because this is the easiest parallel to Luke Skywalker being trapped in a trash compactor. Campbell notes that there is a sense in which any temple interior is a kind of belly of the whale, a place of self-transcendence and initiation. It is only after Angela saves everyone at the funeral and plunges into the tunnel, perhaps significantly inside a small temple-like mausoleum, that Laurie reveals herself and now engages Angela's journey. Passing through the belly of the whale always entails becoming unstuck from a particular worldview or, as Campbell puts it, passing through the "contraries of phenomenality."[16]

It is only at this point that Angela begins to shake herself loose from what she had taken to be her socially established superhero identity—Sister Night, a law enforcement officer working behind a mask—and evolve into her fully authentic superhero identity—one that does not require a badge or a mask.

INITIATIONS AND TRIALS

The belly of the whale marks the beginning of a series of initiations and trials, the next stages in Campbell's monomyth, which liberate the hero from an identity crafted by parental and social expectation. Traditional examples, both mystical and religious, are easy to find, but Campbell translates this stage into "a vocabulary of more modern turn: this is the process of dissolving, transcending, or transmuting the infantile images of our personal past."[17] These infantile images, and self-images, of our personal past are typically acquired from or imposed upon us by our parents or by any figures who embody the authorized socially and culturally sanctioned paradigms—the models by which we come to form our *public* identities. With luck and perseverance, we eventually discover our *true identity* is different from what our parents, or our culture, imposed upon us. As the series progresses, Angela's masked police-work identity is unmasked to reveal her true identity as an authentic hero, and not just another vigilante. Well established in her public, (masked) identity Angela's plot trajectory now requires her to examine how much of this identity is her own and how much is societal imposition.

Here is an opportunity for us to move to "a vocabulary of [a] more modern turn" and reclaim Campbell's insights from his own, historically conditioned and problematic, gender paradigms. The next stages in the hero's journey address this need to move beyond the "infantile images of our personal past," to take off the masks strapped onto us by parental and social expectation and reveal our authentic selves—but Campbell's adherence to the gendered structures of canonical Western mythology, initially, poses a problem.

Campbell identifies the next stage in his treatment of the hero's journey as "meeting with the goddess" and "sacred marriage." Western mythology typically describes a moment when heroes (*male* heroes) encounter a goddess of some kind who tempts them, and Campbell's description highlights his historical frame. "Woman, in the picture language of mythology, represents the totality of what can be known. The hero is the one who comes to know."[18] This sentence explicitly embodies the 4000-year-old Western *Weltanschauung* that the *quest* for knowledge is available only to men. Fortunately, we are no longer bound by these conditions and, I want to say hopefully, neither are Campbell's insights about the structure and function of mythological narrative.

Reconstructed without traditional gender roles in play, we can look to the underlying psychological functions denoted by these metaphors and jettison the constraints imposed by the gender bias inherent to the Western canon—just as *Watchmen* does. These functions are well expressed by replacing Campbell's editorial divisions of "Meeting with the Goddess," "Woman as Temptress," and "Atonement with the Father" with the operationally equivalent headings: "Sacred Marriage" (embracing the reality of our authentic selves), "Temptation" (moving past the temptation to accept the rewards of living a socially prescribed life), and simply, "Atonement" (making peace with the dichotomy between who we are expected to be and who we really are). These sections describe the psychological stages of moving beyond the childhood identity society and parents impose.

SACRED MARRIAGE

If "meeting with the goddess" is problematic, the metaphor of a "sacred marriage" is not. The sacred marriage, operationally speaking, is the hero's moment of embracing the underlying truth of their fate, here understood as their authentic selfhood—their moment of achieving *amor fati*. If we are looking for the mythological chapter in which the hero, on their journey, achieves a mystical marriage, it is an easy matter to find it in *Watchmen*. Dr. Manhattan and Angela begin an affair that Dr. Manhattan, who sees everything trans-temporarily, tells her will end in their marriage. The affair literally ends in marriage: Dr. Manhattan agrees to a ring, not in his nose but in his frontal lobes, in order to become human and move to Tulsa, Oklahoma. And when I say literal, there is the wonderfully delightful scene with Angela and Dr. Manhattan making love in their closet at home so as not to wake up the kids. I'm unable to imagine a better example.

TEMPTATION

If we look at the psychological events that characterize what Campbell describes as "temptation," it is easy to pick out the functional aspects and to notice that none of these is necessarily gender specific. This phase of one's development, understood through Freudian or Jungian lenses, can be characterized as "getting over mom and dad"—or better, "getting over parental and socially sanctioned authority figures." For Angela, Judd Crawford and Laurie Blake provide the temptations of a culturally sanctioned, positively reinforced, and well-rewarded social role. They portray external projections of the hero's internal dialogue with parental and social expectation—and can tempt her to remain within the lines of her chosen profession, the path of law enforcement. Judd is the local false front avatar of law enforcement. Laurie represents an explicit hero's journey—having been a superhero herself and the former lover of Dr. Manhattan—and a path that leads to the highest *socially* sanctioned embodiment of law, the FBI. Both offer Angela socially acceptable (and rewarded) routes forward in life, but, and here's the tricky part, they represent the path as laid out *for her* as distinct from the path *she makes for herself*. The path provided by social sanction is always more tempting (and easier) than, as the Knights of the Round Table did, plunging into the woods where it was darkest and there was no path—the only path to the Grail.

The tension with our relationship to both male and female parental projections, the sanctioned authorities of our culture, "lies in the fact that our conscious views of what life ought to be seldom correspond to what life really is."[19] Angela already knew she was a police officer and a masked police officer at that; this accorded with her conscious understanding of the life she had chosen. But her *true* life wasn't simply to *appear* to be a hero, but to actually *be* one. Had she accepted the imprint of her superiors in the social order—the kind police officer in Vietnam, Judd Crawford, or Laurie Blake—she might have remained a first-rate and even heroic police officer, but she could never have become an authentic, self-actualized hero.

So, how do heroes pass through this stage of their journey? These temptations are typically overcome solely as a result of some inertia (often inherited) in their character[20] and, in Angela's case, this is easy to see: Angela was born disposed to follow the footsteps of her grandfather. Grandpa Reeves himself had veered away from the socially sanctioned and reasonably well-rewarded role for an African American police officer before the civil rights era. He took off the mask of his public uniform to put on a mask that belonged to him alone, becoming the first hero of this story universe: *Hooded Justice*. Angela follows suit. Law enforcement was literally in her blood. The only thing missing, at this stage of her journey, was the knowledge of that inertia—of how her past, her family, and the inevitability of her fate had conditioned her present. Her grandfather supplies this next stage.

ATONEMENT

Campbell describes this stage as "a radical readjustment of his emotional relationship to the parental images. The mystagogue (father or father substitute) is to entrust the symbols of office only to a son who has been effectually purged of all inappropriate infantile cathexes—for whom the just, impersonal exercise of the powers will not be rendered impossible by unconscious (or perhaps even conscious and rationalized) motives of self-aggrandizement, personal preference, or resentment."[21] Once again, we can read between the lines of a 1948 gender bias and find the "at-one-ment" with the true ancestor whose inertia we have inherited and which we must, once again, earn. A regular occurrence in mythological hermeneutics is discovering that what begins as metaphor suddenly appears in blisteringly literal terms. Here, Angela literally becomes One with her grandfather by ingesting his memories via the drug Nostalgia. Even more directly, her grandfather, *qua* mystagogue, had prepared these digestible memories for her: certainly, a clear way to become "at-one" with the (grand)father. The complete truth about her fate is now fully disclosed to her through living and experiencing her grandfather's memories, and this event concludes the stage of initiations into the mystery of her own life.[22]

Having taken Nostalgia, Angela is now fully prepared for the duties that follow, entrusted with the "symbols of office." Translating this stage into a more modern vocabulary, we can say that the just and impersonal exercise of the powers that belong to a person *in virtue of their personhood*, that belong to the hero in virtue of his or her adventure, can be disrupted and made impossible when "motives of self-aggrandizement, personal preference, or resentment" override the call of their true, authentic selves. Angela survives these perils and, through reliving the memories of her grandfather, is entrusted with the symbols of authentic adulthood, if we use the Jungian language. At least, she is now equipped psychologically to endure the rest of her adventure.

I'm struck by the three motives Campbell references: self-aggrandizement, personal preference, and resentment. In the course of most spiritual adventures, there is an ever-present danger posed by *success*—and that is, rather than transcending the limits, the chains, of infantile cathexes in order to grow beyond what society expects (girdled by expectations and choked into an acceptable social construct by the psychological molds of parents and peers), the hero will appropriate this psychological equipment to double down on their role as defined by the limits, and the barbed wire, of their social construction. In the language of *Star Wars*, it is to fall into the power of the Dark Side.

Personal preference and resentment especially recall Nietzsche's critique of ethics—the idea that personal preference, rationalized in and by the structures of social norming, will dictate the possible range of one's desires and aspiration. The problem of course is that being locked into personal preference, preferences established not as a result of the great adventure but as a result of upbringing and social conditioning, the hero can never become who they really are. Resentment is the bitter aftertaste of not being allowed to act on one's infantile, personal preferences. It is a bitter aftertaste people come to love and long for and then impose on others. Angela, however, never falters.

APOTHEOSIS

Campbell identifies the next stage, apotheosis,[23] with the figure of the bodhisattva, an individual who having achieved enlightenment decides to remain engaged in the world to help others on their own journeys. Jennifer Stuller's analysis of contemporary female superheroes observes that these characters "have a Bodhisattva nature" where the hero delays their own nirvana in order to help others along the way.[24] This is the moment when, having set aside their personal egos, compassion for others takes over, and their true nature is revealed—to others as well as to themselves. Nostalgia gave Angela a God's-eye-view of her life, including the generations before her—her own karmic inertia as it were—and she finds herself on a footing similar to Dr. Manhattan's (who is, after all, "God—and he's American"). Even more resonant with this piece of narrative scaffolding, when she recovers from her Nostalgia overdose at Lady Trieu's lab, she finds herself *plugged into an elephant* as part of her therapy. The Hindu elephant god Ganesha is the overcomer of obstacles, and this is another in a series of nods toward the metatextual Hindu themes of deity, which are hidden in plain sight throughout the series (e.g., Dr. Manhattan and Angela are both depicted in the series' advertising in glowing Krishna blue).[25] Initiations, at-one-ment, and apotheosis completed, Angela is now ready for the final stages of her journey, achieving what Campbell identifies as the ultimate boon.

ULTIMATE BOON

Campbell's characterization of the ultimate boon describes the moment when the power to save the world first comes to the hero. It's the moment when Jason grabs the Golden Fleece, when Parzival walks back into the Grail Castle a second time, or that moment when Luke throws down his lightsaber and tells the Emperor he can't be turned. For Angela, this moment occurs when she brings Manhattan ("God," remember) back from his "sleep" as her "husband" and attempts to rescue him from the Seventh Kavalry.[26] We see here her fully formed agency, taking up the power waiting there for her all along. This is an acceptable moment to identify as the boon since "this was the moment," Dr. Manhattan tells us, when he fell in love with her—just before he's captured and at the moment she acts to save the world from the Seventh Kavalry and Lady Trieu. It is the moment that caused him to petition[27] Angela, years earlier in a bar in Vietnam (in Angela's timeline, but at the same time for Manhattan), to marry him and the moment when Dr. Manhattan admits that he can pass on his power and promises it to Angela. As Campbell notes, the deities who possess and/or guard this power "dare release it only to the duly proven"[28] and, at this point, that's Angela.[29]

But now that the imperishable is promised to Angela, she still must bring that back and save the world. This is the return.

RETURN

Re-entry is not always easy. Mythology is littered with examples of heroes who, having achieved the boon (the Holy Grail, the Golden Fleece, victory at Troy) have a hard time bringing it home. Some of these same mythological difficulties confront Angela. Here's one: Campbell notes that it is common for heroes, once they achieve the boon, to refuse the return. Heroes have the opportunity to claim their reward and leave the world behind. This often appears as one of the final temptations along the path. Buddha, after his enlightenment, thought about leaving but decided to stay in the world. Angela does too. But even if you want to go home with the Grail, or just get back to Kansas like Dorothy, it is not always as easy as clicking your heels. Sometimes the hero must return to the world challenged for the powers they now possess, pursued in a "magical flight" or "rescued from without." It is an easy matter to identify explicit analogies to these transitions as *Watchmen* moves toward its conclusion.

THE MAGICAL FLIGHT

In another metaphorically literal plot twist, *Watchmen* gives us a "magical flight" when Lady Trieu teleports the now restored Dr. Manhattan, and the whole cast, to the site of her attempted deification. The analogies to Campbell are a bit less precise here but remain compelling. Campbell describes the flight of Jason, carrying home the Golden Fleece, and how in order to slow down the pursuing king, Medea convinced him to cut up her younger brother so that the following ships would have to stop and collect the pieces. The idea here is clearly that one must sacrifice pieces of whatever is held most dear in order to return safely with the great prize. At the end of this magical flight, Dr. Manhattan himself is sacrificed in order to secure the remaining adventure for Angela.[30]

RESCUED FROM WITHOUT

All that teleporting surely constitutes a magical flight, but *Watchmen* is more explicit in the way it reiterates the theme of "rescued from without." During a lapse in the containment field holding him, Dr. Manhattan transports Adrian, Laurie, and Looking Glass to Adrian's secret hideaway in Antarctica, so that they could save the day—since, of course, Dr. Manhattan had already seen it happen. In order to disrupt the engineered ascension of Lady Trieu—who had been prepared by intellect but not by a hero's journey of her own—Adrian creates an apocalyptic rain, a fusillade of frozen squid, to destroy her machinery. It succeeds. Lady Trieu is prevented from assimilating the unearned power of Dr. Manhattan. She and her minions are destroyed in the squid storm, and the power is preserved for Angela, the true heir to this salvific power—although we don't know it yet.

But we're not quite done.

CROSSING THE RETURN THRESHOLD

On their way home with the boon all heroes must cross a return threshold. In Campbell's language, "the returning hero, to complete his adventure, must survive the impact of the world."[31] Angela endures that impact, literally the impact of a million frozen squid, in the steel-encased "Call-Dr-Manhattan" phone booth. Having endured this impact, she goes down the street to the theater where the entire series began, where she finds her grandfather (her past) and her children (her future) safe and sound. Having begun in the mundane world of policing, here at the end of her journey, now a fully authentic agent of not merely law, but of justice, she finds herself a master of both worlds.

MASTER OF THE TWO WORLDS

When she discovers her grandfather safely ensconced with her children in the theater, the cycle of her journey is complete. The future has been saved and the past redeemed.

In what we could characterize as a very Dr. Manhattan point of view, Angela's return to that theater completes a hero's journey that encompasses both her own chronology and the flashback-fractured chronology of the series itself. The series begins and ends in the same theater. This is the kind of happy recursion—that a theatrical presentation should begin and end, literally, in a theater—we can depend on a graphic novel to make explicit. This is what a successful journey looks like at the end. In Campbell's words:

> The meaning is very clear; it is the meaning of all religious practice. The individual, through prolonged psychological disciplines, gives up

> completely all attachment to his personal limitations, idiosyncrasies, hopes and fears, no longer resists the self-annihilation that is a prerequisite to rebirth in the realization of truth, and so becomes ripe, at last, for the great at-one-ment. His personal ambitions being totally dissolved, he no longer tries to live but willingly relaxes to whatever may come to pass in him; he becomes, that is to say, an anonymity. The Law lives in him with his unreserved consent.[32]

Angela is no longer just a police officer: the law itself now lives in her with her "unreserved consent." This is the true meaning of freedom and the end of the hero's journey.

FREEDOM

After all of this, what about Dr. Manhattan's promised powers? Without those, Angela can never fully act as the person she's become. Then she remembers the egg where Manhattan's powers are stored. In the closing scenes, she goes home, eats the egg, and, in the final moment of the series, begins almost to step onto the surface of her swimming pool—something Manhattan had told her would be important. The audience is left to decide if she's truly able, like Manhattan, to walk on water,[33] but we're given every indication. As she's about to step onto the surface of her swimming pool, the Beatles' "I am the Walrus"[34] plays in the background.

With this gesture, she has returned to the world with the power to redeem the world. Recall that in the series' advertising poster, she is depicted, a bit more than suggestively in retrospect, as blue—just like Manhattan.

CONCLUSION

While Campbell takes great pains to explore the depth and history of classical mythology, it also prompts us to ask where we are today, mythologically speaking. The simple answer is that the story of our relationship to the cosmos, originally provided in the narrative myths of Gods and demigods, is now cast with heroic human beings. Campbell observes, "This is the line where creation myths begin to give place to legend—as in the Book of Genesis, following the expulsion from the garden [. . .] The heroes become less and less fabulous, until at last, in the final stages of the local traditions, legend opens into the common daylight of recorded time."[35] We all live in the shadow of history. Our heroes, just like us, must reflect on where we've been as a culture and how we can move forward.

The HBO *Watchmen* series, like the original graphic novel, steps in to address what mythology has become—it is the means by which we relate ourselves to the world we inhabit, a world no longer conditioned by and subservient to a religiously saturated universe, but a universe now filled with the harder surfaces of economic and social relations. Campbell argues that gods can no longer hide in modern society: "The social unit is not a carrier of religious content, but an economic-political organization. Its ideals are not those of the hieratic pantomime, making visible on earth the forms of heaven, but of the secular state, in hard and unremitting competition for material supremacy and resources."[36] The subsequent sequels and prequels to *Watchmen*, in comics and on television, have continued this tradition of social engagement by engaging human histories while examining the nature of heroism.

We are left with the common daylight of Tulsa, Oklahoma, where Angela's grandfather, the first of these alt-historical heroes, was tucked safely into an escaping vehicle—like Superman—as his birthplace burned. Campbell's work focuses on how the mythological process puts humans into relation to their world—a world once informed by religious concerns but that now, as he points out, has all but vanished: "All of which is far indeed from the contemporary view; for the democratic ideal of the self-determining individual, the invention of the power-driven machine, and the development of the scientific method of research have so transformed human life that the long inherited, timeless universe of symbols has collapsed."[37] This explains why heroes today look like Angela rather than Parsifal, or Herakles, or even Superman. She is more like "one of us," a relatable, altruistic, and principled human.

In discussing the modernity of superheroes, Aldo J. Regaldo observes that superheroes represent "the potential for shirking off the modern forces that constrain us."[38] Angela, like many other superheroes before her, "inspire[s] an unyielding struggle against the metaphorical steel that cages human agency in the pursuit of pro-social agendas."[39] The metaphor is completed when we, as the viewer, see something of ourselves in the hero. Comics writer and erudite scholar of the medium Grant Morrison found such a connection in *Supergods*. As Morrison wrote, "We can divide atoms . . . we can fly across the Atlantic in hours, access any information instantaneously . . . we have online secret identities, other lives, missions. Everyone is special, everyone is a superhero now."[40]

NOTES

1. Kimberly Ricci, "Damon Lindelof Has Launched a Respectful F-Bomb toward Original 'Watchmen' Creator Alan Moore," *UPROXX*, July 25, 2019.

2. Geoff Klock, "The Revisionary Superhero Narrative," *The Superhero Reader*, ed. Charles Hatfield, Jeet Heer, and Kent Worchester (Jackson: University Press of Mississippi, 2013), 117.

3. Richard Reynolds, "Heroes of the Super Culture," *What Is a Superhero?*, ed. Robin S. Rosenberg and Peter Coogan (Oxford: Oxford University Press, 2013), 53.

4. Reynolds, 53.

5. Jeph Loeb, "Making the World a Better Place," *What Is a Superhero?*, ed. Robin S. Rosenberg and Peter Coogan (Oxford: Oxford University Press, 2013), 10.

6. Richard Reynolds, "Masked Heroes," *The Superhero Reader*, ed. Charles Hatfield, Jeet Heer, and Kent Worchester (Jackson: University Press of Mississippi, 2013), 106.

7. Jennifer Stuller, "What Is a Female Superhero?" *What Is a Superhero?*, ed. Robin S. Rosenberg and Peter Coogan (Oxford: Oxford University Press, 2013), 19.

8. Peter Coogan, "The Hero Defines the Genre, the Genre Defines the Hero," *What Is a Superhero?*, ed. Robin S. Rosenberg and Peter Coogan (Oxford: Oxford University Press, 2013), 19.

9. Coogan, 4.

10. Coogan, 6.

11. Sandra Lindow, "To Heck with the Village: Fantastic Heroines, Journey and Return," *Heroines of Comic Books and Literature*, ed. Maja Bajac-Carter, Norma Jones, and Bob Batchelor (Lanham: Rowman & Littlefield, 2014), 4.

12. Lindow, 12.

13. Lindow, 12.

14. Joseph Campbell, *The Mythic Dimension*, New World Library; Reprint Edition (March 14, 2017), 221.

15. Joseph Campbell, *The Hero with a Thousand Faces*, originally published in 1949 (Novato: New World Library, 2008), 14.

16. Campbell, *The Hero*, 77.

17. Campbell, *The Hero*, 84.

18. Campbell, *The Hero*, 97.

19. Campbell, *The Hero*, 101.

20. Consider the number of Greek heroes who turn out to be the children of Zeus or one of the other deities.

21. Campbell, *The Hero*, 115.

22. The senator fails here, when he attempts to take Manhattan's power and is turned into goo, in much the way Phaeton is when he attempts (too soon!) and fails to drive the solar chariot.

23. "To deify" or "to make like a God."

24. Jennifer Stuller, "Love Will Bring You to Your Gift," *The Superhero Reader*, ed. Charles Hatfield, Jeet Heer, and Kent Worchester (Jackson: University Press of Mississippi, 2013), 239.

25. A set of analogies and associations which probably require their own separate article. Google provides a myriad of examples.

26. Taking the Veidt designed ring from his forehead, Angela "grabs the brass ring" so to speak. Obvious puns like this are often symptomatic of a hermeneutic verification.

27. Boon (n.) late 12c., *bone* "a ***petition***, a prayer," from Old Norse *bon* "a petition, prayer," from Proto-Germanic **boniz* (source also of Old English *ben* "prayer, petition," *bannan* "to summon"). Mythological discourse is always startlingly obvious, almost cliché or pun-like, when you see the relevant connections (cited from etymonnline.com, July 2020).

28. Campbell, *The Hero*, 155.

29. Neither the senator (scorched, like Phaeton, by an unfiltered exposure to the power of Dr. Manhattan) nor Lady Trieu (the illegitimate daughter of Adrian Veidt who, like Icarus perhaps, flew too close to the sun) was worthy to receive it.

30. Campbell, *The Hero*, 176.

31. Campbell, *The Hero*, 194.

32. Campbell, *The Hero*, 204–5.

33. Joanna Robinson, "The Final *Watchmen* Easter Egg Goes Deeper Than You Think," *Vanity Fair*, December 16, 2019.

34. "I am the egg man!"

35. Campbell, *The Hero*, 271.

36. Campbell, *The Hero*, 334.

37. Campbell, *The Hero*, 333.

38. Aldo J. Regaldo, *Bending Steel: Modernity and the Superhero* (Jackson: University Press of Mississippi, 2015), 228.

39. Regaldo, 228.

40. Grant Morrison, *Supergods: What Masked Vigilantes, Miraculous Mutants, and a Sun God from Smallville Can Teach Us about Being Human* (New York: Spigel & Grau, 2012), 401.

Chapter 4

"AN EXPENSIVE BIT OF FAN FICTION"

Negotiating Canon and Multiplicity in *Watchmen*

LAURA E. FELSCHOW

In 2018, HBO announced that the next project for Damon Lindelof, popular showrunner of *Lost* (ABC 2004–2010) and *The Leftovers* (HBO 2014–2017), would be the development of a television series based on Dave Gibbons and Alan Moore's *Watchmen*. Fan reaction to this news might have best been described as a collective groan.[1] Zack Snyder's 2009 feature film adaptation of the comic book property received tepid reviews and box office earnings of $186 million.[2] While those numbers may outwardly seem like a box office success, with a production budget of $130 million, its financial and critical performance was a let-down for Warner Bros. studios.[3] Did audiences—and *Watchmen* fans in particular—really want to see another adaptation of the same material so soon?

Lindelof was an outspoken fan of both the original material and Snyder's film adaptation. In the "Re-Reading *Watchmen*" series on the amateur comics news website Comic Book Resources, Lindelof called *Watchmen* "the greatest piece of popular fiction ever produced," credited it as a major influence on all of his own writing, and praised the feature film as the "most married-to-the-original-text version of *Watchmen* that could have been made."[4] However, after HBO's announcement of the forthcoming television series and initial negative fan response, Lindelof took to Instagram and, in a five-page letter, semi-clarified his approach to the material. After apologizing to fans angry at his involvement, Lindelof professes his utmost respect for writer Alan Moore—and to lesser extent, artist Dave Gibbons—and attempts to assuage fans by reassuring them that he finds their ire to be only proof of their love and dedication to the same text that he himself loves. Lindelof then lays out his and his collaborators' creative vision for the television series:

> We have no desire to "adapt" the twelve issues Mr. Moore and Mr. Gibbons created thirty years ago. Those issues are sacred ground and they will not be retread nor recreated nor reproduced nor rebooted.
>
> They will, however, be *remixed*. Because the bass lines are just too good and we'd be fools not to sample them. Those original twelve issues are our Old Testament. When the *New* Testament came along, it did not erase what came before it. [. . .]
>
> To be clear. *Watchmen* is canon.
>
> But we are not making a "sequel" either. This story will be set in the world its creators painstakingly built . . . but in the tradition of the work that inspired it, this new story must be *original*. It has to vibrate with the seismic unpredictability of its own tectonic plates. It must ask new questions and explore the word through a fresh lens. Most importantly, it must be *contemporary*.[5]

I quote this at length because it aptly demonstrates the positioning of the television series in relation to the original text—and importantly, in relation to nothing else. Lindelof prioritizes Moore and Gibbons's twelve issues and disregards all other entries into the *Watchmen* franchise: the feature film adaptation, the prequel *Before Watchmen* comics (DC Comics 2012), and the *Doomsday Clock* sequel comics (DC Comics 2017–2019). In his letter, he doesn't even acknowledge their *existence*, much less rate them any importance. When Lindelof writes that "*Watchmen* is canon," the referent is the original series and the original series only. Similarly, this letter also demonstrates Lindelof's promotion of the series as a new entry into that specific canon, a "remix" set in the same storyworld but not, as he believes, a sequel. In short, Lindelof is outlining the television series as an entry in a new transmedia franchise without explicitly using this terminology, while simultaneously articulating that his series is engaging only with certain parts of the already-existing *Watchmen* comic book story universe.

While *Watchmen* the television series does reference specific events from the original text, such as the rain of squid or elements of the Minutemen material, it does not adapt the majority of the original text, nor its prequels nor sequel comics. It expands on the original *Watchmen* comic book universe familiar to fans while ostensibly still standing on its own as a television program that is also enjoyable to those previously unfamiliar with the *Watchmen* property. Here though, lies the crux of one central issue facing the television series: Who, precisely, is it for? This reverence to canon makes it seem as if established fans will hold a place of privilege in approaching the television text. Lindelof penned this open letter to diehard *Watchmen* fans. He promotes the forthcoming material as "original" while taking great pains to position the series as significantly beholden to Moore and Gibbons's comic book run. The nine produced episodes do little narrative handholding to situate those new to the *Watchmen* storyworld, providing little backstory for continuing characters from the original *Watchmen* comics and taking even less time to explain how all the characters, old or new, arrived at the narrative moment of the series' start. From this angle, the television show seems to be catering to the already existing fan base; if others come along for the ride, then so be it.

However, at the same time as canon is revered, the *Watchmen* television series challenges the ideas of canon in significant ways. It asks those already-existing fans to engage with the series in the same way that comic book readers might engage with comic book narratives: to hold multiple versions of *Watchmen* in mind at the same time, much as Dr. Manhattan can see multiple layers of time unfolding simultaneously. Yes, there is the *Watchmen* that consists of twelve issues of comics and nine television episodes, and at the same time there is the *Watchmen* that exists as original, prequel, and sequel comics, and at the same time there is a *Watchmen* feature film that differs significantly from the original text, and at the same time there is a motion comic of the graphic novel . . . so on and so forth.[6]

The television series also challenges the formation of canon itself in its narrative content and disrupts how canon-making is usually a privilege of white men. The TV series brings to the fore important, real-world historical events that are nearly always left out of the historical canon within the US educational institutions, and it also reframes *Watchmen* itself through a lens that prioritizes Black characters and Black stories while deliberately challenging default assumptions of the unknown identity of superhero Hooded Justice as white. In this way, the question of "who the television series is for" becomes complicated. The gatekeepers of comic book canon are primarily white men, just as the gatekeepers of the historical canon in US schools are primarily white men. By revering canon and at the same time attempting to "remix" it, *Watchmen* is attempting to satisfy different types of audiences: "traditional" comic book readers constructed in public discourse as gatekeeping white male fans, and other comic book fans oft-ignored in this construction; HBO viewers in search of so-called "quality" content that are also constructed in public discourse as gatekeeping white male viewers, and other new, hopefully more "diverse" television viewers previously unfamiliar with the *Watchmen* comic series.

MULTIPLICITY VERSUS CANON

In comic book storytelling, particularly in relation to superhero comics at the Big Two companies of DC and Marvel, the concepts of multiplicity and canon are frequently in tension. Multiplicity refers to myriad incarnations of the same character. In relation to comics, this means that multiple versions of the same character exist throughout a company's history, and/or multiple versions of the same character exist *now*, at the same time, on the shelf in your local comic book store. As fan and comics studies scholar Henry Jenkins states, "Multiplicity allows fans to take pleasure in alternative retellings, seeing the characters and events from fresh perspectives, and comics publishers trust their fans to sort out not only how the pieces fit together but also which version of the story any given work fits within."[7] For example, 2018's superhero comic book movie *Spider-Man: Into the Spider-Verse* demonstrates this idea nicely, centering its entire narrative around the collision of multiple Spider-Men from multiple universes.

Canon, however, labels one of these multiple versions of a character as "the" version, with other interpretations taking on secondary status in different narrative universes. To remain with Spider-Man as an example, in Marvel Comics, Peter Parker is the canon Spider-Man (Universe 616), while Miles Morales is the Spider-Man in the Ultimates universe. What is and is not canon is integral to preserving the idea of continuity—keeping the elements of a character's story consistent across a serialized narrative. In superhero comics, a single character's serialized narrative can extend not months or years but decades, which is often why superhero comics are seen as daunting labyrinthine narratives for new readers to enter.

The head editors at comic book companies themselves are usually the arbiters of this canon and often "re-set" canon with major event series and new #1 issues when it is felt a narrative universe is becoming too unwieldy or when a particular narrative approach is no longer selling to fans. The most recent and much-discussed example of corporate powers deciding the limits of canon is within the *Star Wars* universe. Since the release of the first *Star Wars* film in 1977, decades' worth of story material has been created across multiple media, including comics, novels, animated and live action television programming, live action and animated films, video games, and more. This is referred to as the *Star Wars* Expanded Universe. However, when LucasFilm was purchased by Disney in 2012 and the conglomerate announced plans in 2014 for a new trilogy of films, the thirty-plus years of content created for the Expanded Universe was officially excised as canon.[8] This move on the part of Disney upset legions of *Star Wars* fans who had invested much of their time and money into the Expanded Universe.

Canon is a loaded concept often weaponized at the corporate level to demonstrate to fans where the true power over intellectual property lies. Furthermore, as arbiters of canon at the corporate level are usually white and male, what gets coded as canon often reflects the race and gender of those in power. One need only look back at the previous reference to Spider-Man to see how white Peter Parker is the canonical Spider-Man, while Afro-Latino Miles Morales is the alternate universe Spider-Man. This is the dominant mode within superhero comic properties and attempts to alter canon—for example, canonically promoting Carol Danvers from Ms. Marvel to Captain Marvel, who was originally a male character—is a source of contention within comic book fan communities wherein some contingents of white, male fans vociferously protest any changes to canon that alter the stable of white, male superheroes. At its core, canon predominantly centers whiteness, maleness, and heteronormativity—among many other aspects of identity—and reinforces existing societal power structures. Characters of different genders, races, sexualities, ability, etc. are usually relegated to narrative threads of multiplicity: the alternate universes secondary to the canonized universe that reinforces patriarchy, white supremacy, and heteronormativity.

Canon is also weaponized by fans in order to construct hierarchies within fan communities and to police fandom membership, also in racist and sexist ways. As fan studies scholars such as Suzanne Scott, Bertha Chin, and Bethan Jones have noted, gatekeeping and fan policing is an all-too-common practice that seeks to limit who can and cannot actively take part and "belong" within a fan community. Within comics and comics-related media fandoms, this practice is particularly fraught. In *Fake Geek Girls*, Scott outlines how white male fans act proprietarily over popular culture and purposefully and actively marginalize others unlike them who seek to participate in fandom. Proving one's own encyclopedic knowledge of canon in regard to the object of fandom is one of the commonly used methods of policing fandom participation.

When comic book properties get adapted to or expanded across other media such as film and television, ideas about canon and multiplicity come along in these transitions, and approaches to canon or multiplicity have come to guide corporate strategy. In "From Stories to Worlds: The Continuity of Marvel Superheroes from Comics to Film," David Sweeney articulates some key differences between Marvel and DC's approaches to continuity and multiplicity from the 1940s through the 2010s. Under the guidance of editor-in-chief Roy Thomas, Marvel Comics has historically been more focused on preserving continuity and being perfectly clear in corporate missives as to which storylines are canon and which are not, while DC Comics has frequently let continuity become more unwieldy, often necessitating massive resets of their entire comic line in order to untangle the narrative web.[9] These attitudes toward canonization have also dictated their narrative approaches as they expanded their superhero properties into other media, particularly as the production of superhero media has increased rapidly in the 21st century.

For example, Marvel focused on the creation of the Marvel Cinematic Universe (MCU), bringing its live action feature films, live action broadcast, basic cable, and streaming television programs, short films, and other media in line with a transmedia universe marketed as a coherent canon under the tagline #ItsAllConnected. The extent to which Marvel succeeded in this strategy—and the degree to which it even *tried* to succeed in this strategy—is debatable, but public position was that the transmedia MCU would have its own strict canon, with different films and television shows hopefully drawing audiences into the overarching MCU narrative. Under the auspices of Warner Bros., DC, in contrast, carried over multiplicity into its television and film properties, offering viewers entirely separate narrative universes on film and TV: the DC Extended Universe (DCEU) for film, the fan-dubbed Arrow-verse on broadcast television, and a mix of not-necessarily related programs on basic cable and streaming platforms. DC embraced audience segmentation, with its television programming on the CW starkly different in aim and tone than its feature film offerings, and with little concerted effort to merge these audiences into a larger pool of viewers following all DC properties across multiple media. DC's focus on multiplicity rather than canon has led to an increase in inclusive representation both on-screen and behind-the-scenes. While representation is only one measurement of diversity and arguably not a very effective one, multiplicity does lend itself to increasing different types of representations due to the lack of slavish regard for canon.

I take this space to briefly outline these differing approaches because *Watchmen* is a DC property, and therefore the television series is part of an already-existing corporate narrative strategy. Lindelof's "remix" approach to the original material would most likely not have been greenlit and produced if it were part of an operation focused on creating a coherent transmedia canon. Even though Lindelof, prior to the production of the series, carefully cultivated the appearance of devotion to a "sacred" canon, *Watchmen* actually demonstrates DC's strategic engagement with multiplicity.

WHO WATCHES THE DC UNIVERSE?

The television run of the *Watchmen* series occurred around the same time as the conclusion of *Doomsday Clock*, the comic book sequel series to *Watchmen*, written by Geoff Johns and drawn by Gary Frank. Because two differing versions of "after" the original series were being offered to audiences simultaneously, some fans and critics became preoccupied with the question of canon. Comics news and discussion websites like Bleeding Cool, Comic Book Resources, and ScreenRant spilled much virtual ink on the topic. Which continuation of the Watchmen story would be the "official" sequel sanctioned by DC Comics? Which version is canon, and which is the alternate universe?

Moore and Gibbons's original comics presented an alternate universe in and of themselves, marking time from the late 1930s to the mid-1980s in a world where superheroes had become persona non grata with the public, Nixon was still president, the United States had won the war in Vietnam, and the world was on the verge of apocalypse. Moore and Gibbons's twelve-issue story ends with the death of Rorschach and the release of his journal to the public, which reveals Ozymandias's responsibility for the monstrous alien squid attack on New York City. Both *Doomsday Clock* and HBO's series pick up after this event, with *Doomsday* taking place seven years later in 1992 and the TV series taking place thirty-four years later in 2019.

In *Doomsday Clock*, Ozymandias's plan to prevent nuclear holocaust by bringing people on Earth together to fight an alien invasion has failed. His machinations are revealed to the public by Rorschach's journals and the nuclear arms race between the United States and Russia continues. Meanwhile, Dr. Manhattan has entered the DC Universe in search of the hope that will convince him to aid mankind. The *Watchmen* television series posits a world where Ozymandias's plan succeeded, and the nuclear arms race has ceased. Rorschach's writings have instead been utilized as the manifesto of a nationalist hate group, Seventh Kavalry, with particular venom for minorities and law enforcement. Superheroes are still outlawed, but police have taken to wearing masks in order to protect their identities. Dr. Manhattan is presumed to have left Earth, and it is revealed that Ozymandias is imprisoned in outer space as well.

Neither the comics nor the television series was approved of by Alan Moore (who famously despises any attempts to adapt his work), and neither project received assistance from Dave Gibbons. Therefore, neither is afforded the veneer of creator approval that might label it as canon. In "'Who Makes the World?': *Before Watchmen*, Nostalgia, and Franchising," Kathryn Frank cites media critic Robert Loss and comics studies scholar Benjamin Woo's arguments that all *Watchmen* franchise material, as it has not been approved by one of its main creators, denies creators and co-creators' rights and, in Loss' estimation, is "morally reprehensible."[10] DC Comics may own the copyrights to the *Watchmen* material and may do with it as it wishes, but some will look upon comic book prequels, sequels, video games, and TV series as inherently noncanonical despite DC's corporate stamp of approval anyway, because the original series writer does not wish for his original work to be adapted or expanded upon. Neither DC Comics, Warner Bros., or HBO has publicly weighed in on the canon question.

At New York Comic Con in October 2019, Lindelof called the television series "an expensive bit of fan fiction" and said that "we had to be aware that we were appropriating *Watchmen*, that it was not ours."[11] HBO's publicly presented logline for the show similarly emphasized its "remix" status: "Set in an alternate history where 'superheroes' are treated as outlaws, *Watchmen* embraces the nostalgia of the original, groundbreaking graphic novel while attempting to break new ground of its own."[12] The transformative work of fan fiction is oft-derided, particularly by mainstream media, thus Lindelof's performance of self-deprecation and modesty in front of the NYCC audience was one of supplication. Whether this was a rhetorical move to ingratiate himself to judgmental fans or Lindelof really does look at the television series as noncanonical is debatable, but the statement does publicly renounce a canonical status and instead embraces its place as one of many options for those desiring the story of *Watchmen* to continue.

Other media scholars and critics have embraced this positioning of the program as transformative. As Michael Boyce Gillespie puts it in a *Film Quarterly* roundtable about the television series, "*Watchmen* presents itself as a disobedient adaptation that modifies, extends, and redirects the world-making of its source. [. . .] It elaborates on its source not as a sequel, reboot, or even translation, but rather as an adaptation that substitutes speculation and deviation in place of fidelity."[13] This emphasis on "speculation and deviation" places *Watchmen* in the realm of transformative work. In the same roundtable, media scholars Kristen Warner and Rebecca Wanzo echo Gillespie, with Warner stating that the series is "a really successful piece of fan fiction."[14] Wanzo adds: "*Watchmen* does two things that are very standard in fan fiction: it continues a story beyond the existing material, and it thematically reimagines the conceptual center to address a different set of politics."[15]

Doomsday Clock and its positioning in relation to canon is quite different. Speaking in May 2017, Geoff Johns, writer of *Doomsday Clock* and at-the-time DC Comics's chief creative officer, stated that *Doomsday Clock* "will have an impact on the entire DC Universe. It will affect everything moving forward and everything that has come before. It will touch the thematic and literal essence of DC."[16] According to Susana Polo of pop culture website Polygon, the year-long run was "expected to make good on the most shocking promise of DC's Rebirth relaunch," wherein *Rebirth* #1 introduced Dr. Manhattan into DC's new continuity.[17] Issues with the execution of *DC Universe: Rebirth* due to personnel changes in the month prior to *Doomsday Clock*'s release lessened the impact of *Doomsday Clock*, however, with *Rebirth* branding to be removed from all covers.[18] In addition, as *Doomsday* was designed as a standalone story, it was unclear how *Doomsday* really fit into the larger picture. In conversation with *The Hollywood Reporter* in 2020, DC Comics writer Scott Snyder echoed that the original intent was for *Doomsday Clock* to be official canon, a part of ending the previous continuity of *The New 52* and kicking off the new continuity of *DC Universe: Rebirth*.[19] While Snyder may publicly link *Doomsday Clock* to canon, it is also unclear if Snyder's comments represent the official position of DC Comics, or if this is one writer's personal opinion.

If *Doomsday Clock* is considered canon and *Watchmen* the television series is not continuity but instead part of a multiplicity of *Watchmen*-related narratives, this would again relegate to secondary status a property that attempts to ideologically re-orient itself and highlight different axes of identity that frequently are shunted aside in superhero media. While fan studies scholars, including myself, would argue that "an expensive bit of fan fiction" should not be denigrated, the fact remains that in mainstream media the term "fan fiction" is still used pejoratively. However, "fan fiction" from an award-winning showrunner provided a large budget and star-studded cast on a premium cable network like HBO is worlds away from transformative works offered by other fans without access to such a strong, professionalizing sheen. To say that Damon Lindelof is just a hardcore *Watchmen* fan making "expensive fan fiction" is to downplay all elements of power undergirding and legitimizing the work of a white, straight, male television producer and writer with access to valuable resources afforded to someone of his position.

IS CHALLENGING CANON A POLITICAL ACT?

I expend time and space on the question of canon vs. multiplicity because this question is also at the heart of the narrative content of the television series and again prompts consideration of to which audiences the show is trying to appeal. As Michael Gillespie states and Rebecca Wanzo reiterates in the "Thinking about *Watchmen*" roundtable, *Watchmen* makes a concerted effort to remediate American history in multiple ways. The series begins with the Tulsa Race Massacre of 1921, which, as evidenced by fan and press reaction to the pilot episode, is a historical event little known to US citizens today.[20] As Vanessa Etienne writes for *BET* about the 1.5 million viewers for the series premiere, "the majority of those viewers are assumed to be white men. That explains why #BlackWallStreet started trending on social media shortly after the series premiere . . . *Watchmen* snuck a lesson in Black history right in the opening scene that had many people rushing to Wikipedia."[21] The series also centers on a Black woman, Angela Abar (Regina King), while Dr. Manhattan is revealed to be hiding in the form of Angela's husband, Cal (Yahya Abdul-Mateen II). In the original *Watchmen* comic, the identity of superhero Hooded Justice is left a mystery; in the television series, this canonical gap is filled in with the story of Will Reeves (played as a young man by Jovan Adepo and as an old man by Louis Gossett Jr.). In the television version of *Watchmen*, Hooded Justice is both Black and queer, significantly refocusing Hooded Justice's journey to explicitly be about racial and queer injustice in the United States.

While the aim of this chapter is not to discuss *Watchmen*'s attempts to complicate or challenge dominant historiography, I mention these elements because the show's relationship to canon can and should be considered alongside these narrative moves as part of disruptive efforts. If canon is always-already inculcated with dominant ideologies, if canon—whether comics canon or historical canon—is arbitrated by white men, then what does it mean for the *Watchmen* television series to explicitly embrace its transformative status? At the same time, how is this undermined by Lindelof's public reverence for and the series' reliance on the original text and the original text only?

Many fan studies scholars, including Francesca Coppa, Matt Hills, and Henry Jenkins, have written about the potential of fan works as political acts, speaking back to systems of power and creating space for those excluded by dominant ideologies. *Watchmen* does attempt to disrupt the original text, and it does attempt to disrupt dominant modes in US television that traditionally ignore or minimize Black experiences and do not center on Black characters. However, even the series' star, Regina King, assumes that the majority of the *Watchmen* audience is white, stating of her *Saturday Night Live* hosting gig that "If you're white, you probably know me from *Watchmen*."[22] The *Watchmen* brand also lends more recognizability and built-in fan base that helps the show find a necessary foothold in a crowded television landscape. Nevertheless, the way that the television extension of the original comic run simultaneously re-trenches within canon and attempts to open up beyond canon stifles its ideological promise. The audience *Watchmen* seems to be catering to are already-existing fans who may have felt that the original series, while providing political commentary on US culture in the 1980s, still narrowly represented only certain segments of society, and the television series now offers a broader scope more directly engaged with issues of racism, sexism and misogyny, homophobia, etc.

Furthermore, positioning the television series as "fan fiction" or "remix" implicitly addresses the audience as already familiar with the original series. One can certainly engage with fan fiction or a remix without knowing the original text or texts, but the experience is by nature shallower. While the TV program offers viewers new characters and situations that should ostensibly offer an "in" to the show, understanding even these new characters is deepened by an understanding of the already-existing *Watchmen* storyworld. This is not to charge the show with being entirely inaccessible, but it is certainly predicated on either audience familiarity with *Watchmen* canon or viewer willingness to learn about that canon. This dependence on canon is supported by the existence of promotional material that further contextualizes episodes as well as the copious professional and amateur press discourse dedicated to explaining each episode fully in the aftermath of each airing.

Despite generating much press and discussion from these target audiences—both white, male comic book fans, oft-ignored nonwhite and nonmale comic book fans, and the typical HBO demographics of middle-to-upper-class viewers—ratings for *Watchmen* were merely solid, ranging from seven to eight million viewers across the season.[23] Though not a failure by any stretch in the saturated 21st-century television market, *Watchmen* was a far cry from HBO's most recent ratings hits. *Watchmen*'s decision to center Black narratives most likely drew in demographics that may not have engaged with a property like *Watchmen* otherwise, but the high level of engagement with Moore and Gibbons's work confused both television critics and viewers alike. Entertainment news segments on *HuffPost*, *Slate*, and other outlets published articles attempting to explain the confusing elements of the show, often debating whether wading through this narrative confusion is worth the viewers' effort. *Entertainment Weekly* felt the need to publish a primer for the program for viewers unfamiliar with the comic.[24]

Those unfamiliar viewers often echoed television critics' concerns. For example, film blogger Josh Spiegel chronicled his experience viewing *Watchmen* with no prior knowledge of the comics and came to the conclusion that although the cast and aesthetics were pleasing, he found himself "at a bit of a loss about what is actually . . . y'know, *going on* in this show," stating that he found it challenging "to envision the endgame of this show, both because of where the story has gone, and because of how this show connects to the source."[25] Bloggers on *CinemaBlend* and *ScreenRant* made similar statements.[26] A search of message boards on forums like Reddit, RPG, and Stack Exchange reveal multiple threads of questions from confused viewers, while a YouTube search for the television show yields dozens of by-episode video explainers. While the sheer number of engagements like this demonstrate that some viewers take pleasure in both explaining and being explained to, the comments on these types of videos and in online forums also illustrate that a television series predicated on audience tolerance for confusion may also alienate viewers who don't feel that a television show should require homework.

CONCLUSION

The creative decision to set aside comic book sequels and prequels and rely heavily on the original twelve issues of *Watchmen* is fraught, just as any adaptation or expansion of the *Watchmen* property is by its very nature due to Alan Moore's public disapproval. By prioritizing the 1986–1987 run, the *Watchmen* television series is in its own separate transmedia storyverse that consists of *Watchmen*, the comic, and its "remix" sequel of *Watchmen*, the limited television series. It sets aside the debatable canon of *Before Watchmen* and *Doomsday Clock*, along with other *Watchmen*-related properties like motion comics or video games, and instead offers an alternate universe within an alternate universe.

In treating the original *Watchmen* as sacred and at the same time attempting to "remix" it as commentary on Black experiences in the United States, the television series paints itself into a tough corner wherein its messaging is constrained in both its clarity and reach. Steeped in *Watchmen* canon with little explanation for new viewers who may have been tuning in based on the appeal of a Black superhero program, the television series is quite inaccessible for passive or casual viewers. This is not always necessarily a problem, but when the "remix" aims to broaden representation and engage with critical societal issues, limiting the ability of the audience to engage is contrary to that goal. In the end, *Watchmen* gestures toward multiplicity but is too invested in canon to fully embrace the concept. What's the point of an alternate universe if it's not *really* alternate?

NOTES

1. For example, Sydney Bucksbaum, "Damon Lindelof to *Watchmen* Creator Alan Moore: 'F— You, I'm Doing It Anyway,'" *Entertainment Weekly*, July 24, 2019, https://ew.com/tv/2019/07/24/damon-lindelof-watchmen-hbo-series-alan-moore-tca-2019/; Ray Flook, "'Watchmen' Week: Jean Smart, Tim Blake Nelson Talk Fan Reactions, Importance of Divisiveness," *Bleeding Cool*, October 17, 2019, https://bleedingcool.com/tv/watchmen-week-jean-smart-tim-blake-nelson-talk-fan-reactions-importance-of-divisiveness-interview/; Ben Travers, "'Watchmen': Damon Lindelof Reveals Plot Will Be an Original Story vs. Adaptation, Apologizes to Angry Fans," *Indiewire*, May 22, 2018, https://www.indiewire.com/2018/05/watchmen-hbo-series-original-not-adaptation-sequel-damon-lindelof-1201967479/.

2. "Watchmen (2009)—Financial Information," *The Numbers*, https://www.the-numbers.com/movie/Watchmen#tab=summary.

3. "Watchmen (2009).

4. Atom Freeman and Carr D'Angelo, "Re-Reading *Watchmen*," *Comic Book Resources*, March 11, 2009, https://www.cbr.com/re-reading-watchmen-with-lost-co-creator-damon-lindelof/.

5. Damon Lindelof, Instagram post, May 22, 2018, https://www.instagram.com/p/BjFsj6JHEdq/?hl=en.

6. Please see Mark J. P. Wolf, "World-Building in *Watchmen*," *Cinema Journal* 56, no. 2: 119–25 for a more thorough cataloging of all *Watchmen*-related properties.

7. Henry Jenkins, "The Revenge of the Origami Unicorn: Seven Principles of Transmedia Storytelling," *Confessions of an Aca-Fan*, December 12, 2009, http://henryjenkins.org/blog/2009/12/the_revenge_of_the_origami_uni.html.

8. Bryan Hood, "Why Disney Blew Up More Than 30 Years of Star Wars Canon," *Bloomberg*, December 15, 2015, https://www.bloomberg.com/news/articles/2015-12-15/why-disney-blew-up-more-than-30-years-of-star-wars-canon.

9. David Sweeney, "From Stories to Worlds: The Continuity of Marvel Superheroes from Comics to Film," *Intensities: The Journal of Cult Media* (July 2013): 133–50.

10. Kathryn M. Frank, "'Who Makes the World?': *Before Watchmen*, Nostalgia, and Franchising," *Cinema Journal* 56, no. 2: 143.

11. Noelene Clark, "Fans React to HBO's Ultra-Violent *Watchmen* Debut at New York Comic Con," *TV Guide*, November 11, 2019, https://www.tvguide.com/news/watchmen-panel-new-york-comic-con-reactions/?rss=keywords.

12. Emma Stefansky, "Damon Lindelof's HBO *Watchmen* Series Is Officially On," *Vanity Fair*, August 18, 2018, https://www.vanityfair.com/hollywood/2018/08/damon-lindelof-watchmen-hbo-series-order-2019.

13. Michael Boyce Gillespie, "Thinking about Watchmen: A Roundtable," *Film Quarterly* 73, no. 4 (Summer 2020), published online June 26, 2020, https://filmquarterly.org/2020/06/26/thinking-about-watchmen-with-jonathan-w-gray-rebecca-a-wanzo-and-kristen-j-warner/.

14. Gillespie.

15. Gillespie.

16. Aaron Sagers, "Exclusive: DC Comics' Geoff Johns Reveals Teaser, Details on Watchmen/Rebirth Title Doomsday Clock," *SyFyWire*, May 14, 2017, https://www.syfy.com/syfywire/exclusive-dc-comics-geoff-johns-reveals-teaser-details-on-watchmenrebirth-title-doomsday.

17. Susana Polo, "DC Comics Met Watchmen in The Button, Here's What You Need to Know," *Polygon*, May 18, 2017, https://www.polygon.com/comics/2017/5/18/15469254/dc-comics-watchmen-the-button-explained.

18. Cliff Biggers, "DC's Eventful December," *Comic Shop News*, no. 1584, October 25, 2017.

19. Graeme McMillan, "How 'Death Metal' Became a DC Team's Biggest Story Yet," *The Hollywood Reporter*, February 12, 2020, https://www.hollywoodreporter.com/heat-vision/how-death-metal-became-a-dc-teams-biggest-story-1278849.

20. For example, see Bill Kaveney, "How 'Watchmen' Reminds Us of the Tulsa Race Massacre Before Trump's Oklahoma Rally," *USA Today*, June 15, 2020, https://www.usatoday.com/story/entertainment/tv/2020/06/15/watchmen-reminded-tulsa-race-massacre-ahead-trump-rally/3180156001/; Tambay Obenson, "'Watchmen': How the 1921 Tulsa Race Massacre Influences the Series," *Indiewire*, October 23, 2019, https://www.indiewire.com/2019/10/watchmen-hbo-tulsa-massacre-1202182758/; Jennifer Vineyard, "The Tulsa Race Massacre Happened 99 Years Ago: Here's What to Read about It," *New York Times*, October 21, 2019, https://www.nytimes.com/2019/10/21/arts/television/watchmen-tulsa-race-riot.html.

21. Vanessa Etienne, "HBO's Watchmen Gives America a Black History Lesson It Desperately Needs," *BET*, October 22, 2019, https://www.bet.com/celebrities/news/2019/10/22/hbo_s-watchmen-gives-america-a-black-history-lesson-it-desperate.html.

22. *Saturday Night Live*, Episode #901, NBC, February 13, 2021.

23. Kate Arthur, "TV Ratings: HBO's 'Watchmen' Is a Word-of-Mouth Hit," *Variety*, December 4, 2019, https://variety.com/2019/tv/news/hbo-watchmen-ratings-1203425067/.

24. Sam Adams, ""The Casual Viewers' Guide to WTF Is Going On in 'Watchmen,'" *Slate*, December 8, 2019, https://slate.com/culture/2019/12/watchmen-series-explained-hbo-episode-8-post-credits.html; Bill Bradley and Erin E. Evans, "Why 'Watchmen' Is the Best Kind of Confusing," *HuffPost*, November 11, 2019, https://www.huffpost.com/entry/watchmen-hbo-season-1_n_5dc5c536e4b0fcfb7f662066; Christian Holub, "The Beginner's Guide to *Watchmen*: What You Need To Know Going into the HBO Show," *Entertainment Weekly*, October 20, 2019, https://ew.com/tv/2019/10/20/the-beginners-guide-to-watchmen-hbo-show/.

25. Josh Spiegel, "What It's Like to Watch 'Watchmen' When You Know Nothing about the Original Comic," *Slash Film*, November 13th, 2019, https://www.slashfilm.com/watching-watchmen/.

26. Amanda Hurych, "10 Things That Still Don't Make Sense in HBO's Watchmen (Even If You Read the Comic)," *Screenrant*, December 26, 2019, https://screenrant.com/hbo-watchmen-no-sense-show-comic-book/; Mick Joest, "Watchmen: 6 Thoughts About HBO's Show from Someone Who Didn't Read the Comic," *CinemaBlend*, November 14, 2019, https://www.cinemablend.com/television/2484461/watchmen-6-thoughts-about-hbos-show-from-someone-who-didnt-read-the-comic.

Chapter 5

"FUCKING OKLAHOMA"

Peteypedia as Paratextual Transaction and Its Impact on the Aesthetic Experience of *Watchmen*'s Transmedia Storytelling

ZACHARY J. A. RONDINELLI

"You know, Laurie. President can pardon anybody he wants. Anybody. He could even get your owl outta that cage."[1] Senator Joe Keene of Oklahoma sits at the edge of FBI Agent Laurie Blake's black leather sofa as he speaks these seemingly cryptic words. Quickly, the camera cuts to Blake, her facial features frozen in deep contemplation. Behind her in the frame is an Andy Warhol-esque painting featuring three costumed men. The first (top left) wears an owl headdress with yellow-rimmed black goggles. The second (top right), a blonde man wearing a purple mask and golden Egyptian collar. The third man (bottom left) is differentiated because he wears no costume at all. Instead, he stares blankly out at the viewer from his yellow eyes. He is blue, and bald, and bears a strange mark on his forehead.

There is a fourth square in the bottom right corner obscured by Agent Blake's face. In moments, as the scene ends, the camera will slowly pan towards that final panel passing over her right shoulder to reveal the face of a young woman. This woman, who also wears no mask, is dressed in a yellow blouse with a deep neckline that plunges below the artistic frame. Her features bear a striking resemblance to Agent Blake. Before this though, as she contemplates the investigation that Senator Keene has just told her she will be leading into the suspicious death of the Tulsa, Oklahoma, chief of police, Judd Crawford, Agent Blake closes her eyes. The camera shifts to a close up of her face, a crackling fire in the background. Gently, she tosses her head back and sighs.

"Fucking Oklahoma," she says.[2]

QUIS CUSTODIET IPSOS CUSTODES?

In his 2010 book, *Show Sold Seperately: Promos, Spoilers, and Other Media Paratexts*, Jonathan Gray speaks about the long and formidable shadow that a previous work casts on a new work, particularly as it relates to the paratextual aura of audience discussion surrounding it.[3] This is undeniably true in the case of *Watchmen*, a comicbook[4] often acknowledged as one of the medium's all-time best. In a May 22, 2018, Instagram post, Damon Lindelof, creator of HBO's *Watchmen*, declared that he would not be attempting to adapt the work done by the original creative team of the *Watchmen* comics, but would instead create a remixed variation.[5] The letter, as much a plea for viewers to give the show a chance as it was an outline of his method of creation, serves as Lindelof's recognition of the long, dark, and terrible shadow that he knew the original *Watchmen* would cast upon the television series, as well as how that shadow was bound to affect the production of its new media follow-up.[6] Indicative of *Watchmen*'s position as an outgrowth of the original comic, the show's intertextual existence not only forces it to embody previous collective knowledge about the meaning of the original comicbook that informs our *re-entry* into the world,[7] but it also forces us to grapple with how the show is understood outside of its intertextual context as a viewer's first *entry* into the *Watchmen*-verse.

To further illustrate this dichotomy of entry versus re-entry, let us return to the previously discussed scene from *Watchmen*, episode 3, "She Was Killed by Space Junk." A viewer unfamiliar with the comics material (entering into *Watchmen*'s universe for the first time) would be hard-pressed to identify, let alone make meaning from, the costumed faces of the vigilantes that grace the imaginary Warhol on Agent Blakes's wall or understand the oddity of her having a pet owl. While these viewers might be left questioning these details, their inability to make meaning from them does not prohibit them from comprehending the narrative progression of the scene. Based on knowledge collected from the previous two episodes of the series, the viewer can easily ascertain why Agent Blake, who only minutes earlier demonstrated her prowess as a member of the FBI Anti-Vigilante Task Force, is being assigned to the Crawford case. Finally, her sigh and colorful comment about Oklahoma can be understood as a glimpse into her true feelings about the state; clearly, an unimportant piece of the larger narrative puzzle, right?

For the viewer re-entering the world of *Watchmen* (having previously entered through the comics, or maybe the Zack Snyder–directed 2009 *Watchmen* film), it would be a much easier task to make meaning out of the seemingly inconsequential information provided in this scene. Recognizing Nite

Owl II, Ozymandias, and Dr. Manhattan in the faux-Warhol takes little effort, and the artistic connection made between Agent Blake and Silk Spectre II assists with a critical viewer's ability to recognize/conclude that Agent Laurie Blake and Silk Spectre II (who was previously known as Laurie Juspeczyk) are the same person. Once this connection is made, and the viewer remembers her romantic entanglement with Dan Dreiberg, a.k.a. Nite Owl II, her pet owl also becomes a clear nod to their romantic past.

With this positioning of a viewer as either *entering* or *re-entering* the *Watchmen*-verse, the comics infamous question, "*Quis Custodiet Ipsos Custodes?*" ("Who Watches the Watchmen?"), takes on an entirely different meaning. This focus on the question of readership/viewership is important for *Watchmen* because both the comicbook and the HBO series provide the opportunity for a reader/viewer to explore an assortment of transtextual and paratextual material meaning that neither permit their primary mediums to bear the entire load of meaning-making.

While we can easily recognize *Watchmen* as transmedia storytelling simply by the debt that Lindelof's series owes to Moore, Gibbons, and Higgins's comics series, it is potentially less obvious to detect the importance of the role played by the original comics' paratextual back matter. In the original *Watchmen* comics, every issue would feature supplemental back matter containing files, notes, book excerpts, or some other piece of paraphernalia from the universe that readers could explore to better understand the context of the narrative being told. Though they were always contained within the material comicbook, this acted as a sort of proto-transmedia storytelling since the back matter was never presented as comics, but always some other type of media. As testament to Lindelof's dedication to transmedia storytelling, he commissioned show writer Jeff Jensen to create "Peteypedia," a paratextual online website disguised as FBI Agent Dale Petey's digital collection of personal research, interoffice memos to the Anti-Vigilante Task Force, and other important documents. After each episode, a new folder would be made available on the website containing new documents that would force a critical reader to renengotiate meaning that they'd made previously while watching the show.

With this in mind, Peteypedia must be consciously considered alongside HBO's *Watchmen*-as-television series, not simply as backstory or companion to the series' narrative, but as integral to the aesthetic experience evoked from the negotiation and re-negotiation of meaning across and between texts inherent in transmedia storytelling. This chapter intends to map the *entry vs. re-entry* conversation onto the process of *negotiation and re-negotiation* (paratextual transactions) that occur when considering the implications of

Peteypedia on *Watchmen*'s transmedia storytelling. Utilizing a transactional approach (Rosenblatt 1978), I propose that the aesthetic criteria by which transmedia storytelling should be evaluated rests not within the aesthetic object itself, but rather between the object and the reader/viewer (the aesthetic experience). In order to explore how paratextual transactions inform the evocation of aesthetic experiences in *Watchmen*, Agent Blake's journey will serve as an exemplar and demonstrate that while choosing not to engage with Peteypedia may not detrimentally impact one's comprehension of the narrative, it certainly hinders one's ability to evoke the aesthetic complexity of the transmedia text. Ultimately, I aim to position *Watchmen* as an example of transmedia storytelling that successfully leverages intertextuality and paratextual transactions towards the evocation of a unique aesthetic experience that cannot be achieved independently.

PARATEXTUAL TRANSACTIONS AND THE AESTHETIC *EXPERIENCE* OF TRANSMEDIA STORYTELLING

According to Melanie Bourdaa, we live today in a television environment much different than the ones that have come before.[8] This new environment is proving itself to be profoundly impacted by technological development, but even more so, by the influence of the internet: "The internet has become more central to the TV medium, with both official and illicit downloadable shows, transmedia narrative extensions, and the rise of sites like Netflix and YouTube as alternative ways to view a wide range of programming."[9] As it pertains to transmedia storytelling, the encouragement of active participations from viewers by extending the narrative of a storyworld beyond the material limitations of the medium has been made significantly simpler through the access provided by the internet.

Watchmen is by no means the first to take advantage of transmedia storytelling through paratexts on the internet, but Peteypedia stands as a recent example of how this type of paratext can reveal meaningful information that, though not intrinsic to *enjoying* the viewing experience, inform and reshape how one constructs their *understanding* of the primary text.[10] That said, simply by the reality of its intangible digital design, Peteypedia relies upon a particular type of viewer: one who is determined and dedicated to seeking out, finding, and absorbing as much about the storyworld as they possibly can. This is an experience born of the vicarious desire to blur the boundary line between fiction and reality through an engagement with the fictional storyworld as though it were real. Indeed, the existence of storyworld notes and fictional characters' belongings, writings, or other diegetic material becoming accessible within our "real world" not only confuses the concept of fiction and reality, but also our position within it. We want to uncover more about this world, simultaneously real and imagined; the experience of discovery and the bridging of connections between texts is paramount.

With the addition of HBO's *Watchmen*, the universe in which these stories take place becomes an example of drillable transmedia storytelling.[11] Not only do the original comics series and its paratextual back matter become a part of the meaning making process for the show, providing critical knowledge and material for viewers to use as they build connections across media, but the television series and its associated paratext become linked to the original comics, creating opportunities to renegotiate meaning previously considered concretized from the comics series (William Reeves/Hooded Justice's journey demonstrates this). If the plethora of websites dedicated to "forensic fandom" (i.e., hunting for every possible "Easter egg" within the television series in order to catalogue it for other interested viewers) are not enough to demonstrate this, HBO's very own website for the series, Go Deeper Inside the World of Watchmen,[12] certainly does. By acknowledging this, and recalling its paratextual relationship with both the comicbook and Peteypedia, *Watchmen* can be viewed as a narrative that relies heavily on the drillability of its intertextual and paratextual recesses for the purposes of transmedia storytelling. Furthermore, it can be assumed that the larger aesthetic experience meant to be evoked from the series is heavily reliant on the viewer's engagement with these inter- and paratextual relationships.[13]

For theorist Gérard Genette, paratextuality is described as a "threshold"[14] that blurs the boundaries of the text and opens up a liminal space between the inside and the outside of the textual experience. Gray takes this idea of threshold further by relating paratexts to an "airlock that helps the reader pass without too much difficulty from one to the other."[15] Though both of these metaphors adequately describe paratextual function generally, they fail to appropriately emphasize the importance of paratextuality as it relates to the aesthetic experience of transmedia storytelling. This is because both metaphors describe the space between the two texts while ignoring how they are connected.

In contrast to Genette and Gray, I want to suggest that the "threshold" or "airlock" should not be focused on the paratext as it exists between the text and text, but rather on the *experience* as it exists between the texts and the reader/viewer. In this new conceptualization, the paratext, no longer the physical manifestation of the space between, acts instead as the door/gateway that connects the "airlock" (meaning making space) to, at one end, the text, and, at the other end, the reader/viewer. Without it, there can be only a limited meaning-making experience between/across these two agents (an only partially opened door/gateway) and therefore no transmedia aesthetic experience. Intertexts and paratexts then, when opened/read/viewed, are what permit access to the airlock, creating the space where the aesthetic experience can occur; without engaging with/opening the intertext/paratext/door, the viewer/entrant cannot experience/pass through the meaningful transactional space that fosters the aesthetic experiences unique to transmedia storytelling. The constant opening and re-opening of these doors as one goes back and forth between experiences also better assists in the visualization of the transactional process of negotiation and renegotiation that occurs throughout transmedia storytelling. Though not meant to replace socially oriented paratextual theories surrounding more passive consumption of paratexts within the world (commercials, movie posters, social media ads, etc.), it provides an opportunity to consider the experiences of active participants who choose to engage with all that a transmediated world has to offer.

This proposed repositioning of the paratext may seem trivial, but it has a profound impact on the role that a critical reader/viewer plays within the aesthetic of transmedia storytelling. A focus on active reader/viewer participation through forensic fandom and drillability forces one to position the reader/viewer as a primary agent within both the meaning making process and the aesthetic experience of transmedia storytelling, recentering them within the framework. In other words, this shift places the reader/viewer in the driver's seat; they are in control of their own aesthetic experience. From this perspective, "drilling" one text becomes a process of absorbing new knowledge and critically applying that new knowledge in order to renegotiate previously constructed meanings from other texts rather than passively consuming the "mothership" text as it is brought to us.

Supporting this new position is the transactional theory of literary theorist Louise Rosenblatt (1978). According to her, reading and meaning making can be viewed as an event (or *transaction*) between the reader and the text in the pursuit of evoking an aesthetic response.[16] Rosenblatt believed that neither a "generic reader" nor the text-as-object exists;[17] to recognize either as separate, disconnected entities is to reify the position of one over the other, effectively destroying the two-way, transactional relationship that occurs during the process of reading.[18] Therefore, while the text is viewed as a vital actor within the two-way relationship, it is simply one of the two agents involved. To initiate a transaction between text and reader, and thus evoke an aesthetic experience, both must be active in the process; a reader brings their lived experiences, knowledge, background, (etc.) to the text, constructs meaning from it based on both what they bring with them and what the text offers, leaves the text, learns more, and comes back to renegotiate meaning in light of new experiences/knowledge, etc.

It seems as though transmedia studies has lacked a critical engagement with this type of two-way transactional process, and for that reason has found itself speaking mainly to aesthetic qualities that a text-to-text connection can create *for* the reader, or even *by* the reader, but has less frequently considered the aesthetic qualities that are created *with* the reader. That said, during his search for the transmedia aesthetic, Henry Jenkins has suggested that "seriality" and "world-building" are the textual qualities that best lend themselves to a transmedia experience.[19] In his defense of transmedia against David Bordwell in 2009, this shift towards a focus on the experience of transmedia, as opposed to how it is constructed, becomes more evident: "There are also aesthetic pleasures . . . in suddenly understanding how a bit of information consumed in one medium fits into the larger puzzle being laid out for us in a totally different platform."[20] Though I would agree that seriality and world-building, as principles of transmedia storytelling, assist in the revealing of the unique aesthetic experience of transmedia, they cannot and do not succeed in evoking an aesthetic experience on their own. Only through the transactional process initiated by a critical reader/viewer (facilitated by formal qualities of transmedia) does transmedia storytelling's true aesthetic experience reveal itself. These experiences, not a "lightning-strike moment of sense-making"[21] but rather an ongoing process of two-way negotiation and renegotiation, are how we must evaluate the aesthetic of transmedia storytelling.

If, as Jenkins himself suggests, transmedia storytelling is built upon the foundation of integral elements of a fiction dispersed across multiple delivery channels, then altering the experience of one element by another is the ultimate aesthetic goal. As readers/viewers engage with the many texts associated with any given transmedia narrative, their success or failure *as* transmedia must be evaluated based not on their use of seriality, world-building, or any other formal principle, but rather on how well they foster/encourage the transmedia experience. Though Jenkins believes that, ideally, "each medium does what it does best"[22] in transmedia storytelling, this new positioning divorces transmedia aesthetic from medium-specificity.

Certainly, we can evaluate HBO's *Watchmen* on the basis of its success or failure to evoke the television aesthetic, but how would that help us to understand its success or failure as transmedia storytelling? I suggest that a more appropriate way to test for the quality of a transmedia narrative is to explore how profoundly our experience of one text is shaped, or reshaped, by our experiences with another. In other words, this paratextual transaction, the back-and-forth negotiation and renegotiation of meaning that occurs when a critical viewer communicates with, across, and between the text and its paratextual associations, is where the evocation of the transmedia aesthetic truly resides. In the case of *Watchmen*, I ask, How is my experience of the television show changed by its intertextual relationship to the original comics series and its paratextual relationship to Peteypedia? The remainder of this chapter will answer that question by exploring the journey of Laurie Juspeczyk across the *Watchmen*-verse.

"S'ALL A JOKE": PARATEXTUAL TRANSACTIONS AND THE EVOCATION OF TRANSMEDIA AESTHETIC THROUGH *WATCHMEN*'S LAURIE BLAKE

Watchmen creates opportunities for critical viewers to make numerous paratextual transactions throughout the series. Whether it is re-experiencing the comicbook in light of Hooded Justice's newly revealed origins, Ozymandias's plan for world peace in light of the America we enter into during the television series, or the thrill of seeing Laurie Juspeczyk transformed into FBI agent Laurie Blake, there are many opportunities for meaning making across and between the textual realities of the *Watchmen*-verse. Personally, I find Laurie's journey most compelling, in large part because she is, of all the characters that we meet in HBO's *Watchmen*, the most intrinsically tied to paratextual associations beyond the television show. Though an important and meaningful character as head of the Anti-Vigilante Task Force in the show-only narrative, the true aesthetic experience of her story is uniquely mediated through the paratextual transactions that a critical viewer experiences when bringing together the disparate threads provided through Peteypedia. As such, her story, more than any other, demonstrates the power of the transmedia aesthetic experience.

One example of paratextual transaction that requires the viewer to create meaning in collaboration with the show, the comics, and Peteypedia involves better understanding how Laurie became an FBI agent in the first place. In the final issues of *Watchmen*, the last time we see Laurie and Dan, they are discussing their future adventures as vigilante crime fighters together. When the show opens, Laurie is about as far from a vigilante as she could possibly be as the head of the Anti-Vigilante Task Force. How does one reconcile this drastic about-face?

After the fourth episode of *Watchmen* aired, Peteypedia was updated to include a new file folder called "Contents//File_04," featuring two documents.

The first, schematics for a large blue dildo designed and built by Merlincorp, a company Dan Dreiberg owns, is interesting (mainly because it is called "Excalibur," which hints through paratextual transaction at the identity of Dr. Manhattan in the television show, her "Ex" Cal Abar[23]) but is largely unimportant to Laurie's aesthetic journey.[24] The second file, however, titled "interrogation-juspeczyk," is an FBI interrogation transcript from an interview that occurred after Laurie's capture by police in 1995. This file is, arguably, the most important piece of the puzzle that is Laurie Blake.

Though heavily redacted, there is more than enough readable material in the transcript to, at the very least, infer how the Comedienne (Laurie's alias at the time) became FBI agent Laurie Blake. It seems as though, in one last mission together before they parted ways, Nite Owl and the Comedienne successfully intervened with the Oklahoma City bombing on April 24, 1995 (five years later than the historical terrorist attack), preventing the massacre and causing the death of would-be terrorist Timothy McVeigh in the process.[25] Both Dan and Laurie were apprehended by the FBI for breaking the Keene Act that (still) outlawed vigilante crime-fighting. Ultimately, when confronted with the prospect of prison, Laurie threatens to expose Veidt's false peace by revealing to the world the true events of 11/2, the day Ozymandias murdered 3 million Americans in the Extra-Dimensional Incursion Event (EDIE).

Though this document in particular certainly functions to fill some of the gaps that the show leaves in the thirty-plus years between the comics series and the television series, it actually does so much more than that. As the reader interrogates the document, it becomes clear that while Laurie was all too eager to make a deal to ensure her release from prison, Dan was not. At one point in the interview, FBI agent Lattimer suggests that Laurie may be charged with Timothy McVeigh's "murder,"[26] to which Laurie laughs out loud. When Lattimer's suggests that "Dreiberg didn't find it funny . . . He's not talking to us,"[27] a critical viewer could use this information to renegotiate our previous understanding about Dan's peculiar absence from the show.

Recall the scene described at the beginning of this chapter. In it, Senator Joe Keene pledges to get Laurie's "owl outta that cage" and, at the time, while paratextual transaction between the original comics and the show can assist one in recognizing that the owl being referred to here is Dreiberg, and that Keene is insinuating he is in prison, we don't know why. This transcript, though, suggests one possibility: Laurie talked to the FBI first, got what she wanted, and Dan was sent to prison. What this means is that, at the time of the series' beginning, Dan has spent the past two decades in prison and that Laurie herself might be responsible for it.

This document forces the critical viewer to reconsider the meaning originally made from that scene in brilliant and meaningful ways. We can now ascertain that the only reason she didn't refuse Keene's request to go to Oklahoma is because she believed that a Keene presidency might assist her in rectifying this past mistake. It also changes how we look at her dedication to Who; she isn't just taking care of the owl out of past affection for Dreiberg, but more likely because she is responsible for his true owner's incarceration. While she failed to keep the real Nite Owl safe, she is vehement in protecting his surrogate. (In one of her memos found in Peteypedia she says, "Speaking of Who, I hope you dipshits remembered to bring him his mouse today."[28]) Finally, when she tosses her head back and sighs declaring, "Fucking Oklahoma," she does so because it is exactly where Dreiberg was captured. Even though it is a site of immensely painful memories for her, the prospect of freeing him is worth more to her than the discomfort of going back to where it all went wrong.

This realization completely deconstructs the meaning made for Laurie's character in the show-as-text and forces us to reconsider who she is and what her motivations are. By the end of the series, when we discover that Senator Keene is not a well-meaning presidential candidate, but actually the racist leader of the Seventh Kavalry, we're confronted with the realization that all Laurie has done in the pursuit of freeing Dan from prison was for naught. As she sits, tied to a chair, watching the Seventh Kavalry attempt to atomize Dr. Manhattan, we're witnessing not just the failure of the show's heroes, but also her personal failure. Furthermore, not only will Keene not free Dreiberg from prison, but he's also threatening another of her past lovers. It is a tragic moment for her character that one fails to appreciate without the paratextual transactions to evoke the reconstruction of meaning.

Arguably most important to the aesthetic of Laurie's transmedia narrative is the way that her story's conclusion is woven into her tangled relationship with her father, Edward Blake. Peteypedia makes explicit just how important Laurie's father became to her after the events of the comics series. The very last thing Laurie says in the original series is, "Silk Spectre's too girly, y'know? Plus, I want a better costume, that protects me: Maybe something leather, with a mask over my face . . . also, maybe I oughtta carry a gun."[29] This costume that Laurie describes sounds incredibly similar to her father's costume, and, as we've seen, Peteypedia does confirm for us that between the events of the comics and the television series, Laurie takes up her father's old mantle, becoming "The Comedienne."[30]

This is a fairly shocking revelation considering that the emotional climax of Moore, Gibbons, and Higgins's *Watchmen* comes when Dr. Manhattan reveals to Laurie on Mars that she is the offspring of Sally Jupiter and Edward Blake, the Comedian. It was particularly difficult for Laurie to learn this as she had grown up despising the man who had nearly raped her mother during their time together in the Minutemen: "Blake, that bastard, and my m-mother, they . . . they pulled a gag on me is what they did! My whole life's a joke. One big, stupid, meaningless . . . aw, shit."[31] By the time the television series begins, though, Laurie has clearly reconsidered her position because she has not only restyled her vigilante persona after him, but also established a reputation for herself as "Laurie Blake." In this way, she becomes for the critical viewer a personification of paratextual transaction, one whose very name prepares them for the process of negotiation and renegotiation that will inevitably be required to evoke the full aesthetic experience of her story.

If the interrogation document is accurate, then during Laurie's time as the Comedienne she was still operating under the name Laurie Juspeczyk. It seems as though it was only when this identity was taken away from her after joining the FBI that she began to go by Laurie Blake. This shift signals the importance of her father not just to her transmedia narrative, and it also suggests that her *Watchmen* television journey might be less about her correcting her own past failing and more about correcting one of Blake's many wrongs. Though the show does (eventually) provide a brief explanation about her connection to the Comedian, only someone who has read the original comics series will appreciate the complexity of the relationship and how it has impacted who she is on the screen. This becomes particularly important at the series' conclusion.

In the comics series, the Comedian is one of the earliest people to realize what Ozymandias is planning. He is so disturbed by the plot that he breaks into an old enemy's home and sobs at the foot of his bed while rambling about how "it's a joke. S'all a joke."[32] It is this late-night confession that ultimately leads to Ozymandias murdering him at the start of the series. Though it is tearing him up inside, Blake believes that he can do nothing to stop Ozymandias's plot because, though it is horrendous, it will achieve the goal of world peace . . . and what cost is too high for that? It is a macro sacrifice (the lives of three million Americans) that must be made at the micro level (the personal torture of knowing the truth and being able to do nothing about it). It is this same sacrifice that all but Rorschach agree to make, again, at the comics series' conclusion.

For Blake, this becomes an all-encompassing torment. After years spent as a street-level crime fighter, giving up his life for the country that he held most dear, his work was meaningless. As the Comedian, Blake had, by self-admission, done "some bad things,"[33] including rape and murder of children in Vietnam, but by his logic, he "never did anything"[34] like Ozymandias was planning. The realization that it wasn't the Comedian's dedication to the war in Vietnam or his up-close and dirty defense of the streets that saved America from destruction, but rather an art project by the "world's smartest man" on a distant island orchestrated from his throne at Karnaq in Antarctica, both led him to inaction and broke him. He died defeated and ruined, a shell of the "hero" he once was.

Laurie's decision to take up her father's mantle as the Comedienne meant that she could, possibly, right her father's failure. Indeed, her involvement in stopping the Oklahoma City bombing certainly speaks to difference making as a street-level crime fighter by preventing the loss of what were, in the real world, the lives of 168 men, women, and children. But the ultimate gift to her father, and by extension to herself, comes at the end of the television series when she finally holds Ozymandias accountable for his actions thirty years ago: "You killed three million people, Adrian. You're under arrest."[35] When Adrian scoffs at her, saying, "You've kept this secret all this time and now you're having misgivings," Laurie replies by telling him that "people change," before pausing momentarily and finishing, "At least some of us do."[36]

Though a viewer who has not engaged in the paratextual transaction of negotiating and renegotiating Laurie's journey from Silk Spectre to Comedienne, from Juspeczyk to Blake, might consider her final remark a snide jab at Ozymandias, the emotional pause by actress Jean Smart seems to be more a momentary reflection on the past than a glib shot in the present. I read this moment as Laurie's ultimate victory; she has, after over thirty years of dedicating herself to her father's memory, redeemed his (and her) ultimate failure. As the first one to know about Ozymandias's plan, he could have ended it before it began. Even if he'd failed, he'd have been remembered for trying. Instead, he gave up and died a broken man. In this moment, after years of trying, she has finally righted the wrong that the Comedian allowed all those years ago. It is, therefore, poetic that she is the one to finally bring Veidt to justice.

"Good joke. Everybody laughs. Roll on snare drum. Curtains."[37]

THERMODYNAMIC MIRACLES: REDISCOVERING THE IMPORTANCE OF THE "ORIGAMI UNICORN" ON TRANSMEDIA AESTHETIC EXPERIENCE

In 2006, Henry Jenkins began his "search" for the origami unicorn. This unicorn, an element of the *Blade Runner* director's cut that challenged readers to reconsider the film, is "emblematic of the core principles shaping [Jenkins's] understanding of transmedia storytelling,"[38] his "patron saint"[39] of transmedia storytelling. In 2009, Jenkins assisted in the origami unicorn's "revenge," outlining the seven core principles of transmedia storytelling, as he saw them. Today, I ask us to "reconsider" the origami unicorn and reflect on its original purpose in *Blade Runner*.

What made the origami unicorn so special was its ability to force a critical viewer to renegotiate meaning that the viewer previously thought solidified, to change the viewer's perception of the film's ending and thereby evoke an entirely new aesthetic experience through viewing. It didn't add to the storyworld or perform a serial function, but rather it asked the viewer to open the door to the text once again and enter into the two-way transactional space of meaning making.

In a similar way, Laurie's journey through, between, and across *Watchmen*'s intertextual past as a comic, textual present as a television series, and paratextual existence as online web content, reveals an experience that evokes the aesthetic brilliance of transmedia storytelling. It is an experience that cannot be negotiated by a viewer unwilling to "drill" beyond the permeable borders of a television set to reveal a playground of transactional complexity to explore. This unwilling viewer, not exempt from enjoying or understanding the primary textual narrative witnessed during the runtime of HBO's *Watchmen*, is however locked out of the aesthetic experience that Laurie and her transmedia journey evokes. What this understanding reveals is that the aesthetic criteria by which we evaluate the success or failure of transmedia storytelling must hinge on the experience evoked in partnership with the critical viewer, not on the seriality or vastness of the storyworld established across media.

Maybe it's time for the origami unicorn to pass the baton onto a new emblem for transmedia storytelling, one that might serve to reposition the conversation onto the experience as opposed to the object. Maybe the patron saint for this new era of transmedia storytelling and the aesthetic criteria of experience should be Laurie's big blue dildo instead. Making that happen, though, would require nothing short of a thermodynamic miracle.

NOTES

1. *Watchmen*, episode 3, "She Was Killed by Space Junk," directed by Stephen Williams, aired November 3, 2019, on HBO.

2. *Watchmen*, episode 3.

3. Jonathan Gray, *Show Sold Separately: Promos, Spoilers, and Other Media Paratexts* (New York: New York University Press, 2010), 118–19.

4. I am using the word "comicbook" in its compound form, instead of the more recognizable two-word ("comic book"), variation, in keeping with comics legend Stan Lee's insistence on its correct spelling. In a 2014 blog post on the now-defunct *AMC's Comic Book Men Blog*, Lee said: "People always write it as if it's two separate words. But to me, if it's two separate words, then it means a funny book—a comic book! If you write it as one word, which is the way I do it, then it's a generic term meaning comicbook! So feel everybody ought to write comicbook as if it's one word, because it doesn't mean funny book" (Lubin, 2014, BusinessInsider.com). I have adopted Lee's terminological distinction in my own work and so continue it here.

5. Damon Lindelof (damonLindelof), "Day 140," Instagram, photographs of letter pages. May 22, 2018, https://www.instagram.com/p/BjFsj6JHEdq/?utm_source=ig_embed.

6. Gray, 119.

7. Gray, 42.

8. Melanie Bourdaa, "'Following the Pattern': The Creation of an Encyclopaedic Universe with Transmedia Storytelling," *Adaptation* 6, no. 2 (2013): 202.

9. Jason Mittell qtd. in Melanie Bourdaa, "'Following the Pattern': The Creation of an Encyclopaedic Universe with Transmedia Storytelling," *Adaptation* 6, no. 2 (2013): 202.

10. The first instance of this type of internet paratext was associated with *The Blair Witch Project* in 1999.

11. Mittell describes "drillability" as a type of viewer engagement with complex narratives that is less about "horizontal ripples" that encourage viewers to flock to the text for a short while, and more about a "forensic fandom that encourages viewers to dig deeper, probing beneath the surface to understand the complexity of a story and its telling." By definition, this type of "drillable media" can be expected to engage fewer people, but it can also be expected to occupy those few people that it does engage for a much longer period of time as they endlessly descend into a text's narrative complexities.

12. HBO, "Go Deeper Inside the World of Watchmen," https://www.hbo.com/watchmen/world-building-full-experience.

13. Gerard Genette, *Paratexts: Thresholds of Interpretation* (Cambridge: Cambridge University Press, 1987), 1.

14. Genette, 1.

15. Gray, 25.

16. Louise Rosenblatt, *The Reader, the Text, the Poem: The Transactional Theory of the Literary Work* (USA: Southern Illinois University Press, 1978).

17. Rosenblatt, viii.

18. Rosenblatt.

19. Henry Jenkins, "The Aesthetics of Transmedia: Response to David Bordwell (Part Three)," *Confessions of an Aca-Fan* (blog), September 15, 2009, http://henryjenkins.org/blog/2009/09/the_aesthetics_of_transmedia_i_2.html.

20. Jenkins, "The Aesthetics of Transmedia."

21. Gray, 42.

22. Jenkins, *Convergence Culture: Where Old and New Media Collide* (New York: NYU Press, 2008), 96.

23. Jackson McHenry, "How *Watchmen* Built Out Its Universe with Peteypedia," *Vulture*, December 20, 2019, https://www.vulture.com/2019/12/how-watchmen-made-peteypedia.html.

24. That said, it does inform the viewer that the "happy-ever-after" promised for Dan and Laurie at the end of the *Watchmen* comics series didn't pan out. ("Dan was convinced I was still holding a candle for my ex, so he made me a big blue dildo as a f###-you. Literally.")

25. Peteypedia, "Interrogation (Redactions): Juspeczyk, Laurel Jane (4/25/95)," https://www.hbo.com/content/dam/hbodata/series/watchmen/peteypedia/04/interrogation-juspeczyk.pdf."

26. Peteypedia, "Interrogation."

27. Peteypedia, "Interrogation."

28. Peteypedia, "Memo: What Has One Eye and Loves Evil Plans?," https://www.hbo.com/content/dam/hbodata/series/watchmen/peteypedia/06/blake-memo-actual-work.pdf.

29. Alan Moore, Dave Gibbons, and John Higgins, *Watchmen* #12 (DC Comics, 1987), 30.

30. In "Contents//File_01," uploaded to the "Peteypedia" server following the first episode of the television series, an FBI memo, "rorschachs-journal-memo," reveals that Laurie took on the code name hinted at in the comics and continued illegally working as a vigilante with Nite Owl II (Dan Dreiberg) for years.

31. Alan Moore, Dave Gibbons, and John Higgins, *Watchmen* #9 (DC Comics, 1987), 22.

32. Alan Moore, Dave Gibbons, and John Higgins, *Watchmen* #2 (DC Comics, 1987), 22.

33. Moore, Gibbons, and Higgins, *Watchmen* #2, 23.

34. Moore, Gibbons, and Higgins, *Watchmen* #2, 23.

35. *Watchmen*, episode 9, "See How They Fly," directed by Frederick E. O. Toye, aired on December 15, 2019, on HBO.

36. *Watchmen*, episode 9.

37. Moore, Gibbons, and Higgins, 28.

38. Jenkins, "The Revenge of the Origami Unicorn: Seven Principles of Transmedia Storytelling (Well, Two Actually. Five More on Friday)," http://henryjenkins.org/blog/2009/12/the_revenge_of_the_origami_uni.html.

39. Jenkins, "The Revenge of the Origami Unicorn."

Chapter 6

WHAT'S INSIDE THE CLOSET

Costume as Critique in *Watchmen* and Its Adaptations

ALISIA GRACE CHASE

For fans and fashionistas alike, one of the most pleasurable aspects of literary adaptation is seeing "written garments" come to life. When translated to the screen, what is presumed to be a flatter mode—words—is exchanged for one presumed to be of greater magnitude—costumes—with visual proof of tactility, dimensionality, and vivid color rather than mere linguistic descriptions of the same. But the hybridity of comics problematizes this axiom and refutes Roland Barthes's theory in *The Fashion System* that the "image garment" is imbued with more interpretive possibilities than the "written garment."[1] It does so because the power of the medium lies in the interdependence of image and word; as Scott McCloud theorized, "[In comics] words and pictures go hand in hand to convey an idea that neither could convey alone."[2]

This interdependence is particularly intentional in the original *Watchmen* (1986), and especially regarding superhero costumes, which appear as both "image garments" and "written garments" throughout the comic. When first published, *Watchmen* was embraced by a jaded generation who knew appearances could be deceiving and that "choosing to dress up in gaudy opera costumes and express good and evil in simple, childish terms" was more than a bit atavistic.[3] Moore and Gibbons operated within the conventions of the genre even as they deconstructed its tropes, chief among them the symbolism of the "gaudy opera costumes" that such masked adventurers wear. From the advent of Superman's red tights, audiences had been conditioned to see superheroes' suits as visual shorthand for their particular powers, but *Watchmen* subverted these expectations from the outset.[4] In the first chapter, Gibbons's images foreground the Comedian and Night Owl's secret closets and the impotent, bodiless costumes that hang within, and in the second, Hollis

Mason ponders the practicality of spandex, as well as what wearing skintight outfits might insinuate about a masked vigilante's "proclivities."[5] Costumes are continually called into question, and the resulting paradox—that costume connotes one's heroicism and one's deviance—becomes a dominant theme that critiques the entire genre.[6]

Accordingly, in adapting *Watchmen*, a director would need to finesse such a significant aspect of the text. Zack Snyder, whose feature-length film was released in 2009, said he aimed for a fanboy's fidelity, and Michael Wilkinson, his costume designer, tried to balance stylistic allegiance with sartorial innovation. Damon Lindelof, showrunner of the 2019 HBO series, believed that any attempt that was too faithful to the comic would ultimately fail. As Lindelof stated, "you cannot take these 12 issues and jam them into a theatrical experience. What makes *Watchmen Watchmen* is its density, its slow-burn-ness."[7] Sharen Davis, who designed the pilot's costumes, and Megan Kasperlik, who succeeded Davis as lead costumer, faced similar considerations as Wilkinson, but had the additional challenge of designing for television, which undeniably diminutizes these larger-than-life characters. This chapter endeavors to illustrate that although limited by a far smaller budget and screen, Davis and Kasperlik are more successful than Wilkinson in replicating the legacy text's deployment of costume as critique.

Cinematic costuming—whether meant to clothe a king or a cowgirl—has always been designed to utilize iconography that quickly establishes character—often to the point of stereotype—and convey that character's development over the course of the film. Influenced by the stage, designers in silent-era cinema understood that dress could be used as a mode of speech, describing the character in one symbolic sweep. This methodology held sway even as sound was added, and renowned Hollywood designer Edith Head averred that even if a film's soundtrack was turned off, good costumes could still communicate something critical about character and plot.[8] Wilkinson's costumes follow Head's lead—and do so in true superhero film fashion, as they are hyper-spectacular with little to no nuance. Wilkinson wanted the film to be chromatically faithful, and the tones do match those of colorist John Higgins, whose palette signaled a radical break with comic book tradition. (Instead of using primary colors for heroes and secondary colors for villains, Higgins used a range of secondary colors like orange and brown—closer on the spectrum—to express *Watchmen*'s morally ambiguous world.[9]) But box office apparently trumped fidelity, as the majority of Wilkinson's costumes are techno-modernized and obviously influenced by contemporary cinema and street fashion. This is unsurprising, as designers always incorporate trending silhouettes, but Wilkinson's slavishness to spectacle detracts from his costumes' self-reflexive potential. There is a dramatic difference between the comic's melancholy-colored forms, which are open to wide interpretation given their semi-abstract qualities and the written text that constantly calls their proscribed meaning into question, and Wilkinson's realistically colored, three-dimensional costumes, which tend to be read straightforwardly, according to established codes.

This difference is apparent even in a superficial comparison of the costumes of Nite Owl and Ozymandias in each medium. As drawn by Gibbons, Dan Dreiberg's suit is visually enervated; its mauve and sepia coloring lacks marked contrast and its flatness recalls ballet tights before the invention of spandex, which typically bagged and sagged as much as Dreiberg's tummy does. Yet in Wilkinson's version, Dreiberg's costume makes him a physical peer of the most powerful superheroes of the preceding decade, visually echoing the neoclassical, latex body armor from Joel Schumacher's late 1990s Batman films, as well as the ballyhooed webbing of Tobey Maguire's first Spidey suit. Wilkinson similarly refashioned Ozymandias, whose purple raiment and golden diadem symbolized his fascination with historical royalty and reliance on brains over brawn. But tights and tunic were evidently too effeminate for Snyder's Ozymandias; his most recognizable extradiegetic reference is Schumacher's muscle-laden, uber-masculinity, with pronounced nipples as a perverse addition. That designers must consider the original source costume in the printed comic, the formal and iconographic variations in costume that multiple artists may have brought to the character as they developed in response to societal changes, advancements in printing technologies, the reception of film and television antecedents, *and* how said costume will translate to an individual actor's body is no small task.[10]

In Hollywood, where the human body has commodified exchange value as a visual object, an actor's physique is as critical to conveying character as his clothes, and designers typically consider what the convergence of fabric and flesh will communicate. Given our cultural obsession with idealized bodies produced by merging steroids and surgery, it's unsurprising that Wilkinson's superheroes look so perfectly sculpted. In contrast, the original *Watchmen* foregrounds the unreliability of costume to deify its wearer, and physiques are rarely ideal. This disparity can be shown by comparing one of the more pathos-inducing comic panels to its cinematic equivalent. In Gibbons's drawing of Dreiberg slumped beside the closet in his superhero lair, neither man nor costume seems virile—both hang limply. Of particular note is how flaccid and flimsy Dreiberg's boots appear, better suited for a child pirate than a crime fighter. In the filmic hideout, Nite Owl's numerous suits are the first thing illuminated when he switches on the lights, and the fact that his costumes are displayed like medieval armor in a plexiglass vitrine rather than a closet underscores their spectacularity—they are miraculous objects to be admired. As the camera focuses on the bespectacled, rumpled, and plump Dreiberg, viewers can see the muscularly erect suits standing behind him—so taut they don't even need a body. Dan is definitively pitiful in comparison to his chiseled costumes.[11]

Similarly, Wilkinson modifies the younger Silk Spectre's costume to satisfy audiences but doesn't interrogate the consequential tropes about female sexuality that arise from his changes. Comic Laurie is no wide-eyed ingénue—she's an angry, middle-aged woman with a sharp tongue and a sturdy, wide-shouldered form, still wearing the mini-dress her mother designed. In Wilkinson's hands, however, Silk Spectre is an eternally nubile, latex-clad dominatrix in a scuba yellow leotard cut high on the leg and stiletto heels that are impossible to run in, much less leap from upper-stories. Her costume is clearly influenced by intertextual sources—Alicia Silverstone's Batgirl and Jennifer Garner's Elektra being the most obvious. Paul Petrovic believes Snyder trivialized Laurie's costume as it was originally written, and I concur:

> The filmic *Watchmen* tries to deconstruct notions of the sexualized woman by being overt about this kind of sexual construction, changing Laurie's costume from a short black skirt and yellow gauze material in the graphic novel to a seemingly intertextual gloss of Comic Bad Girl dominatrix garb through her latex and thigh-high boots. However, though it seeks to hybridize the two, Snyder's *Watchmen* loses a clear sense of where postmodern irony is intended and where simple objectification comes into play.[12]

Both the Golden Age costume and its movie counterpart are meant to entice the heterosexual male gaze, and although Silk Spectre's BDSM outfit heightens her erotic potential, it lowers her heroic potential. Costuming a female character to be both is arguably impossible, as a sexualized female is always synecdoche for the submissive—and heroes are always assertive. Perhaps this is why female superheroes are so frequently outfitted in bondage-style clothing, as it undisputedly conveys dominance.

Like its predecessors, HBO's *Watchmen* takes place in an alternate universe where self-made superheroes struggle to make their way in a corrupt society, but it presents audiences with entirely new characters and revises a number from the original. The series "elaborates on its source not as a sequel, reboot, or even translation, but rather as an adaptation that substitutes speculation and deviation in place of fidelity."[13] Paradoxically, this produces a storyline that although as fantastical as the original, is quite conceivable in a number of aspects. By making an African American woman the star, changing the origin story of Hooded Justice, and complicating any facile readings of Dr. Manhattan based on skin color, Lindelof foregrounds our nation's very real history of racial injustice, as well as the omission of the heroic African American in popular culture. Davis and Kasperlik use costume—the conflation of fabric and flesh—to develop and reveal each superhero's character, but also as "second skins" that subtly undermine cultural stereotypes about skin color and what it purportedly communicates. Additionally, by designing outfits that signify the seriousness rather than the sex appeal of the series' women, Davis and Kasperlik refashion visual tropes associated with female superheroes, foremost among them the main character, Angela Abar/Sister Night.

It is tempting to presume that designing costumes for television is exactly the same as designing for the cinema and that primary differences are merely a matter of each designer's vision, and in most cases the process is similar.[14] But even in an era of large-screen, high-definition television, there is still a dramatic reduction in the size of the image from that of the movie screen. As such, TV costume designers must balance filling a much smaller frame with costumes that do not detract from the storyline yet still telegraph information about the character and their narrative arc. In a big budget film, spectacle is the very point—which is probably why the two most visually compelling "costumes" in Snyder's *Watchmen* were made possible by the latest advances in CGI technology.[15] In contrast, and somewhat ironically, given the low status typically awarded to television costume designers and their comparatively miniscule budgets, Davis and Kasperlik's modest creations are far more effective at replicating Moore and Gibbons's deployment of costume as critique. To wit: Red Scare and Looking Glass, two of the series' cops, are anything but valiant, and their sad-sack costumes drive that point home. The former wears a crimson-colored, cheap nylon track suit from the 1970s and a machine-knitted ski mask, and his scrappy appearance hints at his reactionary pugilism. The latter—whose "reflectatine" mask is meant to protect him from psychic blasts—has such a scrawny, ill-clad body that he is more a stereotype of the bedraggled, plainclothes detective than someone able to leap over tall buildings in a single bound. Looking Glass's mask did necessitate using CGI when scenes required a fully legible reflection, as Davis was unable to find a material that stretched comfortably over the actor's face and functioned as a mirror image, but the overall effect still reads as extremely low-tech and is as feature-deforming as the old bank-robber masks made from pantyhose. Like the original Rorschach, Looking Glass's mask is as much a symbol of his enduring psychological trauma as it is a means to protect himself from further abuse. His fluctuating status in the story—also similar to Rorschach—as both brave vigilante and damaged child, is apparent when his police chief, Judd Crawford, tells him to "Come on over here and pull your face down" so that Crawford can use Looking Glass as a mirror to straighten his tie. The implication is that Looking Glass's individuality and, therefore, humanity are irrelevant. His "face," as Crawford dismissively calls it, is only present to reflect the handsome man in power—it's literally self-effacing. Other characters' costumes are equally homespun: Pirate Jenny appears to have simply added a lacy mask to her everyday mash-up of goth, punk, and grunge, while the villainous members of the Seventh Kavalry all wear plaid flannel shirts and self-fashioned Rorschach masks to illustrate their commitment to a redneck, backwoods—and therefore backwards—way of life, where good versus evil and white versus black are not relative—they are oppositions that undergird one's *raison d'etre*. Unlike the original Rorschach's constantly morphing forms, the black and white blots on the Kavalry's balaclavas are static because their politics are fixed.

Fidelity to the original text and the plausibility of this adaptation's fictional world converge in Lindelof's choice to emphasize the DIY aspects of the characters' costumes. As he stated:

> [In the original comic] Rorschach's trench coat had stains on it and stuff, and they showed you how he made his mask from this dress. And you realize, "Oh, he's really only got a couple of these masks." . . . Moth Man or the original Nite Owl was just wearing basically a bathing suit and a domino mask. So I think that the first part of the aesthetic was these people are making their costumes themselves.[16]

Davis echoed this: "They should look like they were all made at home . . . no amazing marble-looking costumes here."[17] So did Kasperlik: "We would go back and reference the source material and [ask], 'How can we move it into . . . 2019?' . . . The vigilantes in the graphic novel made their own costumes. That was the theory, so they're not necessarily the big Avengers with super high-tech costumes."[18] This choice humanizes the characters and reaffirms the source text's proposition that superheroes are not divinities—they're mere mortals battling shady criminals while managing quotidian lives.

Lindelof's mise-en-scène of humble, makeshift realism rather than sci-fi-inspired futurism also fits the new storyline. By situating his narrative in the nondescript suburban sprawl of Tulsa, Oklahoma, Lindelof suggests that these events could happen anywhere, but the city's history also allows him to make the Tulsa Race Massacre of 1921 the genesis of his story. In doing so,

Lindelof both addresses and redresses the erasure of African Americans in our national historical imaginary. As Emily Nussbaum has succinctly stated, "[This] is a show about blackness . . . about the idea of African-Americans playing roles [in both senses] from which they've often been excluded, among them soldiers, cops, and superheroes."[19] By complicating media stereotypes associated with the terms "black" and "white"—as costume hues, skin colors, and/or political identities—Lindelof exposes them as reductive and often erroneous. Indeed, the series illustrates that race, like costume, is a visual construct meant to convey who is powerful and who is not and underscores that viewers must know the codes of one's society to understand exactly what each character is meant to embody, and therefore how the series is critiquing them. This is fitting, as the reductive terms "black" and "white" are arguably inseparable from the visual messaging of costume given their origins in the theater. As Virginia Mason Vaughan writes, "Black-faced characters in early modern dramas are often used . . . to make whiteness visible."[20] Shakespeare's *Othello, the Moor of Venice* of 1604 likely set the stage stereotype of "black," and a decade later, in what appears to be the first use of the term "white" to refer to people of European origin, English playwright Thomas Middleton juxtaposed that visual trope with its dramatic opposite.[21]

Lindelof begins upending racial codes within the first five minutes of the series to show how culturally ingrained yet arbitrary they are. Viewers are situated as the audience of a silent film, and as the piano accompaniment crescendos, a white-suited figure astride a white horse is chased by a figure who is wearing a hooded black cape and riding a black horse. If interpreted along the presumption that light symbolizes the savior and darkness represents the devil, a viewer might presume that the villain is chasing down the hero. But the chase's climax inverts the aforementioned stage paradigm and the successive cinematic codes most likely cemented by D. W. Griffith's *Birth of a Nation* (1915).[22] The figure in the black cape is revealed to be Bass Reeves, the first African American US deputy marshal of Oklahoma, a real-life historical figure who famously arrested over 3,000 criminals. This inversion foregrounds the series' premise that conventions do not apply here: not only is the man in black the hero, but the hero is a Black man.

Such reductive binaries—as well as the stereotypes that typically accompany false oppositions—are most effectively disrupted within the characterization of Angela Abar/Sister Night. Both supermom *and* superhero, Abar is iconoclastic in almost every aspect of her being. She is not only an African American female police officer, but she is also a loving wife and mother by day and an ass-kicking superhero by night. In the same way that the original *Watchmen* deconstructs superhero costumes in order to critique them, so

Davis and Kasperlik's costuming of Abar disrupts audience expectations regarding a Black female superhero in order to examine its tropes. In her pedestrian incarnation, Abar is clad in the uniform of almost all suburban American mothers at the turn of the millennium: an Anthropologie-esque global chic grounded by denim and low-heeled booties. For example, when she is first introduced, Abar's embroidered silk vest with frog closures is reminiscent of historical Asian clothing—an understated nod to her Vietnamese childhood, but also fashionably on point. Other outfits are similarly au courant and quietly tasteful: a long, sleeveless slip dress for the wake, a faux-leather and shearling moto jacket and skinny jeans while digging around a cemetery. By costuming Abar in the same sort of trendy and feminine clothing styles that former first lady Michelle Obama popularized, Abar's body transcends skin color and moves into a postracial sartorial space made possible by class. Indeed, the following assessment of the way in which Obama's position as first lady provided a new model for Black women could easily apply to Abar: "The high visibility of this role gives mainstream Americans a chance to see her as an exceptional mother, a fashionable trendsetter, and a supportive wife."[23] The similarly modest clothing of Lady Trieu and Laurie Juspeczyk also play against gender stereotypes, with the former dressed in monochromatic, architectural silhouettes that signal her vision of a sanitized utopia, and the latter in loose pantsuits and a deconstructed trench that suggest a professional woman of a certain age finally comfortable in her own skin.

In keeping with the series' DIY aesthetic, Abar's superhero costume isn't overly spectacular, but that may be the very point. Unlike the hypersexualized, bondage-inspired suits worn by most female superheroes (of all skin tones), her costume is sober in color and cut, a modified nun's habit dominated by a long, hooded, black leather jacket which flares into a full skirt.[24] This gives the costume the flourish typically associated with a superhero's cape but also keeps it elegant. Diegetically, the habit recalls the convent where Abar was raised and her youthful obsession with the blaxploitation heroine Sister Night, who guards the homeless in Hell's Kitchen. This rupture with stereotypical costuming makes Sister Night's modest costume particularly empowering, visually evoking the monastic life and imparting to Abar the air of a woman devoted to a higher calling.[25] Extradiegetically, it could nod to Whoopi Goldberg's comedic character in *Sister Act*, but it better functions as an allusion to the oft-forgotten but formidable history of Black women in American religious orders. Shannon Dee Williams argues that the history of Black Catholic sisters in the United States is inseparable from and parallel to the African American community's long struggle for liberation and the right to one's bodily integrity. While enslaved, African American women were inordinately subjected to unwanted sexual advances. Therefore, "embracing the celibate religious state was an inherently political and radical act." As Williams further relates, "[These women] wanted to live a 'radical' way of life, one that nurtured Black women's intellectual genius, their spirituality, and their talents. [They] wanted to serve their own communities through education and a host of other social services but outside the traditional confines of marriage and motherhood." [26] Williams chronicles the activist nuns who set up schools to educate former female slaves, as well as sisters who embrace the Black Lives Matter movement and took part in protests in both Ferguson and Milwaukee. Like the Tulsa Race Massacre, the true story of these nuns' social justice work has long been overlooked. Therefore, Sister Night can be seen as a pop culture remediation of this missing history: an African American woman in a nun's habit, living an ethical life in a degenerate world while fighting for the dignity of all humans.[27]

The most impressive aspect of Abar's superhero vestment is the dramatic hood, which outwardly functions to disguise her real identity when crime-fighting. But the hood is also a potent intra- and extratextual reference to African American history. Over the course of the series, it is revealed that Abar's grandfather was Hooded Justice, whose costume consisted of a red hood secured around his neck with a rope, visually summoning the mythic garb of professional executioners, or more grimly, the noose and hood of a hanged man, obliquely referencing lynching. Hooded Justice, living in a time when a Black man was assumed to be the criminal rather than the crime-fighter, also whitened the area around his eyes. This "whiteface" became an integral part of his costume, one that allowed him to "pass" in white society. Unknowingly, his granddaughter creates a costume that closely resembles his—with a big hood that can be used to cloak her face—only updated to reflect a period wherein being African American is not something to hide but to highlight: Abar intentionally darkens, rather than lightens, the skin around her eyes. Abar's hood is also a tribute to that of Bass Reeves, and a repudiation of the white hoods associated with the Ku Klux Klan. The latter is underscored when Abar discovers the KKK uniform of Judd Crawford hidden in a secret closet, and the audience understands that "white" no longer signals salvation. Abar's hood also symbolically refers to the "hoodie," a generic item of athletic clothing that became infamous after the murder of Trayvon Martin, who was identified on account of his grey hooded sweatshirt. As Troy Patterson writes, "[A] generation of hip-hop kids found the hoodie suitable for the important adolescent work of taking up space and dramatizing the self . . . if, in its anti-surveillance capacity, the hood plays with the visual rhetoric of menace, it is heir to a tradition in teen dressing" that is meant to separate one from their stodgy forebears.[28] After Martin's death, however, people of all demographics donned the hoodie as a sign of solidarity with young Black men.

Given that an actor's body is as much an aspect of costume as clothes are, part of what potentiates Angela Abar as a speculative model is not only that she is a brown-skinned superheroine in a nun's habit, but that the overtly female components of her body—breasts and buttocks—are never fetishized. The only aspect consistently highlighted through dress are Abar's muscular arms, which I would argue also alludes to Michelle Obama, whose similarly toned biceps were the object of much commentary during her husband's presidency. In "Michelle Obama's Arms: Race, Respectability, and Class Privilege," Shirley Tate argues that Obama's arms were threatening to the first lady "somatic norm" because they were simultaneously reminiscent of the muscular Black female slave body and a denotation of the upper-middle-class woman who has the money and time to sculpt her body into perfection. To extract the positive from Tate's analysis as it applies to the *Watchmen* TV series, "[Abar's arm] muscles assert active personhood for herself."[29] Arms are the part of the body that do things, that enact change upon the world. Since the exhibition of Sarah Baartman (The Hottentot Venus) in 19th-century Europe, the Black female body has been one inscribed by others' prejudices and desires. Baartman became a body that was *only* breasts and buttocks, a woman who was displayed like a caged animal while alive, and then as parts in a jar after death.[30] This history makes Abar's extremely modest superhero costume—one that signifies chastity—even more meaningful. As written and performed, a woman whose strong, sinewy arms are the only exposed feature of her female form, Abar is unable to be fixed on either side of the Hollywood dichotomy that posits woman as virgin or whore, or—as Donald Bogle and K. Sue Jewell translate these stereotypes to African American actresses—the asexual "Mammy" associated with the breast, or the tempting "Jezebel" associated with the buttocks. It is tempting to read Abar as an echo of the mammy embodied by Hattie McDaniel in *Gone with the Wind*, as Abar is the adoptive mother of her slain partner's white children and has no children of her own. But she is hardly scripted as domestic—the bakery that she wants to open takes a backseat to crimefighting and it is her husband, Cal, who cooks for the family. Abar can thus be seen as a positive remediation of the mammy stereotype, one who enacts the caretaking associated with the maternal Black female without subservience to a master.

A year after the series ended, Regina King, who plays Angela Abar/Sister Night, was interviewed by *Essence* magazine about working with costume designer Sharen Davis. She stressed that Lindelof wanted to keep the cape, but that Davis wanted something sartorially unexpected for such a groundbreaking character. King stated, "[Lindelof] wanted to have a nod to the cape. You know, the caped crusader, the superheroes you know, that always have a cape, but Sharen was like, 'But we gotta make it cool! We gotta make it fly.'"[31] Hence the billowing cape-skirt. Davis' pun—intended or not—was fitting, as from Superman onward capes are what enable flight. But it was even more appropriate for an African American superhero whose costume pays homage to a gun-toting blaxploitation heroine. After all, it was most likely Curtis Mayfield's soundtrack for the 1972 film *Superfly* that begat the use of the term "fly" to refer to someone who is sharply dressed. As cool as her cape-skirt may be, in the series' finale, Abar seemingly abandons her costume after her grandfather counsels her about his erroneous belief that being a superhero would bring about justice. He says, "Did you feel what I felt? Pain . . . anger? You can't heal under a mask, Angela. Wounds need air." At this, Angela begins to weep. Shortly after, her son sees her Sister Night costume hanging in the bakery closet. The shot is clearly meant to reference the images of superhero costumes in the previous *Watchmen*, and Angela's compassionate expression as she witnesses his awe reaffirms the paradox of superhero costumes: while heroic on the outside, they're often just a mask to hide the human pain inside.

NOTES

1. Roland Barthes, *The Fashion System* (Berkeley: University of California Press, 1990).

2. Scott McCloud, *Understanding Comics: The Invisible Art* (New York: William Morrow, 1994), 155.

3. Alan Moore and Dave Gibbons, *Watchmen* (New York: DC Comics, 1986), 8.

4. Barbara Brownie and Danny Graydon, *The Superhero Costume: Identity and Disguise in Fact and Fiction* (London: Bloomsbury Publishing, 2015), 11.

5. Moore and Gibbons, 7.

6. Matthew Levy and Heather Mathews posit that this interplay is "a nod to the reader, who presumably shares enough awareness of superhero comics to understand such passages as a critique and as a potential transformation of the conventions of comic costumes." See "The Abyss Gazes Also: The Self-Referential Cynicism of *Watchmen*," *ImageText* 2, no. 7, http://imagetext.english.ufl.edu/archives/v7_2/levy, accessed 9/02/2020..

7. Alan Sepinwall, "'Nostalgia Is Toxic': Damon Lindelof on His 'Watchmen' Adaptation," *Rolling Stone*, October 17, 2019, https://www.rollingstone.com/tv/tv-features/watchmen-damon-lindelof-interview-896780/, accessed 10/26/2020.

8. "Dialogue on Film: Edith Head," *American Film* 3, no. 7.

9. Michael Edward Taylor, "15 Ways Watchmen Changed Comic Books Forever" *ScreenRant*, September 16, 2016, https://screenrant.com/how-watchmen-changed-comic-books-forever/, accessed 10/21/2020.

10. The designers for *Deadpool* 2, Kurt and Bart, stress the multiple factors considered: "All of the superheroes have had more than one version of themselves as a lot of them have been drawn by different comic book artists over the years. That's why we always look to the source material first and then collectively and creatively we work with the director to determine the direction, what to keep and what wouldn't actually translate to a human versus a comic book character on the page." "Modern Marvel: Dressing the 21st Century Superhero," *French Vogue*, https://www.vogue.fr/fashion/fashion-inspiration/story/superheroes-marvel-costumes-catwoman-wonderwoman-black-panther-deadpool/3167, accessed 10/11/2020.

11. I would argue that the importance of this "establishing shot" in the original as an icon of Nite Owl's bygone youth/virility is doubly confirmed by a replica of this image on p. 22 of *Doomsday Clock*, which apart from a few banalities, such as "spandex society," has no discussion of costume.

12. Paul Petrovic, "The Culturally Constituted Gaze: Fetishizing the Feminine from Alan Moore and Dave Gibbons's *Watchmen* to Zack Snyder's *Watchmen*," *ImageText*, 5, no. 4, http://imagetext.english.ufl.edu/archives/v5_4/petrovic/, accessed 10/14/2020.

13. Michael Boyce Gillespie, "Thinking about Watchmen: A Roundtable," *Film Quarterly* 73, no. 4 (Summer 2020), https://filmquarterly.org/2020/06/26/summer-2020-volume-74-number-4/, accessed 8/24/2020.

14. David Resha, "Designing for Black and White: Edith Head and the Craft of the Costume Designer," *Screening the Past*, http://www.screeningthepast.com/2015/06/designing-for-black-and-white-edith-head-and-the-craft-of-the-costume-designer/, accessed 8/27/2020.

15. Dr. Manhattan's glowing blue body and Rorschach's morphing mask both relied on postproduction computer labor. Erin McCarthy, "The Tech behind Rorschach's Mask in Watchmen," *Popular Mechanics*, October 1, 2009, https://www.popularmechanics.com/technology/gadgets/a12254/4307536/, accessed 9/29/2020.

16. Scott Collura, "Designing the Costumes of HBO's *Watchmen*," *IGN*, November 25, 2019, https://www.ign.com/articles/2019/11/22/designing-the-costumes-of-hbos-watchmen-hooded-justice-sister-black-looking-glass, accessed 10/14/2020.

17. Rob Licuria, "Sharen Davis (*Watchmen*) on Costume Deisgns for the 1921 Tulsa Massacre," *GoldDerby*, August 10, 2020, https://www.goldderby.com/article/2020/sharen-davis-watchmen-costume-designs-video-interview/, accessed 11/03/2020.

18. Josh Weiss, "Costume and Production Designers for HBO's 'Watchmen' Discuss Damon Lindelof's Reimagined Adaptation," *Forbes*, October 20, 2019, https://www.forbes.com/sites/joshweiss/2019/10/20/costume-and-production-designers-for-hbos-watchmen-discuss-damon-linfelofs-reimagined-adaptation/, accessed 9/03/2020.

19. Emily Nussbaum, "The Incendiary Aims of HBO's Watchmen." *The New Yorker*, December 19, 2019, https://www.newyorker.com/magazine/2019/12/09/the-incendiary-aims-of-hbos-watchmen, accessed 10/14/2020.

20. Virginia Mason Vaughan, *Performing Blackness on English Stages, 1500–1800* (Cambridge: Cambridge University Press, 2005), 6.

21. In his 1613 play *The Triumph of Truth*, Middleton's African king looks out on the English audience and states, "I see amazement set upon the faces/Of these white people, wond'rings and strange gazes."

22. Griffith's costumes were based on Thomas Dixon's *The Clansman* (1905), but the hood's resemblance to European Holy Week penitents is purported to be coincidental. The film's success actually resulted in the Klan adopting the film costume as their uniform, selling them in catalogs. See Melissa Fessenden, "The Ku Klux Klan Didn't Always Wear Hoods," *Smithsonian Magazine*, January 13, 2016, https://www.smithsonianmag.com/smart-news/ku-klux-klan-didnt-always-wear-hoods-180957773/, accessed 12/17/2020.

23. Taquesha Brannon, "Media Representations of Michelle Obama," UCLA Center for the Study of Women website, https://escholarship.org/uc/item/1kg651b3, accessed 12/17/2020.

24. It is generally agreed upon that most female superhero outfits derive from the original 1965 costume of the Avengers-associated Black Widow, who wore a blue-black "merry widow" corselet worn over a fishnet unitard, cinched at the waist with a studded belt. The popularity of "merry widows" most likely arose out of the soft porn imagery of 1950s model Bettie Page, known as "the Queen of Bondage," and this predisposition for what is essentially leather or latex lingerie has been one that few comic artists have broken with, most likely for the reasons I propose regarding Silk Spectre.

25. Daniel Gillespie, "*Watchmen*: Sister Night Looks More Like a Nun in Early Artist Rendering," *ScreenRant*, June 29, 2020, https://screenrant.com/watchmen-tv-show-sister-night-concept-art-nun/, accessed 11/28/2020. and Kasperlik's drawings reveal that the first realization was even more reminiscent of a traditional nun's outfit, with a white "wimple"-like mask and a longer white V-shaped insert for her top.

26. Jaimee A. Swift, "Radical Habits: Unearthing the History of Black Catholic Nuns in the Black Freedom Struggle," *Black Women Radicals*, https://www.blackwomenradicals.com/blog-feed/radicals-habits-unearthing-the-history-of-black-catholic-nuns-in-the-black-freedom-strugglenbsp, accessed 1/27/2021.

27. Given the tendency of Hollywood and Netflix to besmirch the Catholic Church, they may have believed an ass-kicking nun would further annihilate any remaining reverence for this religion, but "the cunning of reason," as Hegel called it, seems to have won out here. Making Sister Night into a nun in an era when most Black women in pop culture are portrayed as video vixens affirms that the truly radical choice is living the moral life.

28. Troy Patterson, "The Politics of the Hoodie," *The New York Times Magazine*, March 2, 2016, https://www.nytimes.com/2016/03/06/magazine/the-politics-of-the-hoodie.html, accessed 1/27/2021.

29. Shirley Tate, "Michelle Obama's Arms: Race, Respectability, and Class Privilege," *Comparative American Studies* 10 (August 1, 2012): 226–38.

30. Carol E. Henderson, "AKA: Sarah Baartman, The Hottentot Venus, and Black Women's Identity," *Women's Studies* 43, no. 7, 946–59.

31. Keyaira Boone, "This Black Costume Designer Transformed Regina King into a Superhero for HBO's Watchmen," *Essence*, https://www.essence.com/entertainment/only-essence/sharen-davis-hbos-watchmen/, accessed 10/2/2021.

Part Two

RACE AND AMERICAN HISTORY

While the theme of part 1—adaptation, remediation, and transmedia—has strong roots going back into Alan Moore and Dave Gibbons's original maxi-series, the focus of part 2 is relatively new terrain in the *Watchmen* universe. Race is a relatively nonexistent theme in the 1986 series, which is dominated by the critique of the Cold War and the superhero at large. As initially established by Moore and Gibbons, none of the Minutemen and the Watchmen appears to be black (more on that in a moment). However, African American characters occasionally fill out the periphery, most notably Malcolm Long, Rorschach's psychiatrist, and Bernie, the young comic book fan who frequents his more formal namesake's newsstand to read the newest copies of *Tales of the Black Freighter*. Yet, Moore and Gibbons largely use the racial difference of Malcolm and Bernie symbolically. On the cusp of Ozymandias's faux alien squid attack, Malcolm tries to intervene in a fight between two lesbian characters, and Bernard attempts to shield the boy from the resulting blast. In short, in the face of tragedy, humanity will band together to help one another, regardless of difference.

Yet, race is front and center in the HBO limited series, becoming the Cold War equivalent of a real-world problem in need of a superhero solution. In so doing, Lindelof not only poses difficult questions about systemic injustice and racism, but also about the origins of superheroes across the past century. It is that last sentiment where there is a bit of overlap between the original and the remixed sequel—both texts want to use superheroes in a way to get us to think more critically about the foundational tropes of the genre at large.

For instance, in one of his boldest revisions, Lindelof finally confirms the identity of Minutemen member Hooded Justice. One of the many mysteries on the periphery of the original series, Moore and Gibbons ambiguously suggest that Hooded Justice is a white, German-American man. In the formative scene in which he saves the original Silk Spectre from being raped by the Comedian, Moore and Gibbons give us a hint of his face under the hood: shocked brown eyes, surrounded by white skin. Lindelof, on the other hand, establishes that Hooded Justice is actually Will Reeves, a young, queer, black man who escaped the 1921 Tulsa race riot and became one of the first members of the New York City police force. After joining, Reeves becomes aware that racism is inherently a part of law enforcement, and his disillusionment leads him to don the hood, place white greasepaint around his eyes in a sort of inverse blackface maneuver, and join with the Minutemen. Yet, just like their offspring the Watchmen, the Minutemen ultimately fail to prevent disaster, this time because they are ambivalent about taking on systemic racism because it isn't the kind of crime fighting that makes headlines. The show seems to suggest that here is something radically new: only a Black, queer superhero, forged in the fires of a real atrocity, has the ability to avenge America's original sin.

The seven chapters in this section pick up on these various themes, beginning with Chamara Moore's chapter on how the television series uses speculative elements to both heal intergenerational racial trauma and to "do more overly antiracist work than its original text." In chapter 8, Brian Faucette connects the real-world contexts of the Trump fueled rise of the alt-right and resurgence of white supremacy to the series' interrogation of white masculinity. In the following chapter, Rusty Hatchell analyzes how the show's embrace of racial politics can be analyzed within the context of the HBO's branding as "quality" television. In chapter 10, David and Sarah Pawlak Stanley focus on Lindelof's reframing of Hooded Justice and how it foregrounds the oppressive qualities of "ostensibly-democratic American institutions." Next, Curtis Marez analyzes the interrelationships between the real and fictional locations of *Watchmen* and considers how, despite its explicitly antiracist narrative, its producers have profited from the history and ongoing reality of where the show was shot. In chapter 12, Apryl Alexander approaches the show's focus on intergenerational trauma through the lens of contemporary psychology, arguing that the show asks us to "imagine a nation" where radical healing could occur. Finally, Brandy Monk-Payton builds upon this conception and considers how the television show functions as a form of televisual reparation, or at least a compensation for legacies of anti-Black violence in the United States.

Chapter 7

SISTER NIGHT AND HER SQUAD

HBO's *Watchmen* and the Healing Power of Speculative Fiction

CHAMARA MOORE

In the *Film Quarterly* roundtable on HBO's 2019 show *Watchmen*, Michael Boyce Gillespie describes the TV adaptation as more of a "reprioritizing" rather than a remixing of a large swath of issues regarding race, comics, politics, and American culture.[1] This "reprioritizing" in HBO's *Watchmen* not only redefines adaptation in our current media era, but also exemplifies how TV is starting to utilize the genre of speculative fiction to make larger arguments regarding racial identity and liberation, taking up the legacy begun in literature and comics. While many headlines have said that we're living in an age that Black speculative authors such as Octavia Butler and N. K. Jemisin have predicted, HBO's *Watchmen* uses its speculative elements to not only emphasize the timeliness of Alan Moore's original comic, but also to heal its relationship to marginalized audiences and particularly Black viewership. This chapter argues that by centering Regina King's character Angela Abar in the show's narrative, *Watchmen* centers a healing of not only intergenerational racial trauma, but of the very relationship between adaptation and Black identity, utilizing HBO's television medium to do more overtly antiracist and Black feminist work than its original text. This centering of Black femme embodiment and Afrofuturist vision solidifies Lindelof's show in the legacy of Black speculative fiction to make a larger argument for a new American imaginary informed by an ethic of care and healing pioneered by Black feminist thinkers.

SPECULATIVE FREEDOM

Before I delve into the intersectional strides that Lindleof's *Watchmen* is able to accomplish, I'd first like to make the show's linkage to contemporary speculative fiction more explicit. "Speculative fiction" is a genre term originally coined by Robert A. Heinlein in his 1947 editorial,[2] though in the last twenty years it has become an umbrella term for narratives relating to any of the science fiction, dystopia, supernatural, horror, or fantasy genres. In its most basic sense, speculative fiction is any narrative in which the laws of what's real or possible in our current society are changed, allowing the narrative to speculate on the outcome.[3] *Watchmen* combines science fiction, revisionist history, and dystopia to speculate on what the world would be like if cops were forced to wear masks and restrict their gun use, America had colonized Vietnam, reparations were real, and America has elected a different popular celebrity as president. The show purposely makes the boundaries of these genres less clear by beginning its pilot episode in the real historical event of the 1921 Tulsa Massacre that captures the ways in which America has often felt like a dystopia to its Black citizens. The episode then shifts forward in time to September 8, 2019, luring the audience into a false sense of security with a masked Black officer conducting a simple traffic stop, only to reveal that the world is no less dystopic, showing us yet another Black man attacked by Klansmen only twelve minutes into the episode, though in this case the aggressor is the 2019 version of a Klan member—a Kalvary member in a Rorschach mask.[4]

Another important element of the show's relationship to the speculative is its utilization of the freedom of the genre to comment on matters regarding race and oppression. While earlier speculative fiction was considered exclusionary in its minimal and notably racist depictions of nonwhite people, Black speculative fiction writers such as Samuel R. Delaney, Nalo Hopkinson, Ismael Reed, and Octavia Butler are best known for centering the Black subject in their narratives. These authors helped create a toolkit for healing the relationship between the genre and its Black readership, especially to famous speculative works most known for their racist origins like that of Edgar Rice Burroughs, H. P. Lovecraft, and Ward Kendall to name a few. In *Race and Ethnicity in Science Fiction*, Elisabeth Anne Leonard explains that the majority of speculative fiction outside of Black speculative fiction in particular "deals with racial tension by ignoring it. In many books the characters' race is either not mentioned and probably assumed to be white or, if mentioned, is irrelevant to the events of the story and functions only as an additional descriptor, such as hair colour or height."[5] Rather than fall into this trope, these Black speculative fiction authors write their characters to be unapologetically Black to the degree that it is usually their Blackness itself that allows them to survive, like in Octavia Butler's novel[6] *Fledgeling.*[7] In this way, Butler and many others created the methodology for utilizing the freedom of the genre to "reprioritize," rethink, and remix societies into complex worlds with different relationships to oppression—worlds sometimes free of racial oppression altogether.[8] Black speculative fiction author Nalo Hopkinson describes her own work as "subverting the genre which speaks so much about the experience of being alienated, but contains so little written by alienated people themselves."[9] While the *Watchmen* series isn't necessarily doing the same pioneering work as these Black creatives, it is candidly informed by this rich Black legacy both in the way in which it depicts its Black characters and in its direct communication with Black audiences.

One of the show's many creative decisions that prove its awareness of its racial legacy is its treatment of Dr. Manhattan. By making Dr. Manhattan a Black man, not only is the show literally empowering the image of a Black man as a god, but it is also offering up a racebent character that is innately altered by his adaptation. By this I mean that it solves the "plastic representation" problem,[10] offering the audience a character that is forever changed by being a Black man, rather than acting in the narrative as a white character with a Black face.[11] This change in the character's race is marked by an innate change in the character himself. Cal is the loving and doting partner that Jon never was in Moore's comic. The show even uses speculative elements to make this clearer. In episode 8, Dr. Manhattan must use a device made by Adrian Viedt in order to keep Cal from sharing Jon's memories. He does this because Angela is frustrated by the difference in power in their relationship. She explains that "when you know everything that's gonna happen, what is there to be afraid of? What is there to risk? . . . I'm taking a risk."[12] The suggestion here is that Angela is a Black woman whose life has been shaped by risk, threat, and fear, contrasting with Jon's whiteness. It is in this way that Angela makes clear it is not Jon's powers or perception of time that specifically irritate her like his past girlfriends, it is instead the fact that Jon is attempting to occupy a Black body and a Black relationship without knowing what it means to actually live with the specificity of the threat of racism and anti-Blackness. Veidt even jokes, "This isn't the 80s anymore, Jon. This kind of appropriation is considered quite problematic now."[13] Nonetheless, Jon leaves it entirely in Angela's hands whether he becomes Cal or not. He chooses Blackness for her and because of her. This changes him completely. Dr. Manhattan as Cal is a loving and doting partner in a way in which Jon never was in Moore's comic, fully inhabiting the Black love between Cal and Angela with only Angela and her Black womanhood as the source. In episode 6, Angela even describes him as "a great husband, an amazing father, and . . . the best friend I ever had."[14] The actor who portrays the character on the show, Yahya Abdul-Mateen II, describes it best in his 2020 Emmy's acceptance speech:

> It was also a story about a god who came down to earth to reciprocate to a Black woman all the love that she deserved. He'd offer her sacrifice and support, passion, and protection . . . and he did all that in the body of a Black man and I'm so proud that I was able to walk into those shoes. So I dedicate this award to all the Black women in my life.[15]

As Yahya describes, the show allows Dr. Manhattan to transform into a Black man to properly love a Black woman for her full self, made possible only by this speculative change. The show's narrative even suggests that this permanently changes Dr. Manhattan since he never takes the form of Jon again, even after Viedt's device is removed. Just as loving Angela has permanently changed his life, embodying Cal and living as a Black man has permanently changed his image.

Additionally, by making Dr. Manhattan a Black man, the show is combining the time Alan Moore created in the comic with Afrofuturist time that is nonlinear and cyclical, allowing Black past present and future to all exist simultaneously. This is what happens when the speculative overlaps with the Black imaginary. Aimee Bahng's definition of the speculative from *Migrant Futures: Decolonizing Speculation in Financial Times* "calls for a disruption of teleological ordering of the past, present and future and foregrounds the processes of narrating the past (history) and future science."[16] This overlaps in some ways with Ytasha Womack's definition of Afrofuturism, which she describes as centrally "a highly intersectional way of looking at possible alternate realities through a black cultural lens" in ways that are "non-linear, fluid and feminist."[17] While Afrofuturism "blends the future, the past, and the present," we see this blending of time in how Dr. Manhattan communicates.[18] When he first meets Angela in episode 8, he explains that the way he "experience[s] time is unique, and for [her] particularly infuriating," though he is at that moment "simultaneously in [that] bar having a conversation with [her], and on Europa creating life."[19] Nonetheless, Dr. Manhattan as Cal is still a Black man of the past, present, and future all at the same time, reminiscent of musician Sun Ra or *Black Panther* (in which T'Challa literally outlives death). Imagining a Black man with the power of a blue god is "radical" in the Afrofuturist sense, meaning that it resists the normative expected narrative about Black people or "a limited sense of possibility."[20] As Womack would describe, Dr. Manhattan is literally "a universal being" made ever more universal by embodying the specificity of Black ancestry in Cal's body. *Watchmen*'s speculative vision is what enables this empowerment. This demonstrates how the show is informed by Black writing, and also includes Black directors and creators—such as Stephen Williams, Cord Jefferson, and Stacy Osei-Kuffour—who are continuning the work of their literary predecessors.

HEALING ADAPTATION

Watchmen's relationship to this genre is actually similar to that of its source material. One of the innovative things about the show is how it clarifies things only glossed over in Moore's comic, while simultaneously updating and adapting threads from the comic into fruitful depictions even more relevant for our current times. In an era where adaptation between mediums means an empty racebent or genderbent reboot of a film from the '90s like *Ghostbusters* or *Jumanji*, HBO's adaptation becomes even more important. Lindelof takes small pieces from the comic and turns them into a future in which the American imaginary has the capacity for change regarding reparations and its colonial past.

An example of this is a quick frame from the comic that Lindelof turns into a full plot point. When we see a flashback to the first Crimebusters meeting in chapter 2, the Comedian burns Captain Metropolis's display board of potential issues for them to focus on. In the flames (Figure 1) we can see "promiscuity, drugs, antiwar demonstrations, and black unrest,"[21] thus revealing Captain Metropolis's problematics. The show turns this on its head in episode 6 after it's revealed that William Reeves, who we've only known as Angela's wheelchair-bound grandfather, was in fact Hooded Justice. After William has dedicated his life outside of police work to both the Minutemen and the defeat of the Cyclops organization, he discovers that Cyclops has been "using film projectors to turn Negroes against each other."[22] After this discovery, he calls his friend and lover, Captain Metropolis, to ask for the Minutemen's help, but Metropolis replies, "William, you of all people should know . . . the residents of Harlem cause riots all on their own."[23] If this weren't enough to make Metropolis's biases apparent, he adds: "I'm sorry William, but this sort of thing isn't really the Minutemen's cup of tea. I'm afraid you're going to have to solve Black unrest all on your own."[24] Here, the reference to

Figure 1. The Comedian burns Captain Metropolis's board in Alan Moore's 1986 *Watchmen* comic.

the comic becomes even more obvious, where Metropolis suggests that he can't be bothered with Black issues while simultaneously implying that he sees the Black community at large as an issue. In this way, Lindelof uses some of the Minutemen characters to make clear that the ideal of the superhero is innately both whitewashed and white supremacist, particularly in the examples of Captain Metropolis, Rorschach, and Ozymandias. By upending the racial identity of a character like Hooded Justice, whom *Watchmen* comic fans may have thought they already knew well enough from his assertions that the Crimebusters "should avoid political situations," Lindleof is upending the entire superhero ideal itself in the Watchmen universe.[25]

This is yet another way that he clarifies Moore's views on superheroes. While Moore's comic is not subtle about the ways in which it is critical of comic "heroes" altogether, it wasn't until a 2017 interview that fans knew Moore's exact feelings about the impact of superheroes on popular culture. In his interview with Brazilian writer and editor Raphael Sassaki, he was asked about people's fascination with comic book heroes in our culture, to which he remarked that he found the obsession "embarrassing" and "worrying." He added:

> These iconic characters are still very much white supremacist dreams of the master race. In fact I think that a good argument can be made for D.W. Griffith's *Birth of a Nation* as the first American superhero movie, and the point of origin for all those capes and masks.[26]

This considered, it seems as if Lindelof is using this futuristic remixing of Moore's material to make the ideological root of *Watchmen* clearer, or arguably create new superheroes with a different relationship to white supremacy that have more potential to make complex and liberatory arguments about race than their counterparts in the white imaginary of America's racist reality.

The murky and speculative relationship between the show and its source text is what makes it such an unusual adaptation. Nonetheless, the ways in which Lindelof takes singular elements such as simple phrases, images, or caricatures to expand into entire storylines for the series are what make its relationship to adaptation so refreshing and new, so that it feels more like a "remix" or "reprioritization." In the "Thinking about *Watchmen*" roundtable, Gillespie aptly summarizes that the show "presents itself as a disobedient adaptation that modifies, extends, and redirects the worldmaking of the source . . . elaborat[ing] on its source not as a sequel, reboot, or even translation, but rather as an adaptation that substitutes speculation and deviation in place of fidelity."[27] It is this elaboration on the comic that feels so out of place in a media industry dominated by comic giants like Marvel who change their source material for the silver screen in ways that prioritize clarity and sales, rather than historical truth and healing. It is this unabashed relationship to truth that is at the heart of *Watchmen*'s potential for healing and treating Black audiences with the ethic of care pioneered by intersectional thinkers and activists.

It's additionally unmatched in its intersectional approach to media adaptation, particularly in its method of taking things from the periphery and centering them unconditionally. It even centers Black viewership in a medium where it's not expected. For example, the very first thing that the audience sees in the pilot episode is a silent film, a genre famous not only for depicting Black characters as white actors in blackface, but also for defining "blackness" primarily as minstrelsy. The show's title blinks sporadically as if projected by an old-timey projector, with only "Watchmen" in color, before it transitions into a wide shot of a white man riding a white horse, an image that feels too akin to *Birth of a Nation*.[28] The only thing that separates it visually thus far in the episode is the black-hooded figure chasing the man. To a Black viewer, it seems like something D. W. Griffith adjacent until the hooded figure reveals himself to be "Bass Reeves, the Black Marshall of

Figure 2. Adult Angela Abar embodies her grandfather's memory of concealing his Blackness as Hooded Justice in HBO's *Watchmen*.

Oklahoma" portrayed and embodied by a Black man.[29] At this point the show introduces its speculative nature, while simultaneously defining itself as deprioritizing whiteness. Rather than the racist violence that the audience expects, the show gives us a remixed silent film in which the Black sheriff is cheered on by the white townsfolk.

Centering an inspiring Black image such as that of Bass Reeves and its connection to William as a young Black spectator also reveals the show's emphasis on Black audiences. This is underscored by the assumption that William was so inspired by not only seeing himself on screen, but also seeing Bass Reeves "trust in the law" and survive, so much so that he fashions his own life around it. The show makes this clearer when in episode 6 his wife, June, asks him why he put the hood back on to fight crime.[30] As if to answer the question, William begins describing his favorite silent film, *Trust in the Law!*, which introduced the audience to the world of the show, but this time the camera pushes in to emphasize Bass Reeves and his badge while William narrates that "the townsfolk cheer" before pulling out to see June putting William in his Hooded Justice eye makeup.[31] While it's clear that William likes the recognition that Hooded Justice receives, June reminds him that he can only get justice and remain a hero as long as the proverbial white public "think[s] one of their own's under" the black hood.[32] This is further emphasized by a shot of Angela Abar's face replacing William's reflection wearing the same white face paint (Figure 2), suggesting that Angela is safe

Figure 3. A nine-year-old Angela Abar begs her parents to let her watch the only movie she can find starring a Black woman.

to wear a mask as she chooses in 2019 because William safely wore his and concealed his own Blackness from the public in the '40s.[33]

In this way, Black media representation is equally as important for both characters. Bass Reeves's inspiration makes William so determined to become a police officer that he is willing to endure being tokenized as the only Black officer inducted onto the force in 1938. He even remains on the force after being beaten and threatened by fellow officers and learning that the NYPD is working with the white supremacist Cyclops organization.[34] This intimate relationship with Black media images is something that we learn Angela has inherited as well when she chooses the character from the cover of a VHS tape as the inspiration for her Sister Night persona in episode 7.[35]

Sister Night from the tape (Figure 3) dons a tight dress and a big afro to fight crime in a way that is reminiscent of the iconic *Foxy Brown* or *Cleopatra Jones* films of the '70s. This highlights yet another way in which the show heals Black audiences' relationship to earlier film genres since it only references blaxploitation[36] without ever actually depicting the film or suggesting Angela has ever watched it. Instead, Angela puts her own twist on Sister Night's image, donning a fashionable leather hooded coat and black mask to fight white supremacists throughout the show rather than anything that looks outdated, caricatured, or stereotypical.[37] The audience gets to watch her bring agency to the Sister Night character just as we watch William become Hooded Justice. Similarly, the show transforms Hooded Justice's elusive comic character that "avoid[s] political situations"[38] into a Black man that channels the rage from surviving his own lynching into a lust for racial justice—sleuthing and fighting from behind badge and mask to take down the organization that burned down his entire world when he was just a child. In this way, *Watchmen* allows Black audiences to go on a journey with its characters from seeing their own media images to becoming racist-punching heroes for the audience itself.

BLACK WOMANHOOD AND INTERGENERATIONAL TRAUMA

Another way in which *Watchmen* centers those from the periphery is in its relationship to the Black female body. It sets itself apart using both Angela Abar and her police persona, Sister Night, as its main character in a media landscape where Black women in comic-adaptation fandoms have almost never seen themselves on screen. Making Angela the protagonist means centering Black womanhood and therefore a subject under the double bind of racist and sexist oppression, meaning othered on numerous margins of existence. The history of the Black female body in the American context means a body commodified to the degree of being barred from humanity altogether. Hortense Spillers argues that Black female bodies are "the principal point of passage between the human and non-human world" because of the intricate ways in which they are commodified and objectified.[39] In this way, Black women are so marginalized that it is noticeable when they are centered, particularly without light skin or Eurocentric features. In addition to her appearance, it's important that Angela is a Black female cop since Black women are brutalized and killed disproportionally more than any other racial group at the hands of state violence. Having Angela act as a police officer who seeks justice for racism and tries to sniff out crooked officers feels like a hopeful and speculative choice in a time when police departments in American cities are, justifiably, under more scrutiny than ever. On a show where the chief of police is hanged for being a white supremacist, the choice of Angela's career lands on the lighter side of its argument regarding faith in police departments.

Nonetheless, Angela's "nose for white supremacy" and her fiercely independent nature solidify her as a depiction of Black women's survival.[40] Black feminist thinker Patricia Hill Collins asserts that Black "women have had to exhibit independence and self-reliance to ensure their own survival and that of their loved ones."[41] This is why Angela is the type of officer to keep a shotgun in a hidden compartment in her headboard. In addition to her fierceness, Angela's depiction resists tropes of Black women. She is given the space in the narrative to be flawed but never caricatured. She's painted with the complexity that she deserves. She isn't the "strong Black woman" or the "angry Black woman." She is instead given moments to be both strong and weakened and has glaring lapses in judgement, such as with her friend and superior Judd Crawford. She carries a troubled and traumatic relationship with her family while still maintaining curiosity about her own lineage. In this way, her own journey is centered in the show's narrative without perpetuating the liberal "Black women will save us" trope of our political era. She has the ability to save herself, but is married to a blue god who can zap intruders to New Mexico if anything goes left.

Another important way in which Angela's character is used as a healing depiction of Black womanhood is in the part that she plays in *Watchmen*'s depiction of trauma. The show's speculative move to have Angela take an entire bottle of the drug Nostalgia allows her to physically embody her grandfather William in his most traumatic experiences, while also demonstrating the ways in which trauma flattens time. Trauma theorist Cathy Caruth explains that trauma is "a shock that works very much like a bodily threat, but is in fact a break in the mind's experience of time."[42] This break in time makes it so that Angela feels William's pain from the racist violence of the Tulsa Massacre, William's lynching, and the Minutemen's betrayal all at once. It allows Angela to see William's trauma rather than falling into the trap that befalls many families, that of hiding the painful family history only to reify the trauma they attempted to bury and continue the cycle. This also makes it so that Angela and William can communicate nonverbally, bringing experience to the unspeakable utterance of the trauma itself. The characters speak very little to each other in the show itself, though their relationship remains intact at the end of the series and even seems to be the thing that saves them both. The show lets us deep into the lives of this family and their history to an intimate degree, so that we still root for them at the end.

In addition to Angela's embodiment of her grandfather's trauma, she is depicted in a way that is frequently informed by trauma so that the audience rarely feels like her actions weren't justified in some way. For example, she carries a distrust of nearly everyone around her, but the show gives us her backstory, so that we understand the chip that she carries about family, having witnessed her parents' death at an early age. She breaks into museums and sneaks into dark rooms at funerals for whatever answers that she needs, but the more episodes the audience watches, the more they understand the complexity of her life, to the degree that she could tell no one of the real identity of her own husband. Her feelings, be they anger, skepticism, incredulity, or otherwise, are almost always justified in a way that makes her a fully rounded character whom we are slow to judge. This in itself is healing in a society that requires Black women to make their rage "eloquent" just to survive.[43]

In this sense, the *Watchmen* series is healing in that it augments and creates along a Black feminist ethic of care.[44] This ethical practice doesn't force an understanding or an utterance around trauma, but instead it acknowledges that the Black body (especially when a Black woman) taking up space is in itself an utterance and an argument.

Lindelof's *Watchmen* suggests that Black women are the leaders of the future, much like the long legacy of Black speculative fiction the show is informed by. Nonetheless, it seems like the show is merely extending an argument made by HBO itself. While HBO made news with its contracts with Black creators such as Issa Rae, Mischa Green, and Larry Wilmore, it has long moved towards diverse shows with Afrofuturistic characters and revisionist histories, such as *Westworld* and *Lovecraft Country*. At this point Alan Moore, Michael Creighton, and H. P. Lovecraft are only the beginning of what's sure to be a long line of white men who have had their works adapted to the HBO screen to center dynamic Black women characters. *Watchmen* ends with a Black woman with the potential to become a god, *Westworld* ends with a Black woman robot yielding a samurai sword in the future,[45] and *Lovecraft Country* ends with a Black girl skipping off with her pet monster and clenching her robotic arm.[46] HBO as a network is using speculative fiction to let Black women rule the world, the first steps on a long road of healing for a Black viewership who is just now seeing inspiring, high quality, and big budget speculative projects that allow them to see themselves in a new light.

NOTES

1. Michael Boyce Gillespie. "Thinking about Watchmen: A Roundtable." *Film Quarterly*, June 26, 2020, https://filmquarterly.org/2020/06/26/thinking-about-watchmen-with-jonathan-w-gray-rebecca-a-wanzo-and-kristen-j-warner/.

2. Heinlein coined the term in the American magazine *The Saturday Evening Post* to refer to the science fiction genre, though its meaning has since been broadened.

3. R. B. Gill, "The Uses of Genre and the Classification of Speculative Fiction," *Mosaic: An Interdisciplinary Critical Journal* 46, no. 2 (2013): 71–85. https://doi.org/10.1353/mos.2013.0021.

4. Nicole Kassell, "It's Summer and We're Running out of Ice." Episode. *Watchmen*, season 1, episode 1. HBO, 2019.

5. Elisabeth Anne Leonard, "Race and Ethnicity in Science Fiction," in *The Cambridge Companion to Science Fiction* (Cambridge University Press, 2003), 253–63, https://doi.org/10.1017/CCOL0521816262.020.

6. Octavia E. Butler, *Fledgling* (New York: Seven Stories Press, 2005).

7. In Butler's 2005 novel *Fledgling*, the protagonist Shori survives because she is the first vampire with Black melanated skin, which allows her to survive daylight unlike her white elders (Butler 2005).

8. Gillespie, 4.

9. Leonard, 1.

10. Kristen J. Warner, "In the Time of Plastic Representation," *Film Quarterly* 71, no. 2 (2017): 34–35. "Plastic representation" is a term coined by Kristen Warner to describe the phenomena in which characters of color are introduced into a narrative to "look like meaningful imagery" but are ultimately "hollow and cannot survive close scrutiny" and merely "serve as visual identifiers for specific demographics in order to flatten the expectation to desire anything more."

11. Kristen J. Warner, "In the Time of Plastic Representation." *Film Quarterly* 71, no. 2 (2017): 32–37.

12. Kassell, 23:42.

13. Kassell, 27:55.

14. Kassell, 53:17.

15. Television Academy, "72nd Emmy Awards: Yahya Abdul-Mateen II Wins for Outstanding Supporting Actor in a Lim Series/Movie." YouTube. Primetime Emmys, September 20, 2020, https://www.youtube.com/watch?v=qsHCopYgZc4.

16. Aimee Bahng, *Migrant Futures: Decolonizing Speculation in Financial Times* (Durham, NC: Duke University Press, 2017), 8.

17. Stephen W. Thrasher. "Afrofuturism: Reimagining Science and the Future from a Black Perspective," *The Guardian*, December 7, 2015, p. 2, https://www.theguardian.com/culture/2015/dec/07/afrofuturism-black-identity-future-science-technology.

18. Thrasher, 2.

19. Kasell, 4:58–5:04.

20. Thrasher, 3.

21. Alan Moore and Dave Gibbons, *Watchmen* (New York: DC Comics, 2005), 11.

22. Stephen Williams, "This Extraordinary Being," Episode. *Watchmen*, season 1, episode 6, HBO, 2019, 46:23–27.

23. Williams 2019, 46:36–40.

24. Williams 2019, 47:23–32.

25. Moore and Gibbons, 5.

26. Raphael Sassaki. "Moore on Jerusalem, Eternalism, Anarchy and Herbie!" ALAN MOORE WORLD, November 18, 2019, https://alanmooreworld.blogspot.com/2019/11/moore-on-jerusalem-eternalism-anarchy.html.

27. Gillespie, 2.

28. Kassell, 0:00–0:09.

29. Kassell, 0:59–1:07.

30. Williams, 24:19–30.

31. Williams, 24:57–26:03.

32. Williams, 26:31–43.

33. Williams, 26:48.

34. Williams, 15:45–16:26.

35. David Semel. "An Almost Religious Awe." *Watchmen*, season 1, episode 8. HBO, 2019, 4:37.

36. Blackploitation is a film genre from the 1970s most known for being often produced by white studios while centering and featuring characters as harmful stereotypes such as pimps, drug dealers, and gangsters in an effort to create cinema that appealed to Black audiences.

37. Craig Lambert. "The Blaxploitation Era," *Harvard Magazine*, November 17, 2009, https://harvardmagazine.com/2003/01/the-blaxploitation-era.

38. Moore and Gibbons, 5.

39. Hortense J. Spillers, *Black, White, and in Color: Essays on American Literature and Culture* (University of Chicago Press, 2003), 207.

40. David Lindelof, *Watchmen*. United States: HBO, 2019.

41. Patricia Hill Collins, *Black Feminist Thought: Knowledge, Consciousness, and the Politics of Empowerment* (New York: Routledge, 1990), 159.

42. Cathy Caruth, *Unclaimed Experience: Trauma, Narrative, and History* (Baltimore: Johns Hopkins University Press, 1996), 61.

43. Brittney C. Cooper, *Eloquent Rage: A Black Feminist Discovers Her Superpower*. First edition. (New York: St. Martin's Press, 2018).

44. A. Maihofer, "Ethic of Care," in *A Companion to Feminist Philosophy*, ed. A. Jagger and I. Young (Oxford: Blackwell, 2000).

45. Lisa Joy, Jonathan Nolan. *Westworld*. HBO, 2016.

46. Mischa Green. *Lovecraft Country*. HBO, 2020.

Chapter 8

"IT IS DIFFICULT TO BE A WHITE MAN IN AMERICA"

White Male Supremacy and the Alt-Right in HBO's *Watchmen*

BRIAN FAUCETTE

The Unite the Right rally that took place in Charlottesville, VA, in 2017 was a weekend of horror that shocked the nation with images of hundreds of young white men wearing khaki pants and white dress shirts and carrying tiki torches at night across the campus of the University of Virginia. They marched in formation shouting, "Jews will not replace us" and "Blood and soil" in a scene reminiscent of Nazi Germany in the 1930s. The march was supposedly in protest of the statue of Confederate general Robert E. Lee being removed by the city. Yet, when looking at the actions, speakers, and the rhetoric used over that weekend, it is clear what that event represented was the unveiling of the alt-right and the return of white male supremacy as a concern for the nation. This concern animated discussions about race in America and the danger of alt-right groups like the Proud Boys and Boogaloo Boys, along with Neo-Nazis and the Klan. Such groups and their hate-filled ideology increasingly are the focus of news reports, books, articles, and documentaries. Their need to rewrite history through the lens of white male supremacy is disconcerting and dangerous because of their sense of grievance and anger that motivates them. Their appearance and the country's shifting focus to issues of race recenter questions about white masculinity and the dangers associated with it at a time of great change that seems to threaten the idea of white patriarchy.

The dangers of white male supremacy in connection with violence and insidious disguised racism are tackled in the Emmy-winning HBO limited series *Watchmen*.[1] It is the series' willingness to tackle these issues using the world of the acclaimed graphic novel from the 1980s that led some young white men to criticize the series as "woke propaganda" on reddit and 4chan: sites often associated with the spread of alt-right ideology and conspiracy theories associated with groups like QAnon.[2] These groups and the white men that comprise them sociologist Michael Kimmel notes are the result of what he refers to as "angry white men" who espouse a feeling of "aggrieved entitlement" that he defines as a form of entitlement "that can no longer be assumed . . . [I]t's about rear guard actions of bitterness and rage . . . trying futilely to hold back the surging tide of greater equality and greater justice."[3] This constant need to reassert white masculinity is addressed directly in the series through plotlines about the Seventh Kavalry, the Cyclops Organization, and the horrific Tulsa Massacre of 1921 depicted in the first episode, "It's Summer and We're Running Out of Ice" (10/20/19).

In the opening scenes depicting the Tulsa race massacre, the episode captures the terrors that in particular some white men are capable of when they feel threatened. Kristin Warner notes how the episode's opening is "a very potent attempt at televisual remediation" that can be celebrated for its use of "microdosing racialized remediation" in order to "center and set the course of this story around not just blackness but a historical moment of blackness that is not celebrated enough."[4] Yet, it is not only Blackness that is presented, as the viewer is presented with scenes of armed white men in long shots and medium close-ups wearing Klan robes confidently marching through the area of the city known as "Black Wall Street" summarily killing any black person that they see and burning down homes and businesses with the help of the US military. Whiteness and the violence associated with it is also presented as the episode depicts the real events that were sparked by the rampant rumor in the city that a young Black man had raped a young white woman the day before.[5] The fear of white women being raped by Black men struck a deep chord with white men who in this period and throughout American history "were obsessed with the connection between manhood and racial dominance."[6] This idea of American manhood and masculinity being linked to questions of superiority, Kimmel argues, is the foundation of the male experience such that "manhood is less about the drive for domination and more about the fear of others dominating us, having power or control over us. Throughout American history American men have been afraid that others will see us as less than manly, as weak, timid, frightened."[7] It is these fears of loss of control and the changing nature of society after World War I and the events of the "Red Summer" where many African American men home from fighting for democracy in WWI began to clamor for equal rights and the end of Jim Crow that serve as a backdrop to the events in Tulsa and those of the HBO series.[8] The horrors presented are seen not only by the viewer but also by a young Black boy whose father, a veteran of WWI, makes the ultimate sacrifice and sends his son away in hopes that the boy will survive and find a better life. It is an origin story that mirrors that of Superman. It is a connection the series acknowledges later when the young boy, now a grown man named Will Reeves (Jovan Adepo) asks a news vendor what he is reading, and in his hand the vendor holds *Action Comics* #1, released in 1938.

The dangers of white supremacy and its connections to white masculinity in a contemporary context are addressed in a later scene that resituates the traffic stop encounter which has been fraught with danger and serves as a reminder of racism for so many African Americans in the United States.[9] Here, the stop involves a white man dressed in a plaid shirt, jeans, and a baseball cap in a pickup truck who ironically is listening to hip-hop when he is stopped. The first thing he does is to turn down the music and then place his hands on the steering wheel at 10 and 2. All his actions are familiar as they are ones that African Americans often recall doing when stopped by the police. Events escalate when the white man smirks at the officer, a clear sign of disrespect, because the cop is Black and is wearing a mask to protect his identity. The cop then asks the man what is in the bed of his truck and asks for permission to search the vehicle, but the white man does not want to comply. The reason for his unwillingness is highlighted when the cop sees a mask in the man's glovebox, which he tries to hide. The scene ends with a medium close-up of the white man hurling a head of lettuce through the broken windshield and into the cop's lap, as if the officer is nothing but trash that white men must remove to maintain their power. What we see is an angry white man acting out his anger and his inability to accept the authority of the cop. As shown later in the episode, he has found a sense of belonging by joining the white supremacist organization Seventh Kavalry and wearing a Rorschach mask. They are a group whose rhetoric and need to hide their faces resembles that of the Klan. Kimmel notes when the Klan was established in the late 1860s that there was a focus on "manly character and courage, and initiation rituals were punctuated by prayers that 'God give us men.'"[10] The linkages between white masculinity, religion, and control over minorities that Kimmel locates as a driver of Klan rhetoric can also be linked to the rhetoric espoused by the Seventh Kavalry in the show.

The Seventh Kavalry adopts the mask associated with the figure of Rorschach, an original member of the Watchmen who is killed and leaves behind a journal that is shown to have been dropped off at the neoconservative newspaper *New Frontiersman* in the last issue of the graphic novel, which takes place thirty years prior to the events depicted in the show. The Seventh Kavalry send the Tulsa PD after the shooting orchestrated by one of their own a video that resembles the now common terrorist videos associated with Al-Qaeda and ISIS. The men in matching Rorschach masks stand before a cross and outline their vision for America: "soon the black filth will be no more. And the streets of Tulsa will turn into an extended gutter overflowing with liberal tears. Soon all the whores and race traitors will shout, 'Save us.' And we will whisper, 'No.' We are the Seventh Kavalry. We are no one and everyone. We are invisible. We will not compromise. Do not stand between us and our mission or there will be more dead cops. There are so many deserving of retribution." What the viewer sees and hears is a manifestation of white male anger at its extremes motivated by fears that society is changing in a way that challenges their authority. The language used in the video corresponds with how today "many Alt-Americans freely fantasize about their desire to execute liberals, terrorists, 'race mixers,' and other traitors" to the point of elimination in order to remake the nation healthy.[11] The video's message is striking and disturbing and mirrors David Neiwert's argument about the rise of the alt-right in light of Trump's candidacy and presidency. "The American radical right—the violent, paranoid, racist, hateful radical right—was back with a vengeance. Actually, it had never gone away."[12] Chief Judd Crawford (Don Johnson) makes this same point about the Kavalry, "Three years we convinced ourselves of peace. That they were gone, but they were just hibernating." The idea that white supremacy is something that can be easily eradicated has been perpetuated for decades in the United States. The norms of Black success and aspiration first seen in the opening scene of Tulsa Massacre and its aftereffects are explored throughout the rest of the series even as it shows how white male supremacy is always lurking to counter, destabilize, and destroy those gains. "White Americans are encouraged to invest in whiteness, to remain true to an identity that provide them with resources, power, and opportunity" argues George Lipsitz.[13] Neiwert labels citizens of "Alt-America" who view race as "essentially a zero-sum proposition: if one race gains in status or power, then another must lose concomitantly."[14] These ideas are echoed by Kimmel in his reading of contemporary white masculinity as emasculated as a result of changes in society, home, and in the workplace. Such feelings of emasculation, he argues, were the fuel for extreme right groups to mold some white men into believing that the only way to reclaim their "manhood" was to embrace white supremacist and far-right ideologies.[15]

The ideological dangers of far-right rhetoric are displayed in the scene where Chief Crawford is listening to right-wing talk radio in his truck. The host of the program and his manner of delivery recall Rush Limbaugh as does his manner of derision as he advocates for the candidacy of the senator of Oklahoma against President Redford. One of the key factors in the development of the alt-right and right-wing populism Neiwert identifies is right-wing media, especially talk radio. He notes that "right-wing media began appearing as a new propaganda type that openly eschewed the journalistic standards of mainstream news organizations: in a classic use of 'Newspeak,' they declared themselves 'fair and balanced.'"[16] The brief scene is a bit shocking as earlier Crawford has been shown to be against the forces of white supremacy like the Seventh Kavalry and friends with his lead African American detective Sister Night/Abar (Regina King). Later in "An Almost Religious Awe" (12/1/19) FBI agent Blake (Jean Smart) confronts Crawford's widow Jane (Frances Fisher) as she investigates his death. She states, "I wouldn't be doing my job if I didn't entertain the idea that the Chief of Police of Tulsa was a secret white supremacist. It has to make you wonder about his friends."

Even more shocking is the discovery after Crawford's death Detective Abar makes when she finds a Klan robe with a badge on it proudly displayed in Crawford's closet next to a photo of a man in a Tulsa police uniform. The image is jarring because it challenges the earlier images of Crawford as an antiracist. Moreover, it forces viewers to question their own thinking about the nature of police and policing and race in America at a time when the growing calls for police reform and movements like Black Lives Matter have focused attention on the reality that white police officers' interactions with minorities are marked with violence and death. The elderly African American Will Reeves (Louis Gossett Jr.) tells Abar, "He had skeletons in his closet. There is a vast and insidious conspiracy here in Tulsa." The origins of that conspiracy that he references and its connection to the dangers of white male supremacy are explored in the penultimate episode of the series, "This Extraordinary Being" (11/24/19).

The episode captures the dangers of white supremacist thinking and conspiracies when Abar takes a lethal dose of Nostalgia, a pill form of Will's memories that enables her and the viewer to experience his life as a Black cop in NYC in the 1930s by suturing her and the viewer into Will's memories. It is one of the most visually striking episodes of television that uses a style akin to a comic book to force viewers to grapple with the historical realities faced by Black America. Will is seen at the graduation ceremony for the NYC police cadets of 1938 and pride is evident on his face.[17] Yet, that pride is soon shown to be misplaced after the white police officer delivering the remarks and awarding the men their badges intentionally skips Will. Instead, he receives his badge from one of the city's oldest African American officers who provides him with the advice to "Beware the Cyclops. Do us proud and be safe out there."

Will's safety and ability to be recognized as a legitimate officer are highlighted in the following scene when he confronts a white man who has fire-bombed a Jewish delicatessen. The man smirks at Will when he tries to arrest him and asks, "Who are you boy?" and then blows cigar smoke into Will's face. He then tells him, "I got to get home to listen to *Amos 'n' Andy*," a reference to one of America's most popular radio shows in the 1930s that was known for its degrading depiction of African Americans voiced by white actors. Will does make the arrest, but in the process he discovers a truth that shatters his own belief in law and order. During booking, the man tells another a white officer that "this spook is accusing me of a horrendous crime. Who you gonna believe, me or him?" One of the white male officers appears to defend Will and demands that the suspect apologize, which he does. The white male officer then explains that he will handle the arrest, and as he takes the man away, he flashes a hand gesture above his eyes in the shape of a circle. The moment is striking because it recalls the current conversation about how white nationalists and members of alt-right have appropriated and used the "okay" symbol, a hand gesture now classified as a symbol of hate and racism by the Anti-Defamation League.[18] Later Will sees the man back on the streets and demands to be told what happened, but the white desk sergeant pleads with him "to let it be." Will asks the desk sergeant about the hand gesture, and he is told "it's going to be the hole in your head, if you don't let it be."

Will's tenacity and unwillingness to accept the idea of white superiority are directly addressed in three key scenes in the episode. Off duty, Will is targeted by his fellow white male officers who are also off duty after he declines their invitation to go out for a beer. They corner him in an alley at night, and the three men begin to beat him mercilessly using their batons. They then drag his unconscious body into the waiting car and drive out into the countryside where they put a noose around Will's neck and a black hood over his head before stringing him up in a tree to scare him. The scene, shot in black and white, captures the terror of Black individuals as the viewer is forced to identify with Will and is sutured into his body to experience the horrors of the lynching. It is another moment where history is made real as the viewer confronts the reality that, for many African Americans, white Americans and especially law enforcement represented a threat that often ended in death. In this case, Will is spared when the officers cut him down. The one officer who flashed the hand gesture in the station house says with an evil grin, "You keep your black nose out of white folks' business. Or next time we won't cut you down." The scene illustrates the terrible reality that explicit racism in law enforcement was quite normal. As time has passed the feeling that racism too has passed is one that animates much of the discussion towards how America grapples with race relations. Yet, as Michael German notes, "Explicit racism in law enforcement takes many forms, from membership or affiliation with violent white supremacist or far-right militant groups, to engaging in racially discriminatory behavior toward the public or law enforcement colleagues, to making racist remarks and sharing them on social media."[19] German's definition, along with the fact that since 2000 there have been hundreds of law enforcement officials involved with white supremacist groups or far-right militias, is a startling, reminder of how pervasive white supremacy is within the United States and that even within the very institutions that are supposed to protect the public, racism is prevalent. Neiwert documents how in 2011 the organization Constitutional Sheriffs and Peace Officers Association was formed by former sheriff Richard Mack to persuade other members of law enforcement to support his views, arguing that county sheriffs are the "last line of defense against a tyrannical federal government." Neiwert connects Mack's organization and philosophy to the rise of the alt-right and white supremacist ideology.[20]

The ideology of white supremacy and its impact on law enforcement are addressed once more in the episode when Will is asked to help investigate why a group of African Americans in a movie theater started a riot, which led to violence, the theater being burned, and deaths. The lack of respect and care for the victims by white law enforcement is emphasized when a beat cop tells Will, "Same thing that always happens when you put a bunch of animals in the same cage." He then explains that he needs Will's help because "we need someone who speaks the language." Will watches as the officers focus their energy on using their batons and arresting people rather than helping them. It is a scene that feels overly relevant in light of the shooting of Breonna Taylor and the BLM protests that have swept the nation since the election of Trump. Through further investigation Will learns that the events at the theater were caused by a white nationalist organization called Cyclops whose goal is to use subliminal messages and flashes of light recorded in films to hypnotize and change the behaviors of African Americans to kill one another in a manner like what Will saw in the theater. He single-handedly dismantles the organization in NYC, sets the building on fire, and then walks away. Throughout the episode the viewer experiences Will's story, so that in the end when Will is shown using Cyclops' techniques against Chief Crawford to force Crawford to kill himself, Will's actions are not as mysterious and feel somewhat justified because he continues to police the dangers of white male supremacy even as an old man.

The connection between the Tulsa Massacre, the Seventh Kavalry, and white male supremacy is revealed in "Little Fear of Lightning" (11/17/19). The senator from Oklahoma, Joe Keene (James Wolk), reveals his connection to the white supremacists when he interrogates Wade/Looking Glass (Tim Blake Nelson), who has been lured by the Seventh Kavalry to an abandoned mall that they are using to stage their plans. Keene removes a Rorschach mask and then outlines his involvement along with Crawford's as an effort to maintain the peace. The moment highlights the hypocrisy and danger of politicians like Keene who are willing to align themselves with conspiracy groups and white supremacists in order to gain power and again reflects on the current concerns that Trump and Republicans have embraced white nationalism in an attempt to garner votes and power. Keene threatens Wade and Abar, telling them, "Angela threatens to disrupt the aforementioned peace . . . serve her up that way I don't have to ask these racist Okies to go to her house and kill her entire family." Keene's words reveal him to be another example of an "angry white man" who has embraced white supremacist ideology and toxic masculinity to push back against progressive advancements for women and minorities. A point that he makes explicit when he tells agent Blake after she is kidnapped by the Seventh Kavalry, "We are not racists. We are about restoring balance in these times when our country forgets about the principles on which it was founded. Because the scales have tipped too far." Keene's words echo Kimmel's argument that some white men who have seen their places in the world upended by change view their purpose to restore a balance where men are in control and everyone else returns to a pre-civil-rights-era position. His rhetoric is also striking in how it resembles the argument made by the alt-right and Trump with his slogan, "Make America Great Again." Unfortunately for Keene, Blake and Abar are powerful, confident women as Blake makes clear when she challenges Keene's notion of himself and the word saying, "It was your legacy to grow up and be the most powerful racist fuck in the nation" and then calls his plans silly.

Keene then tells Blake, "It is extremely difficult to be a white man in America right now. So now I am thinking I might try being a blue one" (reference to Dr. Manhattan who Keene and Seventh Kavalry's plan to kidnap and take his power). Keene's words and the actions of the Seventh Kavalry illustrate Kimmel's version of contemporary America where "angry white boys (rampage school shooters); or scions of hate radio, Tea Partiers, and pre-Trump supporters; or men who murder and assault women; or the misogynist Men's Rights Activists," all espouse a feeling of "aggrieved entitlement, a sense of righteous indignation, of undeserved victimhood in a world suddenly dominated by political correctness. The rewards that these white men felt had been promised for a lifetime . . . of playing by the rules . . . had suddenly dried up . . . the water had been diverted to far less deserving 'others.'"[21] Thus, for men like Keene, the option that they embrace to "restore balance" in the nation and to become masculine is to use violence or adopt white supremacist philosophies.

The kidnapping of Dr. Manhattan by the Kavalry for Keene is disturbing and also shows how Keene is willing to break the law to achieve his ultimate goal: total power. Indeed, when Keene gloats over Manhattan's capture, "I got you," as he looks at the blue body trapped in a cage, it is a visual reminder of how Black bodies have been terrorized, beaten, stolen, and misappropriated since 1619. As Keene begins to remove his clothes, a smile beaming on his face, the viewer grasps the danger of the Kavalry's plot to Tulsa and the world. Keene explains, "First, he took our guns. And then he made us say, sorry. Sorry over and over again. Sorry for the alleged sins of those who died decades before we were born. Sorry for the color of our skin." His argument that Redford is a puppet president whose liberal policies like Redforations, gun control, and a willingness to accept the horrors of white supremacy in America echo the rhetoric of the alt-right, who "see time as cyclical, something that can be brought back, the far right celebrates an idealized past where the white man was master of his home and the colonized world."[22] Yet, it is not only history that Keene relies on when he explains their actions: "Start ourselves a little culture war. And if we control both sides of it, I can come riding up on a white horse and into the White House." His reference to culture war as a political tactic for gaining political support and maintaining it is one that alludes to decades of American political fights, especially in light of the shifting dynamics of the two major parties. Equally important is Keene's usage of the rhetoric of the cowboy and the Western hero which have been crucial in shaping America's ideals around masculinity since Teddy Roosevelt's notion of "strenuous manhood." In effect, Keene's speech implicitly connects his mode of masculinity to whiteness and heroism.

Once Keene is completely naked, he jabs at Blake and the other people present for what feels like a ceremony of "aggrieved entitlement." He gloats, saying, "I am about to become the most powerful man alive. Waving my dick in people's faces is just overkill."[23] Keene's boast in a sense echoes Scott Melzer's notion that "penis size and performance are inextricably tied to contemporary American manhood." Melzer connects the need for contemporary men to be "in essence 'dick proud' to American politics and in particular Donald Trump's taunting of Marco Rubio."[24] Keene's comment serves to critique how Dr. Manhattan was known for walking around naked with his penis exposed, as is shown several times in the series. What is striking in Lindelof's reimagining of *Watchmen* is that Manhattan is an African American man, and the actor playing Manhattan, Yahya Abdul-Mateen II, proudly displays his penis. In displaying his body, especially in the scenes where he is caged, the series recalls images of African slaves on the auction block displayed as chattel for whites to peruse. Moreover, the duality of Manhattan's complete nakedness is seen as "overkill" by Keene, whose jab can be read as a moment of a white man stealing the power of an African American man and his body. In effect, Keene hopes to appropriate Manhattan's body and power to serve the interests of white supremacy and to restore what they perceive as an imbalance in culture and power relations, as illustrated when he chants "Yeah now, let's get blue," as if he were an athlete about to take the field in a competition. It is because of Keene's indifference and racist words that when he is killed trying to steal Manhattan's powers that viewers are able to see the events as justified. Indeed, such a feeling is also marked when all the members of the Kavalry and the original members of Cyclops are killed after Will's statement is read: "You have plundered and pillaged and murdered in the name of white supremacy." The inability to acknowledge their crimes or racist tendencies is brutally displayed when Crawford's widow haughtily says, "Just do it," before they are all killed.

Over the course of nine episodes, the limited series forces viewers to grapple with the dangers of white male supremacist thinking in American history, culture, and politics. Lindelof willingly engages with the hidden truths and legacies of American history to expose how dangerous the rhetoric and beliefs of white supremacists have been to America's well-being. By portraying the terrors of the Greenwood massacre and then exploring the long-term impacts of such an event on America's Black population and how some white men have attempted to reverse progressive efforts in this country using intimidation, violence, and rhetoric, *Watchmen* challenges viewers to engage with the hidden, untold, and more complex version of America and its people rather than the "city on the hill" or a "melting pot" too often cited as examples of American exceptionalism. These ideas have been corrosive and dangerous because, as the series shows, too often white men have relied on them in order to assuage any notion that America is a nation founded in paradox, inequality, and racism. To better understand that legacy of racism also requires the development of more shows like *Watchmen* that grapple with how white Americans, especially men, have used white supremacist ideology to maintain control and power. Indeed, as Will tells Abar, "wounds need air," and it is the airing of America's original sin of racism that is required for the nation to heal and become more unified and to combat the negative and dangerous impacts of white supremacists and movements like the alt-right.

NOTES

1. See Carol Anderson, *White Rage: The Unspoken Truth of Our Racial Divide* (New York: Bloomsbury, 2016).

2. Kevin Fallon. "Comics Fanboys are Pissed about HBO's "'Watchmen': It's 'Woke' Propaganda!". *Daily Beast*, October 25 2019, April 12 2022, https://www.thedailybeast.com/hbos-watchmen-pisses-off-comics-fanboys-its-woke-propaganda#:~:text=Comics%20Fanboys%20Are%20Pissed%20About,%3A%20It's%20'Woke'%20Propaganda!&text=The%20series%20has%20been%20%E2%80%9Creview.

3. Michael Kimmel, *Angry White Men: American Masculinity at the End of an Era* (New York: Nation Books,S 2013), xxii.

4. Michael Boyce Gillispie, "Thinking about Watchmen with Jonathan W. Gray, Rebecca A. Wanzo, and Kristen Warner," *Film Quarterly* 73, no. 4, 52.

5. See Alfred Brophy *Reconstructing the Dreamland: The Tulsa Riot of 1921* (New York: Oxford University Press, 2002); Scott Ellsworth *Death in a Promised Land: The Tulsa Race Riot of 1921* (Baton Rouge: LSU Press, 1992); Randy Krehbiel, *Tulsa 1921: Reporting a Massacre* (Norman: University of Oklahoma Press, 2019).

6. Gail Bederman, *Manliness and Civilization: A Cultural History of Gender and Race in the United States, 1880-1917* (Chicago: University of Chicago Press, 1996), 4.

7. Michael Kimmel, *Manhood in America: A Cultural History*, 4th ed. (New York: Oxford University Press, 2017), 6.

8. See Cameron McWhirter, *Red Summer: The Summer of 1919 and the Awakening of Black America* (New York: Henry Holt and Company, 2011).

9. Joselyne L. Chenane, Emily Wright and Chris L Gibson. "Traffic Stops, Race, and Perceptions of Fairness." *Policing and Society* 30, no. 6 (March 5, 2019): 720–37.

10. Kimmel, *Manhood in America*, 95.

11. David Neiwert, *Alt-America: The Rise of the Radical Right in the Age of Trump*, New York, NY: Verso (2017), 100.

12. Neiwert, 12.

13. George Lipsitz, *The Possessive Investment in Whiteness: How White People Profit from Identity Politics* (Philadelphia: Temple University Press, 2018), vii.

14. Neiwert, 82.

15. Michael Kimmel, *Healing from Hate: How Young Men Get Into—and Out of—Violent Extremism* (Berkeley: University of California Press, 2018), xiii.

16. Neiwert, 15.

17. See Jonathan W. Gray "*Watchmen* after the End of History: Race, Redemption, and the End of the World," *ASAP Journal*, February 3, 2020, April 12, 2022, http://asapjournal.com/watchmen-after-the-end-of-history-race-redemption-and-the-end-of-the-world-jonathan-w-gray/.

18. Bobby Allyn, "The OK' Hand Gesture Is Now Listed as a Symbol of Hate," *NPR.org*, September 26, 2019, April 12, 2022, https://www.npr.org/2019/09/26/764728163/the-ok-hand-gesture-is-now-listed-as-a-symbol-of-hate.

19. Michael German, "Hidden in Plain Sight: Racism, White Supremacy, and Far-Right Militancy in Law Enforcement." *Brennancenter.org*. August 27, 2020. https://www.brennan

center.org/our-work/research-reports/hidden-plain-sight-racism-white-supremacy-and-far-right-militancy-law.

20. Neiwert, 336–39.

21. Kimmel, *Healing from Hate*, xii–xiii.

22. Louie Dean Valencia-Garcia, ed., *Far Right Revisionism and the End of History: Alt-Histories* (New York: Routledge, 2020), 6.

23. See Peter Lehman's *Running Scared: Masculinity and the Representation of the Male Body* (Detroit, MI: Wayne State University Press, 2007).

24. Scott Melzer, *Manhood Impossible: Men's Struggles to Control and Transform Their Bodies and Work* (New Brunswick, NJ: Rutgers, 2018), 81.

Chapter 9

"WHO WATCHES THE WATCHMEN"

Situating HBO's *Watchmen* as (Post)quality Television

RUSTY HATCHELL

The 2010s marked a turning point in HBO's programming slate. The premium cable channel's flagship drama series of the 2010s—*Game of Thrones*—ended in May 2019 after an eight-year run as one of the world's most prominent and discussed television series, amassing 160 Emmy Award nominations (winning fifty-nine of them) and recording viewership numbers in the tens of millions for most of the series' run. Showrunners David Benioff and D. B. Weiss had attained cult authorship status through *Game of Thrones*, and, in 2017, HBO announced development plans for the pair to write and produce an alternate-history drama entitled *Confederate*. Described as "slavery fanfic" by writer Pilot Viruet and generally lambasted by the broader public, the discourse surrounding two white showrunners developing a series in which slavery would exist in the American present aligned with the ambivalence of the entertainment industries and their storytelling operations outside of the very real contexts of race, racism, and white supremacy in the United States.[1] The project was "shelved indefinitely" in the midst of the backlash and was officially a dead project when the men signed a $200 million deal with Netflix in August 2019.[2]

By the end of the decade, HBO's original content slate began to look remarkably different. In their attempts to simultaneously extend the zeitgeist of *Game of Thrones'* success and to diversify the programs distributed on their various platforms, HBO has signaled a significant shift in their programming decisions. Not only are Black actors leading some of HBO's most prominent shows—such as Thandie Newton and Jeffrey Wright of *Westworld* (2016–present) as well as Zendaya of *Euphoria* (2019–present)—but HBO has also become home to the productions of many Black—especially Black women—creators, notably Issa Rae of *Insecure* (2016–2020), Robin Thede of *A Black Lady Sketch Show* (2019–present), Michaela Coel of *I Will Destroy You* (2020), and Misha Green of *Lovecraft Country* (2020). This notable turn for HBO correlates with demands from the media industries for higher rates of representation and inclusion both in front of and behind the cameras. Yet, it is the adaptation of *Watchmen* (2019) that exhibits a case study of how much more complex the conversations and solutions to these narrative and industrial calls can and should be—especially considering the social, political, and cultural ramifications that media can have when portraying race and racism in the United States and beyond.

When HBO's *Watchmen* debuted on October 20, 2019, viewers were stunned not only by the graphic opening sequence but also in their discovery that it was based on true events. The opening imagery—a historically accurate and visceral depiction of the oft-forgotten Tulsa Race Massacre of 1921—quickly ignited conversations regarding the premise and direction of the graphic novel adaptation as well as critical reflections on the intentional erasure of Black history in the American education system. Many national media outlets responded not only with reviews of the first episode but also informative essays further detailing the worst incident of racial violence in American history. The Tulsa Massacre not only captured the attention of viewers who did not expect the series to foreground such visceral reenactments of Black trauma but also set the tone, pacing, and theme of the entire nine-episode run, subtly answering the question of how showrunner Damon Lindelof, who has identified as Jewish and white, was going to *remix* the original material—an assertive strategy in which Lindelof would not "directly translate" the 1986–1987 series penned, drawn, and colored by Alan Moore, Dave Gibbons, and John Higgins, respectively.[3] Lindelof's caution in remixing the source material allowed him to tell a fresh story within the established boundaries of the graphic novel's storyworld and gave Lindelof the opportunity to recruit and hire a diverse writers' room that would not adapt the material but instead would "disrupt" it.[4]

By utilizing the graphic novel's storyworld and narrative logics, HBO's *Watchmen* was initially framed as another entry in the expanding ecology of superhero television. However, the series also marked itself as different and distinctive from others in its association with HBO, through its attachment to a notable showrunner figure, and in its structure as a miniseries. More pointedly, the presence and significance of *Watchmen*'s focus on Black characters—particularly Black superheroes and vigilantes—should not be understated. After the cancellation of *M.A.N.T.I.S.* (FOX, 1994–1995), Black superheroes adapted from comics for television were largely only seen in animated programming aimed at teenage and young adult audiences. *Static Shock* (The WB, 2000–2004), *Justice League* (Cartoon Network, 2001–2004), *Teen Titans* (Cartoon Network, 2003–2006), and *Young Justice* (Cartoon Network, 2010–2013; DC Universe, 2019; HBO Max, 2021–present)—all notable productions that were based on characters and stories from DC Comics—helped spark the contemporary boom of superhero television programming in which many more Black superheroes have appeared.[5]

As a superhero drama, *Watchmen*'s inclusion of and focus on Black characters is significantly different from the rest of what can be termed as contemporary superhero television. While some of these texts—particularly *Luke Cage* (Netflix, 2016–2018) and *Black Lightning* (The CW, 2018–2021)—present majority-Black casts through narratives that blend superhero narratives and thematic issues such as police brutality, other superhero programs have included Black superheroes in a manner that Kristen Warner has termed "plastic representation."[6] Warner's central argument that the contemporary discourse of diversity and representation has become "synonymous with the quantity of difference rather than with the dimensionality of those performances" highlights the industry's deep misunderstanding of the demands in representing authentic Black narratives and the Black experience on American television.[7] While whitewashing and race-swapping discourses continue to guide particular casting and narrative choices across DC Television's productions, *Watchmen* is explicitly anchored in its Blackness, particularly with original characters Angela Abar, Calvin "Cal" Abar, and Will Reeves, played by Regina King, Yahya Abdul-Mateen II, and Louis Gossett Jr., respectively. Thus, the trajectory from *Smallville* (The WB, 2001–2006; The CW, 2006–2011) to the programs that currently populate The CW's primetime slate—colloquially known as the Arrowverse—to HBO's miniseries showcases a progression from mere presence to meaningful portrayal.

The decision to situate the narrative of *Watchmen* within the thematic frameworks of racism and white supremacy in the United States forced Lindelof and his writers' room to embrace meaningful storytelling through the dual lenses of Jim Crow racial segregation and contemporary injustices faced by Black Americans. That Lindelof and company would utilize these moments in conjunction with the anti-Reagan revisionist history carried over from the graphic novel marks a distinction for *Watchmen* to stand out in the increasingly crowded field of what is argued throughout this essay as quality television. Although the term quality television lacks a clear definition beyond subjective evaluations, I argue that *Watchmen*'s authorial lineage from Moore as well as the position of Lindelof as showrunner; the large ensemble cast, which allows for multiple plotlines; the foregrounding of racial politics; the accolades the show received; as well as its distribution on HBO's platforms contribute to a theoretical discursive positioning of *Watchmen* as quality television.

Additionally, this narrative framework aligns with the current rise of social and political movements advocating for a range of systemic solutions for a wide range of systemic issues facing Black Americans, including police brutality; racial bias in education, employment, and health; and inequalities and injustices throughout the entertainment industries. This multifaceted distinction—one that I would pitch as an indicator of a new type of television that pushes beyond the discourses of quality television—is the site of critical analysis in this chapter and one that allows both the discussion of Black narratives and the Black experience largely being ignored by quality television discourses and also a theorization of a new post-quality television, specifically centering and focusing Black narratives and characters previously marginalized in televisual spaces and the American television industry.[8] In this chapter, I challenge the historical discourses of quality television and assert *Watchmen* as a distinctive entrant within a crowded ecology by highlighting what sets this series further apart from the rest of the canon of quality television.

By retracing the historical trajectory of quality television scholarship to the contemporary moment, I hope to identify and address the current moment anchored by *Watchmen* as a distinctive one deserving of critical attention. First, I look at the various attempts to stabilize the definition and characteristics of quality television as well as the manner in which Black-oriented strategies in the industry are largely absent in the historicity of quality television. Second, by concentrating on individual elements that have been used to describe quality television, I implore deeper critical reflections on these characteristics and the relations between audience, author, and text to discursively understand the differences between the texts that are typically canonized as quality television. Additionally, my positioning of *Watchmen* as postquality television is framed by the social, cultural, political, and industrial frameworks of the contemporary moment—the amplification of Black Lives Matter and other racially invested activist movements in the wake of the murders of George Floyd, Ahmaud Arbery, and Breonna Taylor; the calls for the entertainment and media industries to reflect on the overwhelming whiteness of screen media; the mass resistance against a presidential administration and right-wing partisan politics that has energized fringe movements based in racism and white supremacy; and the calls for institutional reform that protects communities of color, from public health and education to law enforcement and social services. *Watchmen* exists focally at the center of all of these overlapping and intersecting discourses, and I argue here that *Watchmen* moves the barometer of quality television beyond our previous understanding of the terms to prioritize these social, cultural, and political frameworks as well as narrative and industrial frameworks that have largely shaped the historical conversations from the 1960s to today.

QUALITY DEMOGRAPHICS IN AMERICAN TELEVISION

As the Hollywood television industry peaked with 532 productions in 2019, it becomes increasingly important to wade through the hundreds of high-budget, high-quality productions with high-caliber casting, complex narratives, and notable showrunners to revisit the scholarly conversations about quality television to characterize the present age of television.[9] Although the definition and deployment of the term has been subject to debate for decades, "quality television" is generally conceptualized as a means of making distinct a group of television programs from the general mediascape of television in terms of aesthetics, narrative complexity, language, subject material, and socio-cultural and political contexts. More pointedly, Robert J. Thompson notes that "the precise definition of 'quality TV' was elusive right from the start, though we knew it when we saw it."[10] This persistence for television scholars to define and organize the canon of quality television has been subject to scholarly debate, with the need to separate the "quality" texts from the rest of "regular" television seemingly as the only constant among a spectrum of other variables.

The term "quality television" dates back to Jane Feuer's popularization of it in relation to MTM Enterprises and the shifts in televised comedies in the 1970s. Used more for the segment of the audience that would tune into a particular series—a "quality demographics"—than the text itself, quality is used descriptively from a logic of understanding audiences.[11] Production teams behind the programming at the Big Three national networks—CBS, in particular—clashed with network executives as the former attempted to embed "a sense of quality and social responsibility" in their programs through political critiques while NBC and ABC still needed to court advertisers and avoid alienating their potential viewers.[12] As the spectrum of American distribution further expanded to include more broadcast networks, cable channels, premium cable services, and streaming platforms in the United States, original series production—particularly hour-long dramatic content aimed at more niche demographics—began to rise. HBO—a premium service whose subscription logics differentiate itself from broadcast and the rest of cable television—also started aggressively focusing on hour-long dramas, starting with *Oz* (1997–2003) and *The Sopranos* (1999–2007). Along with HBO's long marketing claim of "It's not TV. It's HBO," these programs suggested a new model of quality television that hinged on its ability to use "cultural snobbery" to create "buzz" on its offerings that are available nowhere else.[13] Placed in conversation with the synonymy of broadcast television and the mainstream, HBO's "antitelevisuality" is a branding strategy that allows HBO the ability to co-opt broadcast series formats while simultaneously giving them the "privileged position" of quality.[14] HBO's subscription format allowed the premium service to directly appeal to subscribers, who are "willing to pay extra for more specialized and more highbrow fare."[15] While this may be, the idealization of an upscale demographic depends on some variables that haven't been fully unpacked in the conversations about quality demographics beyond the allure of sponsors to affluent consumers-to-be.

In the mid-1990s, for example, network executives began targeting a more socially progressive "psychographic market," which Ron Becker dubbed as "slumpies: socially-liberal, urban-minded professionals" with programming that incorporated more gay and lesbian characters into their primetime programming.[16] Specifically marked by whiteness and their higher education, slumpies and other upscale demographics became targeted by television executives, who in turn have largely stabilized their focus on an affluent segment of a white consumer base and ignored those who didn't fit the model. By aligning the mostly white gay and lesbian characters of the late 1990s with the viewership networks desired, executives made primetime network decisions based on the affluence and whiteness to whom more advertising could be targeted. For viewers of color, particularly Black audiences, the drive for quality television on both HBO and network television seemingly left their interests aside for the more socially upscale and white viewers. Framing the historicity of American television with race, Sasha Torres notes that American television "tended historically to anchor its depiction of raced bodies—and has meant, for the most part, African-American bodies—to particular social conditions which it understands to be both undesirable and inextricably linked to racially marked communities."[17] Torres also notes that a link between "racial representation and the social problem" in 1970s quality programming—particularly the sitcoms produced by Norman Lear's Tandem Productions—was "established despite, or more accurately *because* of these series' 'liberal' intentions," thus fusing the seemingly disparate histories of quality demographics and quality television with the production of race-as-problem in American television.[18] So as liberal politics drove decisions for quality programming in the 1970s and 1980s, the dominant economic imperatives to court advertisers (for network executives) and to increase subscription revenue (for HBO's executives) remained a top priority across the television industry, leaving Black audiences largely undervalued by the industry's trends in programming and in fair and realistic representation. Yet, it was notable sitcoms *The Cosby Show* and its spin-off *A Different World* that helped guide Black representation on-screen in more nuanced and meaningful ways. After criticism that the creative forces behind *A Different World* were not accurately depicting life at historically Black colleges and universities (HBCUs)—which served as the primary backdrop for the series—Debbie Allen was hired on as the primary creative figure for the series. Key to Allen's strategy was her prioritization of the Black experience. By presenting *A Different World* as a polysemic text encoded with complex layering of different narrative and visual signifiers, Allen ushered in a production strategy that "present[ed] forms of cultural knowledge and political struggle in new ways, accessible to both Black and non-Black audiences," while also "resist[ing] the impulse to be the 'Blackness tour guide.'"[19] In this sense, Allen presented a different type of quality to American television, one that understood a more complex nature of audience beyond demographic targeting.

WATCHMEN AS POSTQUALITY TELEVISION?

On September 20th, 2020, in a remote format driven by the circumstances of the COVID-19 pandemic, the Emmy Awards were held at the Staples Center in Los Angeles, California, and hosted by Jimmy Kimmel. Previous to the awards ceremony, *Watchmen* had been nominated for twenty-six awards, including in categories for Creative Arts Emmy Awards as well as the mainstream Primetime Emmy Awards.[20] The series walked away from the evening with the most wins by any series—eleven—including Outstanding Lead Actress in a Limited Series or Movie for Regina King, Outstanding Supporting Actor in a Limited Series or Movie for Yahya Abdul-Mateen II, Outstanding Writing for a Limited Series or Movie as well as Outstanding Limited Series. Building on its reputation for nearly a year, *Watchmen* had become one of the year's most celebrated and awarded programs on television. While HBO's reputation for award-winning miniseries and limited series is built upon the successes of *Band of Brothers* (2001), *Angels in America* (2003) and *Elizabeth* (2005), these awards bring "a great deal of prestige and publicity" to the premium service.[21] This prestige fuels HBO's continuing dominance in the limited series category and frames these series as distinctive quality television. These miniseries also illuminate social issues, such as the case with *Angels in America*, whose focus on the AIDS epidemic in the 1980s was framed by the social and politic climate of the Reagan era.

Similarly, the importance and reputation of *Watchmen* was carried through the George Floyd protests that were magnified by the national media in May and throughout the summer of 2020. The symbiotic relationship between the fictional series and the very real and visceral responses to the violent oppressions that Black Americans face from state apparatuses—predominantly local and state police but also the judicial and carceral functions which also unjustly target minorities across the United States—has demonstrable potentiality in reflection and reformation of the discourses that have traced and documented the subjective evaluations of quality television over the past fifty years. Ultimately, it remains improbable for an objective set of criteria of quality television to be set and agreed upon, yet some scholars have attempted to set some guiding principles, fully acknowledging the subjectivities inherent within them.

Thompson frames his criteria of quality as an emergent "profile" that is "defined by what it is not. It is not 'regular' TV."[22] Yet, the criteria exemplifies what Jason Mittell has asserted as "the slippage between notions of value, prestige, and audience and the need for quality to assert its equally vague opposite of assumed 'low quality' or worth less television."[23] The characteristics in which Thompson proposes as inherent of quality constitute distinctions of aesthetics ("the only artful TV is that which isn't like all the rest of it"), audience ("the upscale well-educated urban-dwelling young viewers advertisers so desire"), postmodernism ("creolized generic heritage"), authorship ("the writing is usually more complex"), subject matter ("the overall message almost always tends toward liberal humanism"), and criticism ("awards and critical acclaim").[24] Given *Watchmen*'s high level of critical acclaim, HBO's embrace of a prized demographic, Lindelof's decades-long career in complex televisual writing and production, and the inherently political messaging of *Watchmen*'s themes and narrative, the miniseries firmly fits within the mold of quality television.

In his seminal study on the visuality and style of television, John T. Caldwell asserts that the rise of a high-style "*televisuality . . . emerged during the very same years*" as the breakdown of the main audience into more niche segments and demographics.[25] This led to a push for a more cinematic style in television, assisted in large part by the migration of Hollywood filmmakers into the American television industry during the 1980s and 1990s. While this cinematic attribute was mainly credited to directors, art directors, and editors, by the early 2000s, "the 'source' of television authorship was re-attributed to the showrunner," a writer-producer figure who is tasked with the production and management of a television series and also liaises with network executives and production companies associated with their series.[26] The seeming ubiquity of showrunners in American television in the 2000s was not by accident; indeed, Derek Kompare argues that one facet of a showrunner is to heighten a network's profile through the distinction of showrunners and their signature programs "in order to gain market share in their targeted demographics."[27] While some showrunners have amassed household name status and others have curated smaller but loyal cult followings, the industrialization of showrunner branding has helped networks, cable channels, and streaming platforms keep viewers engaged through the distinct and quality programs offered by these creatives. There is certainly a relationship between quality demographics—those who view programming that is socially and politically distinct, among other qualities—and showrunners, whose positionality as brand ambassadors of networks and their respective programming is forefront. Lindelof's continued presence as a trusted showrunner for HBO—particularly after his critically acclaimed run on *The Leftovers* (HBO, 2014–2017)—secures the relationship between himself, HBO, and the intended audience for *Watchmen*.

Yet, the series is also constitutive of attributes that set the series as distinct from the canon of quality television itself. While a showrunner figure helps brand a particular series with certain characteristics, it is ultimately the collective authorship in a writers' room whose craft merits any deserving accolades and the label of quality television. In the acceptance speech for Outstanding Writing for the episode "This Extraordinary Being," co-writer Lindelof did not speak and physically stepped back and positioned himself slightly behind fellow co-writer Cord Jefferson, in an implied act of decentering himself—as a white, male showrunner—from the limelight. Months earlier, in an acceptance speech at the Peabody Awards—also accepted remotely—Lindelof explicitly decentered himself as well, despite the discursive branding of Lindelof as the central creative figure and showrunner of the series. These actions showcase Lindelof's cautious journey as a white showrunner of such an impactful narrative that was not his story and not intended for an audience that looked like him. Lindelof not only frequently acknowledged the Black and female writers as partners in the writers' room—rather than subordinates of Lindelof—but he also used his platform to push for the rehabilitation of lost and covered history, explicitly the Tulsa Race Massacre in this case. For as much as quality television discourses have favored socially and politically relevant content, very few televisual texts have so much attempted to foster what Kristen Warner terms a "televisual remediation" on the level of *Watchmen*.[28] Additionally, Rebecca Wanzo notes the inherent difference marked by *Watchmen* in terms of remediating the superhero with race and culture in mind:

> Creators have been reimagining the myths of the superhero through the Black experience for some time. People have objected to racebending and to racism becoming the subject of comic-book story lines. Some fans are much more comfortable with the allegorical representations common in comics that don't require confrontation with the realities of discrimination.
>
> But I think this is a profoundly "playing in the dark" iteration of the Black superhero, not by recasting superheroes through Black experience but by saying that a racialized nationalism is important to the foundations of vigilantism, heroism, and alienated citizenship at the core of this myth.[29]

Speaking directly about the events of the sixth episode, "This Extraordinary Being," Warner asserts that the relation between the fictional representation of Hooded Justice as a white superhero on the diegetic television series *American Hero Story* and the unveiling of Hooded Justice as a Black superhero whose origin story and visual signifiers are tragically linked to the attempted lynching of him by his white New York Police Department colleagues serve as a "site of racial disruption" that is unpacked throughout the episode and the overall series.[30] Wanzo highlights this episode's revisionist history and how it "changes the audience's relationship with the original text."[31] The episode's use of Hooded Justice's origin story as a lens for the contemporary moment—through the aesthetic conflation of Jovan Adepo's Will Reeves and Regina King's Angela Abar as subject—collapses the temporality and historicity of the episode's setting in late 1930s New York City into the present day of Tulsa to showcase an omnipresence of white supremacy as villain and a simultaneity of the Black experience over centuries of oppression that pushes the boundaries of what is potential in televisual narratives and aesthetics today.

Mittell and others—notably Michael Newman and Elana Levine in their book *Legitimating Television: Media Convergence and Cultural Status*—have written about the discursive practices that attempt to uplift and connect certain television programming "to more legitimated media such as cinema and literature, instead of focusing on specific attributes unique to television."[32] *Watchmen* is a particularly interesting case to consider, as it adopts formal traits from across multiple media.

The first episode starts with the visual and aural characteristics of a traditional film projection system as it plays a silent black-and-white film with live piano accompaniment and a square aspect ratio. Soon after, the camera pans over the dark interior of a theater where a young Will Reeves (Danny Boyd Jr.) watches enthusiastically while his mother struggles to keep calm while playing the piano—implying that she knew of the impending danger in Tulsa that day. The events of the day—centering around Will Reeves and his survival—unfold for the duration of the opening scene, which is shakily filmed and filtered with sepia tones. Formally, the series heavily utilizes production techniques typically associated with cinema throughout the series. "This Extraordinary Being" is perhaps the most cinematic in its execution, using various techniques that grapple with perspective and time. Director Stephen Williams and cinematographer Gregory Middleton use point-of-view shots to situate the viewer within Reeves's perspective during the attempted lynching of his body. They also use stop-motion cinematography as Laurie Blake (Jean Smart) attempts to pull Angela Abar out of the hallucination she is experiencing after taking her grandfather's Nostalgia, a personalized drug that allows users to reenact memories and flashbacks. And as if the production of the episode was during the same era of the episode's setting—the late 1930s—Williams and Middleton use simple camera tricks rather than digital effects to switch Adepo and King in and out of the subject position.

The series also makes aesthetic ties to its graphic novel source, particularly in the manner the episode titles are shown against the mise-en-scène of the series. Although the vivid block letters of the episode titles are not diegetic to the narrative world, they do mimic the chapter titles in the graphic novel. Lindelof and his team explicitly avoid the replication of panels, gutters, or any other aspect of comic book design in his series; however, many panels from the graphic novel are recreated, most likely to connect to those fans of the series who are most familiar with the source text.[33] Additionally, the inclusion of the diegetically fictional *American Hero Story*—which plays frequently on screens throughout the series—and the jarringly unconnected scenes of Adrian Veidt (Jeremy Irons) at his manor in an undisclosed location (later revealed to be a moon of Jupiter), operate similarly to the paratextual content included in the graphic novel.

In the series' fluctuations between cinematic and comic book properties, *Watchmen* eludes the notion of a hierarchy of legitimation, and in doing so, maximizes the potential of it as a distinct television production and series. Perhaps legitimating television using any of the previously aforementioned criteria or frameworks is too messy; however, there remains a sense of distinction that at least carries the residual nature of quality television discourses. Perhaps *Watchmen* helps move the conversation beyond the confines of those discourses; perhaps *Watchmen* is a postquality text.

CONCLUSION

As *Watchmen* helped HBO beat its competitors at the Emmy Awards in 2020, it became apparent that high-caliber programming featuring Black characters and centering the Black experience would shift the discourses of quality television moving forward. In 2020, *Lovecraft Country* debuted in a similar manner to *Watchmen* the year prior. Mixing elements of supernatural horror with historical elements of the Black experience—including the Tulsa Race Massacre—*Lovecraft Country* strengthens the argument that HBO is invested in programming and personnel that center Blackness on the premium cable channel (HBO) and streaming platform (HBO Max). In a similar manner in which *Watchmen* educated viewers about the reality of the Tulsa Race Massacre and the effects it had on the genealogies of Black Americans throughout the 20th century, the 2020 series highlighted the dangers of existing while Black during the height of 1950s Jim Crow America. For instance, viewers learned about sundown towns, or "towns where Black folks were relatively free to roam during the daylight hours, but once the sun went down, they were arrested and sometimes killed—simply because of the color of their skin."[34] Shows like *Watchmen* and *Lovecraft Country* have begun to embrace a mode of historical reflection that informs viewers about various aspects of the Black experience that have been largely left out of textbooks and classrooms in the United States. They are series that have also collapsed history into the present, evaporating the perpetuated gap of Jim Crow from the contemporary moment, despite a rise in right-wing violence and state-sanctioned violence against Black Americans negating that gap. This restoration of Black America's past through genre television may just push the discourses of quality, value, and legitimation in American television to not just include but center the experiences and reality of Black America.

NOTES

1. "'Confederate' Writers Defend Modern U.S. Slavery Show as Scary but Real," *Reuters*, July 21, 2017, https://www.reuters.com/article/us-television-confederchaptate/confederate-writers-defend-modern-u-s-slavery-show-as-scary-but-real-idUSKBN1A628Y.

2. Lesley Goldberg, "'Game of Thrones' Creators Close $200M Netflix Overall Deal," *The Hollywood Reporter*, August 7, 2019, https://www.hollywoodreporter.com/live-feed/game-thrones-creators-close-200m-netflix-deal-1230119.

3. Graeme McMillan, "Damon Lindelof Explains His Vision for HBO's Watchmen in Heartfelt Letters to Fans," *The Hollywood Reporter*, May 22, 2018, https://www.hollywoodreporter.com/live-feed/damon-lindelof-posts-open-watchmen-letter-instagram-1114216.

4. McMillan, "Damon Lindelof Explains His Vision."

5. Notable Black superheroes in contemporary live-action superhero programming include John Diggle/Guardian (David Ramsay) and Curtis Holt/Mr. Terrific (Echo Kellum) in *Arrow*, Wally West/Kid Flash (Keiynan Lonsdale) and Nora West-Allen/XS (Jessica Parker Kennedy) in *The Flash*, J'onn J'onzz/Martian Manhunter (David Harewood) in *Supergirl*, Kory Anders/Starfire (Anna Diop) in *Titans*, and Vic Stone/Cyborg (Joivan Wade) in *Doom Patrol*, among others.

6. For more on *Black Lightning*'s storytelling, see Pilot Viruet, "In *Black Lightning*, There's No Right Way to Fix a City," *The Atlantic*, February 13, 2018, https://www.theatlantic.com/entertainment/archive/2018/02/black-lightning-the-cw-review/552947/.

7. Kristen J. Warner, "In the Time of Plastic Representation," *Film Quarterly* 71, no. 2 (Winter 2017): 33.

8. Although this chapter concentrates on *Watchmen*'s distinction as quality television centering Black characters and the Black experience in the United States, it should be noted that HBO programs *Oz* (1997–2003), *The Wire* (2002–2008), and *Treme* (2010–2013) serve as precedents to *Watchmen*'s anchoring of the Black experience in its own narrative.

9. Jean Bently, "Has Peak TV Reached Its Summit? Industry Insiders Weigh In," *The Hollywood Reporter*, February 14, 2020, https://www.hollywoodreporter.com/live-feed/has-peak-tv-reached-summit-industry-insiders-weigh-1279196.

10. Robert J. Thompson, "Preface," in *Quality TV: Contemporary American Television and Beyond*, ed. Janet McCabe and Kim Akass (London: I.B. Tauris, 2007), xix.

11. Jane Feuer, "MTM Enterprises: An Overview," in *MTM: Quality Television*, ed. Jane Feuer, Paul Kerr, and Tise Vahimagi (London: BFI, 1984), 4.

12. Feuer, "MTM Enterprises," 22.

13. Janet McCabe and Kim Akass, "It's Not TV, It's HBO's Original Programming: Producing Quality TV," in *It's Not TV: Watching TV in the Post-Television Era*, ed. Marc Leverette, Brian L. Ott, and Cara Louise Buckley (New York: Routledge, 2008), 85.

14. Deborah Jaramillo, "The Family Racket: AOL Time Warner, HBO, *The Sopranos*, and the Construction of a Quality Brand," *Journal of Communication Inquiry* 26, no. 59 (2002): 65.

15. Jane Feuer, "HBO and the Concept of Quality TV," in *Quality TV: Contemporary American Television and Beyond*, ed. Janet McCabe and Kim Akass (London: I.B. Tauris, 2007), 147.

16. Ron Becker, "Prime-Time Television in the Gay Nineties: Network Television, Quality Audiences, and Gay Politics," *The Velvet Light Trap* no. 42 (Fall 1998): 38.

17. Sasha Torres, "Television and Race," in *A Companion to Television*, ed. Janet Wasko (Malden, MA: Blackwell Publishing, 2005), 396.

18. Torres, 397.

19. Robin R. Means Coleman and Andre M. Cavalcante, "Two *Different Worlds*: Television as a Producer's Medium," in *Watching While Black: Centering the Television of Black Audiences*, ed. Beretta E. Smith-Shomade (New Brunswick, NJ: Rutgers University Press, 2012), 40.

20. Joe Otterman, "'Watchmen' Leads Emmys Winners; HBO Tops Networks and Streaming," *Variety*, September 20, 2020, https://variety.com/2020/tv/news/watchmen-emmys-hbo-scorecard-1234776656/.

21. Avi Santo, "Para-television and Discourses of Distinction: The Culture of Production at HBO," in *It's Not TV: Watching TV in the Post-Television Era*, ed. Marc Leverette, Brian L. Ott, and Cara Louise Buckley (New York: Routledge, 2008), 25.

22. Robert J. Thompson, *Television's Second Golden Age: From "Hill St. Blues" to "ER"* (New York: Continuum, 1996), 13.

23. Jason Mittell, *Complex TV: The Poetics of Contemporary Television Storytelling* (New York: New York University Press, 2015), 212.

24. Thompson, *Television's Second Golden Age*, 13–16.

25. John T. Caldwell, *Televisuality: Style, Crisis, and Authority in American Television* (New Brunswick, NJ: Rutgers University Press, 1995), 11 (emphasis in original).

26. Derek Kompare, "More 'Moments of Television': Online Television Cult Authorship," in *Flow TV: Television in the Age of Media Convergence*, ed. Michael Kackman, Marnie Binfield, Matthew Thomas Payne, Allison Perlman, and Bryan Sebok (New York: Routledge, 2011), 98.

27. Kompare, 99.

28. Michael Boyce Gillespie, "Thinking about *Watchmen*: With Jonathan W. Gray, Rebecca A. Wanzo, and Kristen J. Warner," *Film Quarterly* 73, no. 4 (2020): 52.

29. Gillespie, 52.

30. Gillespie, 53.

31. Gillespie, 54.

32. Mittell, *Complex TV*, 214.

33. u/AlexLocksmith, "HBO Watchmen Comic Panel Recreations," Reddit post, November 26, 2019, https://www.reddit.com/r/Watchmen/comments/e22q6g/hbo_watchmen_comic_panel_recreations/.

34. Lawrence Ware, "*Lovecraft Country*'s Premiere Captured the Horror That Almost Killed My Grandfather," *Slate*, August 19, 2020, https://slate.com/culture/2020/08/lovecraft-country-hbo-sundown-towns-real-history.html.

Chapter 10

REINSCRIBING RACIAL POWER WITHIN HBO'S *WATCHMEN*

DAVID STANLEY AND SARAH PAWLAK STANLEY

Alan Moore's watershed[1] graphic novel *Watchmen* (1987) grittily deconstructed superheroes, critiquing the glorification of the masked vigilantes who reinforce institutional state power. Created by Damon Lindelof, HBO's sequel series, *Watchmen* (2019), continues this deconstruction, incisively critiquing the glorification of the masked vigilantes—and masked police—reinforcing hegemonic white power. Painstakingly layered with allusions, the series simultaneously evokes and thematically expands upon its source material, transformatively reconceptualizing racial representation within the realm of Moore's landmark narrative. The original obsessively engages with temporality, luxuriating in the nuances of cause-and-effect through which are born "thermodynamic miracles," the unlikely confluences of events that "distill" our reality from "chaos." HBO's series recontextualizes this temporal obsession, exploring the cyclical nature of racialized intergenerational oppression, through which the oppressor artificially limits the possible realities imposed upon the oppressed.

Moore's *Watchmen* redefined the quintessential "comic book" experience, creating a "morally ambiguous" world "full of semiological complexity" distinguished "from the clear-cut semiotics of Siegel and Shuster's *Superman*."[2] Lindelhof's *Watchmen* remediates[3] that redefinition, pushing the implications of the graphic novel's moral ambiguities further while using televisual techniques to riff on its "semiological complexity." Moore's text fixates on the authoritarian ramifications that cohere through the extrajudicial application of justice, in both service to and opposition against the system. Lindelof's series intensifies these ramifications, explicitly framing them as emerging from within the context of the continuing American legacy of institutional racism, wherein even the legal justice enacted upon Black bodies *through* "the system" represents authoritarian overreach. Visualizing connections between racist policing and the white vigilantism of the Ku Klux Klan, the show recontextualizes the default whiteness of the Minutemen, the inaugural class of costumed heroes within the *Watchmen* universe. A master class in "resistant reading,"[4] the series deftly exploits the gaps within Moore's graphic novel, reimagining—without, in derogative comic book terms, "retconning"—the backstory of Hooded Justice. Lindelhof recasts the universe's first masked avenger as a 1930s Black cop dissatisfied by his inability to change the system from within, who, in his extralegal crimefighting must pass for white—even among vigilante colleagues—to remain a "hero." His social dissent co-opted by wealthy, white, privileged men, Hooded Justice becomes bleached of his own legacy, the antiracist roots of his vigilantism obscured. Through this reframing, the series spotlights the implicit oppressions ostensibly democratic American institutions perpetuate by policing (in)visibilities of Blackness.

The series counterpoises the performative whiteness empowering Hooded Justice against the performative Blackness through which Dr. Manhattan temporarily divests himself of godlike[5] power. One of the foremost figures defining the graphic novel, Dr. Manhattan, formerly nuclear physicist Jon Osterman, was deprived of his humanity through an atomic accident. This unintentional transformation grants Jon a "unique" perspective of time. Experiencing nonlinear, temporal simultaneity, he gains semi-omnipotence, but only over his own life. More than any of his manifold powers, this alien experience of time, and the detachment it spurs, dehumanizes Jon. The graphic novel's conclusion leaves the isolated Dr. Manhattan, whose "last connection to humanity" was "severed" by his girlfriend's abandonment, to leave Earth in search of a galaxy "less complicated than this one." Picking up thirty-four years later, Lindelof's *Watchmen* circuitously reveals that Jon, having secretly returned to Earth, has spent the last ten years "playing house" with a Black human woman. But making their relationship work requires "playing human" as well. Through the gift of temporary amnesia, he is able to abdicate knowledge of his powers, finding a sense of the simplicity he had erstwhile sought among the stars. Presenting the human-appearing Jon, disguised as the Black "Cal," *Watchmen* (2019) carefully threads the needle between inclusivity and appropriation. Eschewing the assimilationism inherent to Hollywood colorblindness,[6] Lindelof refrains from updating Jon's backstory, opting to present a white-man-turned-blue demigod, in the guise of a Black man. Given the series' overt explorations of racism, this diegetically literalized blackface[7] might be interpreted as a white appropriation of disempowerment, coinciding as it does with the obscurement of Jon's superpowers. However, the show is distinguished by its multiculturalist engagement with the complexities of alterity, deconstructing racism by complicating rather than simplifying our shared legacy of racial strife, its "world-making insist[ing] on the messy interconnectedness" of American identity and "the potential (for success and failure) enabled by uncertainty."[8] Jon ultimately *becomes* a Black human man shortly before his death, passing his powers to his wife. Transforming from appropriative, performative Blackness to embodied Blackness, he self-divests his privileged position as oppressor. Jon's de-apotheosis invokes Blackness as a signifier of the oppressed, simultaneously gesturing toward the transformative potentialities of recusing oneself from white privilege[9] and of offering the power it has granted at the feet of the authentically oppressed.

"MY ORIGIN STORY"

Watchmen (2019) immediately eschews the compulsive, "neo-literalist hyper-fidelity"[10] of Snyder's adaptation. Opening in brightly lit Tulsa rather than among rain-darkened skyscrapers, without a costumed-adventurer in sight, the series initially feels tonally out-of-joint with its source material. Where Moore's graphic novel immediately orients readers within the New York of its gritty, neo-noir alternate 1985, Lindelof's initial scenes deliberately disorient viewers, leaving them wondering what relevance the 1921 Greenwood Race Massacre could have on a franchise formerly defined by its whiteness. *Watchmen* (2019) delights in Mooreian seminonlinear narrative, and in thematic allusions to both real and diegetic intertexts, slowly revealing the significance of its surprising origination point. Despite its differing tone and emphasis, Lindelof's adaptation succeeds where Snyder's fails. Rather than defanging Moore's critique of authoritarian justice, *Watchmen* (2019) raises its stakes by reframing this critique through the lens of systemic racism, reconstituting Hooded Justice as a disillusioned Black police officer lynched by white colleagues.

Moore's original text leaves the secret identity of Hooded Justice deliberately ambiguous. The first masked hero within the setting's alternate timeline, he diegetically remains the center of historical speculation and conspiracy theories. Exploiting its existing uncertainties, Lindelof's series expands Hooded Justice's backstory, narratively justifying its most significant divergence from the original. Including few named Black characters, each embodying specific Black stereotypes, race appears to be an afterthought within the graphic novel. Visually, Hooded Justice (nicknamed "HJ"), appears white. That is, the few inches of exposed skin surrounding each of his eyes suggests as much. HJ's identity remains doubly concealed: his "real" identity protected by his literal disguise and his homosexual identity by his publicly telegraphed sexual relationship with Silk Spectre. The open secret of his sexuality is insinuated throughout the graphic novel, most explicitly surfacing in the diegetic tell-all autobiography of his colleague. However, Moore never suggests that HJ's racial identity is other than it seems. Confirming the implied homosexual relationship between Captain Metropolis and Hooded Justice, Lindelof roots his representation within the story's existing canon, legitimizing his series' signature expansion of Hooded Justice's origin. Where Moore's HJ is doubly masked, that of the television adaptation is trebly so, hiding not only his identity and sexuality, but also his race.

Moore's Hooded Justice is characterized by two costume pieces, his eponymous hood and the noose around his neck, whose significance is never divulged. *Watchmen* (2019) resignifies the original iconography of Hooded Justice. In 1930s New York, Will Reeves becomes the only Black police officer in his graduating class, allegedly hired only for the "publicity." After stumbling on the orchestrations of a secret KKK offshoot, Reeves is stalked, beaten, and eventually lynched by white officers from his own precinct. Tying his hands and feet, they cover his head with a black hood, wrap a noose around his neck, then hang him from a tree. This sequence is shot as though from Will's point of view. A gauzy black veil obscuring all but the silhouettes of his assailants, the camera's focus blurs and darkens before fading to black, signifying his diminishing consciousness. Between shots, Reeves—momentarily having passed out—is cut down by the officers assaulting him. As the shot comes back into focus the camera, still mimicking his perspective, remains partially veiled as one of the officers kneels. Unhooding Will and holding a knife before his eyes, the man threatens, "Keep your black nose out of white folks' business, N----r. Or, next time, we won't cut you down," before abandoning him.

Shaking with adrenaline, continuing to clutch the black hood, Will stumbles back into the city visibly dazed. Awakened from his fugue by screams, Will observes a woman and her date being violently mugged. Given a spontaneous opportunity for exorcizing his pent-up rage, and instinctively putting the hood back on to conceal his face, he intervenes. Saving the couple almost inadvertently, Will continues brutally beating the assailants. The three white muggers function as explicit proxies for the three white officers by whom Reeves was lynched only minutes earlier. Will's immediate trauma stems from that physical attack, his vengeance projected upon the bodies of these thugs. But Will is also possessed by a less immediate, psychological trauma that has been building since he joined the force. From being publicly snubbed by the commissioner during his academy graduation, to having his arrests of anti-Semites actively dismissed, the long-denigrated Reeves has seen his attempts at equally enforcing the law openly undermined by white-supremacist cops. Will's most significant arrestee, a prominent white businessman whom he witnessed setting a Jewish deli ablaze, is released without charges by the same three officers who shortly thereafter attack him. The layers of signification inherent to Will's first taste of extralegal justice are thus multifold: the violent white muggers function as metonymies of the three officers, the three officers themselves functioning as synecdoches of institutionally racist policing. Sublimating his desire for revenge beneath the flimsy pretext of protecting the mugging victims, Reeves's initial act of vigilantism becomes an outlet for his pent-up feelings of impotence.

Being helplessly dangled from the tree literalizes the precinct's denials of Will's agency and authority. Cutting him down, the officers intend to solidify his demoralization. But, combined with his emboldening success against the muggers, their actions instill resolve rather than resignation. Their arrogant assumption of his powerlessness leaves them vulnerable. Like all fascists, these white supremacists are "condemned to lose" because they are "constitutionally incapable of objectively evaluating the force of the enemy." Their failed intimidation is most apparent in Reeves's subversion of the symbols by which they had sought to oppress him. Encountering the muggers, Reeves appears unaware of the noose remaining round his neck, donning the hood because it is what comes to hand. After he is heralded as a hero by the morning papers, and urged by his future wife, June, Will embraces vigilantism as a cause rather than a discrete incident. In doing so, he totemizes both the noose and the hood, subverting them from symbols of oppression into symbols of his determination. If Bruce Wayne were to incorporate his mother's pearls into his costume, he would have no better physical manifestation of his motivation, as these totems transcend Will's own experience of persecution, extending to his entire race. While the lynching catalyzes Will to act on his anger, his trauma-born rage has been seething since childhood, driving him to become an officer of the law in the attempt to change the system from within.

Watchmen (2019) opens with Will's childhood trauma, deliberately downplaying its connection—and his—to the Mooreian setting until more than halfway through the series. Emulating Moore's technique, *Watchmen* (2019) integrates a range of multimodal diegetic texts and real-world allusions, functioning as temporal anchors, thematic gauges, and subtle foreshadowings. Following the limited perspectives of its characters, the graphic novel's narrative moves haltingly forward, interspersed with frequent flashbacks that continually recontextualize their identities and motivations. These piecemeal revelations are thematically deepened, and sometimes outright communicated, through Moore's deftly interwoven metatextual allusions and multimodal diegetic texts, a style Lindelhof flawlessly replicates. Understood in this context, the show's beginning paradoxically alludes to, even as it conceals, the significance of its immediate focal point, the Tulsa Race Massacre of 1921, as experienced through the eyes of a then-unidentified child.

The series' opening shots depict scenes from a fictional silent film, *Trust in the Law!*, which frames Will's experiences of racialized violence, and, thus, Lindelof's remediation of Hooded Justice. As *Watchmen*'s first episode begins, *Trust in the Law* nears its climax, the distinctive 4:3 aspect ratio of a silent film[11] comprising the entirety of the show's initial frames. The camera focus slowly shifts, pulling back from the cinema screen itself to reveal an all-but-empty theater, its only occupants a small Black boy in the front row and his mother, playing the film's piano accompaniment. Reverentially mouthing the lines, the captivated child has clearly seen this film multiple times. Depicting the exploits of Bass Reeves, "the Black Marshal of Oklahoma," the film concludes with his arrest of a corrupt white sheriff. The black-and-white picture destabilizes the normative cinematographic color coding through which "good guys" wear white hats and "bad guys" wear black. Clad entirely in white, the sheriff at first appears the victim of the hooded black horseman who has dragged him from atop his own white steed. Lassoed and dragged along the ground, he is brought before his townsfolk as they emerge from church to decry his treatment. To excited murmurs, Bass reveals the sheriff's corruption and his own identity, exposing the man as a cattle thief in the same instant as he exposes his own unmasked Black face. The white mob cries "String him up, string him up!" The medium of silent film, dependent on intertitles, allows the episode to uncomfortably linger on the uncertainty over to whom the citizenry refers. However, it becomes apparent they mean the cattle-thief, whom Reeves ultimately saves, chiding them, "No! There will be no mob justice here today. Trust in the law."

Without breathing space, the episode abruptly transitions away from this patently fictitious celluloid ending as the reality of the escalating Greenwood Race Massacre outside the Williams Dreamland Theater crashes in upon its lone viewer. The scenes that follow graphically depict the broad-daylight murders of innocent Black folks in the streets of downtown Tulsa. Clutched by his desperate parents, the little boy is shepherded through an ordinary shopping district turned hellscape, where he witnesses white men wantonly killing his Black neighbors as other white men gleefully ransack and torch the surrounding Black businesses. Some of these men are clad in the uniform of the Ku Klux Klan, their white robes evoking the white apparel of the on-screen sheriff. But unlike in the movies, these white criminals—who were tacitly abetted by the National Guard[12]—will go unpunished. Whether real or fictional, white folks have the privilege to "trust in the law," one the legacies of Jim Crow and Klan oppression make clear does not extend to people of color. Juxtaposing the story of Bass Reeves against the Greenwood Massacre, *Watchmen* (2019) establishes the tensions at stake in the narrative that follows: between the simplistic black-and-white idealization of "justice" and the messy realities of its inequitable enforcement. These tensions eventually coalesce in the identity of that little boy, whose future assumed name will combine elements drawn from his favorite theater and his cinematic idol.

The boy's parents are unable to escape Tulsa with him. After narrowly navigating the chaos enveloping Greenwood Avenue, Obie and Ruth arrive at a shop where a friend remains, urgently ladening his car with valuables. As the mechanic insists there "ain't no room," they implore he take "just the boy, then." Hurriedly saying goodbye, his mother lies "[they]'ll be right behind [him]," as his father scrawls a message on a well-worn slip of paper. Lifting his son into a trunk affixed to the vehicle's rear, Obie carefully tucks the paper into his pocket, reprimands him for sucking his thumb, and exhorts that he "be strong." As the car pulls away, bullets whiz through the upper edge of the trunk, creating an eyehole through which the child peers at the continuing destruction of his world. The frame shifting to match the child's perspective, glimpses are revealed of Black bodies dragged behind a moving vehicle. This evokes an image of Bass Reeves dragging the corrupt white sheriff behind his horse, but inverts its meaning. Where the mythical Bass apprehends the criminal, the real-life white vigilantes torture the innocent. Where the mythical Bass protects the white criminal from the white lynch mob, the real-life Black innocents of Tulsa are denied justice and persecuted by just such a mob. Will Reeves's parents are, like Thomas and Martha Wayne, violently killed when their son is a child. Bruce's trauma is deepened by witnessing his parents' murders, his insatiable desire for vengeance driving his need to become Batman. Will's own trauma is magnified through the juxtaposition of what he has seen with what will remain forever unseeable. He has witnessed dozens of murders, seen Black Wall Street burn, and barely dodged several bullets himself. But Will is not present to witness his parents' certain murders, that absence creating a trauma born of ambiguity. Where Bruce is left to replay his parents' deaths, Will is instead left to imagine them, denied the memory without being spared the trauma. And, of course, the two boys will have vastly different experiences of orphanhood. However violent, a back-alley mugging could never dent the Wayne fortune. For Will, however, whatever small earnings his parents might have attained through their hard work now lie plundered or in ashes. Like Batman, Hooded Justice is driven by his desire for vengeance, itself an outward manifestation of his anger. *Watchmen* (2019) recontextualizes this anger as a natural response to the racialized violence he has survived.

Despite thematic connections to Batman's origin story, Will's narrow escape more directly remediates Superman's. Both Kal-El and Will are saved through their parents' sacrifices, sent alone into the unknown in the hope they will survive the dying of their worlds. Both boys emerge from their pods in darkened cornfields. The white Kryptonian refugee becomes adopted by paragons of unconditional love, Bible Belt righteousness, and patriotic Americanism. But there are no analogues of Ma and Pa Kent to welcome the displaced Will Reeves. As a Black child in Jim Crow America, he has already been alienated to a greater extent within his own native country than Kal-El will ever be as a literal extraterrestrial. In the lonely darkness, Will emerges from the trunk, which has been thrown clear of the overturned automobile. Amongst the strewn remains of looted belongings, he discovers the corpses of the mechanic and his wife. Looking for direction, Will unfolds his father's note; it enjoins, "Watch over this boy"—but there are no adults left alive to read its message. He then hears a baby, also thrown clear of the wreck, begin to cry. Picking her up, Will tonelessly murmurs, "You're okay," externalizing his own need for reassurance at the same time as he displaces his father's directions, to "watch over," onto the infant. Glancing backward at the orange glow of the inflamed Tulsa skyline, he resolutely carries her away with him—meeting his father's injunction to "be strong." Denied a childhood, the Black Superman figure must save not only himself, but the child that in other versions he would have been.

The visualization of this infant, swaddled in an American flag, strengthens the Superman allusion. In the first version of his origin story, he is discovered wrapped in Kryptonian cloth, symbolizing his parents' sacrifice. *Watchmen* (2019) subverts this symbolism. Notably, baby June's parents had not intended to send her out into the world alone. Filling their vehicle with valuables, they abandoned their friends to certain death, almost refusing to save their son. Doing so, June's parents embrace not only American rugged individualism, but also the material realities required for sustaining the "pursuit of happiness" represented by the flag in which they wrap their daughter. While their actions appear selfish and materialistic, the mechanic and his wife are clinging to their hard-won wealth, without which they will be less empowered to protect the liberty of their child. But the wealth with which they seek to safeguard their family ultimately makes them a target. The context through which Will discovers baby June subverts the flag's symbolism, affirming the discrepancies between the ideals of liberty and equality it represents and the lived experience of Blackness in America.

But Will continues investing in American idealism despite his long-held anger. Seeking change from within, he joins the police force to personally ensure the equal application of the law. Instilled with the disillusionment stemming from her parents' fractured American dream, however, June scoffs at his decision, already recognizing the uniform will offer him no greater protection than the flag had once offered her. Being lynched by his fellow officers physically embodies the impossibility for Will, as a lone Black beat cop, to change the system from within. But it is not until catalyzed by June that he attempts to change it from without. The morning after his assault, June insists, "You ain't gonna get justice with a badge, Will Reeves. You gonna get it with that hood." But she also warns, "If you wanna stay a hero, townsfolk gonna need to think one of their own's under it," applying makeup to cover the exposed skin around his eyes, concealing Will's Blackness. Though his origin story invokes that of Superman, Will's race means that he is more greatly othered than this alien superhero. Superman chooses not to wear a mask as a symbol of accessibility and transparency, but because of his race Will possesses no such choice. As a Black cop, his efforts at law enforcement have been undermined. If he were outed as a Black vigilante, he would be outright criminalized.

As remediated by *Watchmen* (2019), Hooded Justice literalizes Du Boisian "double consciousness." Will's fractured psyche is communicated through repeated scenes of his gazing at himself in the mirror while wearing this makeup, embodying Du Bois's words of "always looking at [him]self through the eyes" of the racist white society by whose perceptions he remains bound. Will continues "measuring [him]self by the means of a nation that look[s] back in contempt."[13] Through his self-erasure, Will temporarily displaces white contempt when fighting crime, but by doing so further internalizes his self-contempt, preventing him from fighting injustice.

FIGHTING ALONE

Hooded Justice's solo career is soon interrupted when wealthy playboy Nelson Gardner, aka Captain Metropolis, recruits Will to join the new crimefighting team he is putting together. "The Minutemen" is composed of costumed avengers he has inspired. Gardner insists that the presence of the inciting hero will "legitimize the whole enterprise." Nelson ultimately lures Will into his organization through the dual promises of solidarity and sexuality, entreating, "Why fight alone, when you could have *true* companionship?" (emphasis in original). Gardner's *double entendre* simultaneously "recruit[s] Hooded Justice into the Minutemen—and Will Reeves into his bed."[14] Though her warnings can be mistaken for jealousy, June insists that Nelson is merely using Will, which eventually proves true.

During his recruitment efforts, Gardner implies that his team will help HJ dismantle the KKK plot against the Black community. Yet, he makes it clear that not even their fellow Minutemen members must become aware of Will's true racial identity, commanding that "the mask stays on." Acquiescing to this continued concealment as the white-presenting Hooded Justice, Will subsequently becomes complicit in white discrimination, as typified during a later press conference functioning as little more than an ad campaign. When reporters ask Hooded Justice about his crime-fighting plans, Captain Metropolis silences Will, preventing him from publicizing his antiracist agenda. Redirecting the press's attention, Metropolis describes the unrealistic supervillain plot the Minutemen are working to foil. Disgusted, Reeves becomes inattentive, the camera panning left to mimic his distracted gaze, which rests upon a print ad for the bank bonds they are currently shilling. The ad depicts a racist, caricatured "Negro" criminal being waylaid by another costumed hero. Despite his disgust, Reeves appears unaware of the ideological continuity between this mythologized image of "law and order" and Klan rhetoric.

Like the KKK, the Minutemen remains an institution of white vigilantism, invested in reinforcing the status quo. Seduced by Gardner's claim he would no longer fight alone, Reeves has become more isolated than ever, alienating his wife and sidelining his quest for racial justice. Nelson increasingly downplays the significance of Will's personal investigation, deeming it beneath the Minutemen. Yet to recognize his lover's manipulativeness, once Reeves uncovers the Klan's plot he reveals it to Gardner, imploring his aid. Instead of simply refusing, Nelson gaslights him, insisting that Blacks need no provocation to riot, asking if Will has "been drinking," and cajoling him to just "come over." Despite promising they will figure it out together, Nelson has made it irremediably clear that his asymmetrical interest in Will extends only to what he can gain from him.

Finally, Will recognizes that the Minutemen has been—like the police force—simply another oppressive system, from within whose confines he cannot affect change. Catalyzed by this realization, Reeves immediately afterward murders the white business owner whom the law could not reach, as well as his fellow Klansmen, which include the officers by whom Will had been lynched. The collapsing of Will's competing identities is literalized as he puts the hood on over his police uniform. Ceasing to see himself through the eyes of the racist white society that has the privilege to "trust in the law," Will transforms from the white-presenting Hooded Justice who leaves criminals to the police into the antiracist avenger who enacts justice the system would never impose. Having alone disrupted the Klan's plot, Will returns home only to see his son trying on his hood. Misdirecting the anger he feels toward himself, Reeves violently stops his son from whitening his skin with makeup. Now externally visualized, he can recognize the self-erasure he has performed, dismayed he has promoted it within his child. But this abusive outburst severs his relationship with his family. Despite joining the team, HJ has spent years fighting alone, the toll of so doing ultimately leaving him by himself.

HELPING EACH OTHER

Given his history, it is no wonder that when Will is approached decades later by Dr. Manhattan he reacts hostilely toward the proposed team-up, scoffing, "Want me to put on a goddamn mask, huh?" Responding simply, "No," the subtlety of Jon's answer belies its significance: he does not want Will to hide his race and identity. Incredulous, Reeves asks Manhattan, "What the hell you want with me?" Jon again offers a straightforward answer: "Nothing." Immediately this distinguishes him from the solipsistic Gardner. Jon seeks "to form an alliance" not for his own sake, but for that of his lover, Angela, the granddaughter whom Reeves has been hitherto unaware of.

Their experiences of power mirroring one another's, the two men form an influential partnership. Previously, Reeves's white-masked alter ego, HJ, had granted access to the social power denied by his race. Inversely, Dr. Manhattan's Black-masked alter ego, Cal, will subsequently grant him freedom from the social power of his own identity and from the superhuman power he has inadvertently obtained. Both men have been alienated by their individuated experiences of time. Manhattan exists in a perpetually liminal state of untethered temporality, simultaneously experiencing his own past, present, and future. Reeves, instead, remains so tethered to his own past that he cannot progress. Seared into his psyche, the embers of Greenwood Avenue continue to burn within Reeves, his inescapable trauma incinerating his present and future. Will Reeves's ultimate tragedy is that his anger-fueled fight against white power has isolated him from would-be allies against oppression, including his wife. His preoccupation with exacting revenge for the loss of his family of origin isolates him from the new family he and June have made. Through their alliance, however, both men exorcise their toxic temporalities.

At the culmination of Moore's graphic novel, Jon explains, "I can change almost anything . . . but I can't change human nature." Having single-handedly ensured American victory in Vietnam, he has committed atrocities in the name of a salvation he now understands he is neither capable, nor desirous, of delivering. Applied to the context of Lindelof's narrative, this accounts for Manhattan's inability to end racism; for what remains more endemic to human nature than the capacity for Othering? Unable to change human nature, Jon instead changes his own. Collaborating with Reeves to "ensure an optimal outcome" in the "uncertain" future, Jon uses his "limited" ability "to influence events." Sacrificing his godhood, Jon aids Reeves in attaining the justice he struggled toward alone. Doing so provides the closure for Reeves to move forward even as it binds Jon to the now-inescapable present and his ensuing death. De-deified, Jon ceases to merely look like a Black human, instead becoming one as he regains his long-absent humanity. Beforehand, however, he bequeaths his power to his wife, leaving Angela the agency to decide whether or not to accept it. While possessing that power, Jon remained an outsider, unable to uplift the Black community from within. Offering Angela his abilities, he abdicates the role of white savior he had once played for the South Vietnamese, instead leaving the work to be achieved by, rather than for, the oppressed. Unlike the "white liberals and progressives" Kenneth W. Stikkers criticizes, Jon recognizes the "causal link between [his] own advantages and the disadvantages of others," realizing that "racial equality" cannot be "achieved without . . . pay[ing] any price."[15] Bypassing the inherent whiteness of American institutionalism, Jon forms with Reeves an alliance between individuals, rather than members, through which he will eventually entrust his power to Angela.

Recursively structured, the show interweaves the narratives of both oppressors and oppressed, mediating their interactions through characters' relationships with Dr. Manhattan. The ultimate symbol of power, Jon Osterman functions as the narrative's invisible, if not truly absent, center. Because of the "unique" way in which he experiences time, Dr. Manhattan exists paradoxically as both oppressor and oppressed, as both the cause and the effect of the story as it unfolds. Remediating the past from within the present, Jon partners with Will Reeves to achieve the justice heretofore denied him. Atoning, through sacrifice, for his own complicity in cultural hegemony, Jon submits to an inverted apotheosis that literalizes the Blackness he had unconsciously performed during his marriage to Will's granddaughter. Leaving his power to Angela, Jon gives her the chance to do what he could not, to "do more."

NOTES

1. Blair Davis, "Beyond Watchmen," *Cinema Journal* 56, no. 2 (2017): 114. Davis describes the impacts of its "narrative complexity and formal intricacy," which "had both an immediate and an enduring influence on the comics industry."

2. Richard Reynolds, *Super Heroes: A Modern Mythology* (Jackson: University Press of Mississippi, 1994), 114.

3. See Jay David Bolter and Richard Grusin, *Remediation: Understanding New Media* (Cambridge, MA: MIT Press, 2003).

4. See Judith Fetterley, *The Resisting Reader: A Feminist Approach to American Fiction* (Boulder, CO: NetLibrary, Inc., 1999).

5. *Watchmen* criticism is frequently dominated by divisive interpretations of the complex symbol of Dr. Manhattan. Kathryn Imray reads him as "the equivalent to God in the *Watchmen* universe" in "Shall Not the Judge of All the Earth Do Right? Theodicies in Watchmen," *Journal of Religion and Popular Culture* 29, no. 2 (2017): 121. We contend this misses the point.

6. Herman Gray, *Watching Race: Television and the Struggle for Blackness* (Minneapolis: University of Minnesota Press, 2005), 85–87.

7. Some might demur that his actions do not constitute "blackface" because his appropriation does not function as racist entertainment for white audiences. Catherine M. Cole and Tracy C. Davis explore the "potent and slippery" history of blackface which has been "notoriously difficult to control as signification" in "Routes of Blackface," *TDR: The Drama Review* 57, no. 2 (2013): 7.

8. Nicole Simek, "Speculative Futures: Race in *Watchmen*'s Worlds," *symploke* 28, no. 1–2 (2020): 403.

9. Without which Osterman's accident could not occur.

10. Aaron Taylor, The Continuing Adventures of the 'Inherently Unfilmable' Book: Zack Snyder's *Watchmen*," *Cinema Journal* 56, no. 2 (2017): 126.

11. Lindelof riffs on Richard Donner's *Superman* (1978) opening; however, the silent film here exists diegetically, influencing characters, whereas the *Action Comics* issue remains a nondiegetic plot device, transporting viewers to Metropolis.

12. Hannibal B. Johnson describes the "order" restored by the National Guard, "includ[ing] a declaration of martial law, the internment of Black Tulsans, and some still-mysterious burial processes that may have included mass graves" in "Tulsa, Then and Now: Reflections on the Legacy of the 1921 Tulsa Race Massacre," *Great Plains Quarterly* 40, no. 3 (2020): 182.

13. See W. E. B. Du Bois, *The Souls of Black Folk: Authoritative Text, Contexts, Criticism*, ed. Henry Louis Gates (New York: Norton, 1999).

14. See John Orquiola, "Watchmen Reveals Hooded Justice's Identity (& Breaks from the Comic)," *ScreenRant*, November 25, 2019, https://screenrant.com/watchmen-hooded-justice-identity-will-reeves-comic-change/.

15. Kenneth W. Stikkers, "' . . . But I'm Not Racist': Toward a Pragmatic Conception of 'Racism,'" *The Pluralist* 9, no. 3 (2014): 10.

Chapter 11

"PLENTY OF ROOM TO SWING A ROPE"

Watchmen and the Racial Politics of Place

CURTIS MAREZ

In Spring 2020, I taught *Watchmen* to students of color in an undergraduate ethnic studies class at the University of California, San Diego. Because of the COVID-19 pandemic we met over Zoom. The program took on new significance as the quarter progressed, in part because of the contrast between the wearing of masks by both white nationalists and the police in *Watchmen*'s alternative history and the viral image of an unmasked white man screaming at masked police in the Michigan state capital as part of an armed protest against quarantining.[1] Spring also witnessed the 99th anniversary of the Greenwood Massacre represented in the show. Finally, students were struck by the resonances between *Watchmen* and the vigilante and police killings of Black people; masked Black Lives Matter protests against police violence and white supremacy; and the toppling of Confederate monuments.

The experience of teaching *Watchmen* online, with all of the spatial distancing and dislocation that virtual classes presuppose, also suggested to me the topic of this chapter: the relationship between screen settings and real places. The program's first episode begins with the 1921 massacre, where over the course of two days white supremacists murdered as many as 300 Black people and destroyed businesses, homes, and churches in the Greenwood neighborhood of Tulsa. When it first aired in October of 2019, the episode sparked extensive media discussions of racial violence in US history. The episode re-emerged in public discourse after the May 25, 2020, police murder of George Floyd, and again fifteen days later after Donald Trump announced a rally in Tulsa, within walking distance of Greenwood. As if trolling Black people there and everywhere else for the pleasure of his white nationalist base, Trump first scheduled the rally for Juneteenth, but he ultimately rescheduled it in response to public outrage. By contrast, to celebrate Juneteenth, HBO made *Watchmen* available for free during the president's rally weekend. At the same time, Washington DC painted "Black Lives Matter" in large block letters in front of the White House, while other localities followed suit, including Tulsa's Greenwood neighborhood. These BLM paintings appeared to mimic the color and typeface of *Watchmen*'s distinctive title sequences, leading *Watchmen* creator Damon Lindelof to suggest that the DC mural could open one of the show's episodes.[2]

In what follows, I focus on a related but distinct set of relationships between screen settings and real places in the making of *Watchmen*, analyzing the program as an expression of the forms of racial capitalism that shape both its content and its interventions in real places.[3] Although *Watchmen* is set in Oklahoma, New York, and Saigon, it was filmed in Georgia to take advantage of state subsidies for TV and filmmakers. An increasing number of films and TV series are produced in impoverished places such as Georgia, where they profit from conditions that result in racial inequalities.[4] By enabling accumulation at the expense of poor people of color, state programs that divert tax money from social welfare to Hollywood constitute forms of state violence.

As an example of such violence, I focus on *Watchmen*'s production in Georgia, arguing that the show reimagines its locations in contradictory ways. On the one hand, it indirectly calls critical attention to the forms of white supremacy connecting different settings and locations. Those connections are suggested by the many Confederate monuments surrounding the program's Georgia locations, articulating the state to other settings and places subject to histories of white supremacy. Although TV series often suppress their locations so as to maintain the fiction of the worlds they create, *Watchmen*'s material conditions of production bleed into its content, shaping and extending its critical representation of white racial violence. On the other hand, I argue that *Watchmen* disavows its own complicity in the reproduction of racialized inequality in its Georgia locations. Introducing a gap between setting and location, the series displaces from view and critical reflection its conditions of possibility in racial inequality.

The Walking Dead (*TWD*) is also filmed in Georgia, and its recent history draws into critical relief the relationship between setting and location at stake in *Watchmen*. The final season of the popular program about a zombie virus was transformed by the spread of COVID-19 in Georgia. The showrunners faced a dilemma: state subsidies made shooting there attractive, but it was also potentially dangerous for large numbers of actors to come into close contact as part of zombie herds. The virus thus changed the narrative of

TWD's final season, forcing producers to focus on individual character arcs and stories requiring as few actors as possible.[5]

COVID-19's effect on the program's narrative structure opens a window onto the workings of racial capitalism in Georgia. Material inequities there ensure that the virus disproportionately affects the state's Black and Latinx residents.[6] Georgia has the second lowest level of state spending for social welfare in the United States, and the percentage of people of color in Georgia living below the poverty line is significantly higher than the national average. As a result, people of color in the state have been more vulnerable to the virus because they live in crowded housing, perform essential yet low wage and dangerous work, have limited access to health care, and suffer from the negative health consequences of experiencing racism.[7] The COVID-19 pandemic is a unique, once-in-a-lifetime crisis with unprecedented consequences for life and labor, yet the exceptional global disaster has drawn into relief the local, quotidian conditions that make people of color especially vulnerable to illness. The dangers of shooting *TWD* during the pandemic are novel, but they remind us that Georgia is Black and poor even in "normal" times, and those conditions are part of what enables the state to attract Hollywood media makers.

While providing scant support to poor Black people, Georgia nonetheless gives film and TV producers tax breaks and other subsidies. Outpacing even California by some measures, the state has become the world's leading filming location.[8] Georgia spends more on its tax credit program than any other location in the world ($606 million in 2016), and unlike other states it does not limit the amount of its annual tax credits.[9] Also unlike other states, Georgia's program even subsidizes compensation for actors, writers, and directors.[10] Tax money enriches the most privileged TV workers from outside the state but generates relatively few local jobs. Economist John Charles Bradbury recently surveyed existing research on the topic, as well as conducting his own study, and concluded that film and TV incentive programs "divert tax revenue to the film industry from other economic sectors (public and private) without generating corresponding economic growth." He concludes that in some cases, the programs even have a negative impact on local economies.[11]

In the case of *Watchmen*, the employment of extras is the exception that proves the rule. The show employed a number of local Black and white extras for the Greenwood Massacre scenes and Vietnamese extras for the Saigon suicide bomber scenes. The work description of a *Watchmen* extra suggests one definition of racial capitalism: low-wage jobs of limited and uncertain duration requiring people of color to recreate traumatic and traumatizing histories of racial violence. Because the industry depends on the upward redistribution of wealth from poor, racialized taxpayers to Hollywood, programs such as *Watchmen* benefit from tax subsidies at the expense of Black lives. Hence the state's lopsided budget priorities—incentives for Hollywood while starving social welfare—result from long histories of white supremacy and anti-Black racism in both Georgia and Los Angeles.

Set in Oklahoma, *Watchmen* was mostly made in the Peach State, and its story sheds light on the history of racist violence that has indirectly helped make Georgia financially attractive to media makers. At the center of *Watchmen* are the intergenerational origin stories of Will Reeves as Hooded Justice (Jovan Adepo) and his granddaughter, Angela Abar, as Sister Night (Regina King), two masked Black heroes who fight the Klan. The program "imagines a redemptive narrative for superhero origins," according to Rebecca A. Wanzo, "both by writing a black man into the origin story and by making state-ignored (and state-generated) white supremacy the enemy."[12]

Reflecting critically on our present reality, the series projects an alternate world where the police and the Klan are effectively the same institution. The Order of the Cyclops, for example, is depicted running the New York Police Department in the 1930s, while the Seventh Kavalry has infiltrated present-day police and government from Tulsa to DC. The emphasis is on anti-Blackness, but naming the Oklahoma Klan after Custer's genocidal unit also draws attention to settler colonial racism. Viewers discover in one episode that white nationalist senator Joe Keene (James Wolk) has given the chief of police and Seventh Kavalry member Judd Crawford (Don Johnson) a painting titled *Martial Feats of Comanche Horsemanship* as a sort of settler colonial trophy. Keene is compared to a cowboy, and Judd wears a cowboy hat, suggesting the entanglement of white supremacy and settler colonialism.

This analysis of cowboy Klansmen helps explain *Watchmen*'s references to the Rogers and Hammerstein musical *Oklahoma!*, which, I argue, speaks to the show's participation in racial capitalism. Episode 1, for instance, depicts a Black cast performance of *Oklahoma!* in the Dreamland Theater, with Judd, his wife Jane (Frances Fischer), and Angela in the audience. Later, when the Crawfords join the Abar family for dinner, Jane explains that Judd "hated" the performance because he was "jealous," having played the lead character Curly when he was in high school. Pressed to perform, Judd croons "People Will Say We're in Love" from the musical. At the episode's end, when an elderly, wheelchair-bound Reeves (Lou Gossett Jr.) uses the Klan's mysterious mesmeric technology to make the white supremacist sheriff hang himself from an oak tree in revenge for his own prior near-lynching at the hands of white supremacist police, *Oklahoma!*'s "Poor Jud Is Dead" plays on the soundtrack, a song in which Curly attempts to convince his romantic rival to commit suicide. The title of episode 1, "It's Summer and We're Running Out of Ice," is the song's last line, suggesting the difficulty of preserving Judd's corpse. Finally, after taking refuge in the Dreamland Theater near the end of *Watchmen*'s final episode, Will, Angela, and her children emerge from the *Oklahoma!* venue to the tune of "Oh What a Beautiful Morning."

Like *Hamilton*, to which it seemingly alludes, Judd's jealousy over the Black cast version of *Oklahoma!* suggests a racialized struggle over who can represent the nation. The musical's title song can be understood as a popular anthem of settler colonial Americana. "Oklahoma" enumerates the territory's attractions while ignoring Indigenous displacement and genocide. Instead, in the song it is the settlers who "belong to the land." "Oklahoma" also conjures images of lynching, celebrating land with "plenty of room to swing a rope." Indeed, a number of the images in Detective Wayne Tillman's (Tim Blake Nelson) white-supremacy-detecting slide show would be at home in a production of the musical. Some of our most lively discussions of the program in my ethnic studies course were focused on *Oklahoma!* because so many of its mostly people of color students knew the musical from high school productions, intimating that the play continues to serve for many as an influential introduction to a white nationalist structure of feeling.

Watchmen's references to *Oklahoma!* represent a critical commentary on the history of that state but also an unconscious reference to the TV show's filming location and an indirect acknowledgment of the appeal of state subsidies. The title song effectively celebrates the travel of outsiders to a "Brand new state!/Gonna treat you great!," with promises of access to bountiful resources ("Gonna give you barley, carrots and pertaters/Pasture fer the cattle, spinach and termayters"). Read against the grain, *Watchmen*'s *Oklahoma!* interpolations are the disavowed traces of Georgia's financial incentive program and the accumulation by dispossession it presupposes.

While shooting for *Watchmen* commenced on the 97th anniversary of the Greenwood Massacre, the primary locations for the series opening was in Georgia.[13] The first episode begins during the massacre, in the same venue as the Black-cast production of *Oklahoma!*, a Black-owned movie theater that is attacked by Klansmen as a young Reeves watches a silent movie featuring his heroic namesake, the Black sheriff Bass Reeves. The setting is based on the actual theater named the Williams Dreamland Theater in Greenwood, owned by John and Loula Williams and destroyed by white rioters. Interior scenes were filmed in Macon's Douglas Theater, located blocks away from two Confederate monuments, one representing a giant generic Confederate soldier holding a rifle atop a tall pedestal and shaft, and the other a "Monument to the Women of the Confederacy" in the form of a large obelisk flanked by sculptures of two white mothers. The more extensive exterior scenes representing airplanes dropping firebombs, white looting, the murder of Black people by Klansmen, and the destruction of the theater were filmed a few blocks from another large memorial representing a Confederate soldier with a gun, in the historic white commercial district of Cedartown, Georgia.

Cedartown is about an hour northwest of Atlanta and home to a larger-than-the-national-average percentage of Black and Latinx people living below the poverty line.[14] Its current residents work for Walmart, corporate call centers, and office furniture manufacturers, but historically Cedartown was a segregated cotton mill town. Before the passage of the 1964 Civil Rights Act, Black workers were excluded from the mills and hence also from company housing.[15] Cedartown is named for a regional fort that was used as an internment camp for Cherokee people along the "Trail of Tears." The Georgia location's origins in anti-Black, anti-Indigenous racism thus anticipates the representation of settler white nationalism in *Watchmen*'s Oklahoma setting.

Cedartown's white leaders have resisted efforts to remove the marble "pedestal-shaft-soldier" memorial to the Confederacy located between the town's two courthouse buildings.[16] Complementing monuments to "great men" like Robert E. Lee, such statues depicting individual citizen soldiers are common in the region, where they were inexpensively mass produced and often the only piece of public art in many small towns. The basic statue of a soldier resting on a rifle while on watch depicts the Confederacy as defensive rather than aggressive. It also promotes a populist view of Confederate soldiers, balancing their commitment to a larger cause with their individual integrity as white men. Such statues symbolize and enforce race and class inequality in the town's past and present by putting everyday white supremacy on a superhero pedestal.[17]

Confederate memorials were mostly erected in two waves: around the turn of the 19th century, under Jim Crow, and as complements to "lost cause" narratives about the Civil War; and during the late 1950s and early 1960s, in reaction to the African American civil rights movement. According to Dell Upton, they represented white supremacist historical revisionism: "those who fought for the white cause in the Civil War fought for 'their' state in a 'second war for independence'; the Confederacy is an important part of the south's 'heritage' and hence its monuments are sacred; the War was not about slavery; and 'soldiering is inherently honorable' regardless of the cause."[18] Their erecting in front of courthouses and city halls symbolizes white supremacist state power as a means of terrorizing Black people. In addition to its courthouse monument, Cedartown's Greenwood Cemetery includes the graves of almost sixty Confederate soldiers. Because, as Upton writes, "the very evidence of defeat provided by the graves suggested martyrdom in the cause of righteousness," cemeteries have often been chosen as homes for Confederate memorials.[19] Surrounded by hundreds of Confederate graves and memorials, it would be hard to make a TV series in Cedartown without noticing its many monuments to white supremacy.

Watchmen's other Georgia locations are also surrounded by Confederate memorials. The episode 3 scene where FBI agent Laurie Blake (Jean Smart) talks to Dr. Manhattan in a big blue phonebooth was filmed in Decatur's East Court Square, steps away from the courthouse with its obelisk monument to the Confederacy, which would likely have been visible to cast and crew while shooting. Dispensing with personifications of the Confederate foot soldier, the obelisk can be read as an extreme expression of abstraction, the sculptural depiction of revisionary claims that the lost cause wasn't about slavery but valor and principle. *Watchmen* returns to East Court Square and its nearby obelisk in the series finale.

Sherriff Crawford's funeral in episode 3 was filmed in two Confederate cemeteries. Exterior scenes were shot at Atlanta's historic Oakland Cemetery, which includes a Confederate Memorial Ground where approximately 7,000 soldiers are interred, as well as two large memorials to the Confederate dead.[20] Interior scenes, however, were filmed in the Decatur Cemetery, which includes a Confederate memorial cross, erected by the United Daughters of the Confederacy in 1984, as well as numerous Confederate graves.[21] Episode 6 is set in New York but shot in Macon. The scenes where Reeves discovers a Klan plot to pit Black film audiences against each other were filmed in Macon's Hargray Capitol Theater, steps from the massive Confederate soldier statue and the Confederate mothers' memorial mentioned earlier. The scene of a Klansman burning a Jewish deli in that episode was shot nearby, on the same street. The town of Newnan, the location for the Hoboken carnival in episode 5, includes a granite memorial to William Thomas Overby, the "Nathan Hale of the Confederacy," erected in front of the local county courthouse in 1952, as well as one of the mass-produced statues of a generic Confederate soldier originating in 1868.[22] And in episodes 7 and 8, US-occupied Saigon was played by Griffin, a town with a Confederate soldier memorial and the Stonewall Confederate Cemetery. Finally, many other scenes were filmed at Atlanta Metro Studios. As a local reporter recently noted, the state capital is home to numerous anti-Indian monuments and "a mother lode of Civil War and segregationist artifacts."[23] Confederate monuments are increasingly objects of vandalism, and Black people and their allies have agitated for their removal, yet Georgia's white ruling elite remain committed to preserving them as contemporary reminders that they are in charge.[24]

Although as far as I can tell none of the memorials I've described is visible in the show, in many ways *Watchmen* is in dialogue with the Confederate monuments that dot the map of its Georgia locations. The program reframes the figure of the masked vigilante from comic books as a kind of memorial to the Confederacy and the white nationalism it embodies. Alan Moore, author of the *Watchman* graphic novel, has argued that with their hoods and capes, Klansmen were models for comic book heroes, while historian Chris Gavaler has argued that *Birth of a Nation* helped inspire golden age comics.[25] The TV show draws on those histories with its depiction of the Order of the Cyclops and the masked members of the contemporary Seventh Kavalry. As part of a test to determine if a suspect is a white supremacist, Detective Tillman monitors their vital signs while they watch a slide show of monuments to American whiteness—fields of wheat, a milk advertisement, a man on the moon, a cowboy with a lasso, a Confederate flag, Mount Rushmore (with the addition of Richard Nixon), *American Gothic*, and photos of George Armstrong Custer and Klan rallies. Recalling Macon's statue of a larger-than-life Confederate soldier, *Watchmen* visually links settler colonial white supremacy to an aesthetics of white male monumentalism.

In the premiere episode, members of the Seventh Kavalry live in a trailer park called "Nixonville" decorated with a large statue of the president atop a pedestal in the style of a Confederate memorial, thus reminding us of Nixon's law and order, "silent majority" racism. Episode 3 prominently features a CGI-modified image of the Washington Monument, which was partly built by slaves to honor a slaveholder in the form of a giant obelisk, thus anticipating many Confederate monuments. As revealed in the final episode, Klansman and US Senator Keene dream of stealing the massive powers of Dr. Manhattan in order to enforce white global domination. The avatar of such aspirations for white nationalist world domination is the Order of the Cyclops, named for the *Odyssey*'s giant one-eyed monster. In these ways, *Watchmen* suggests that the white supremacist monumentalism associated with the South has characterized US nationalism as such.

Watchmen's representation of white supremacy and the Vietnam War is more problematic. In its alternate history, the US won the war, and Vietnam is now a US state. In a *Washington Post* editorial titled "How 'Watchmen's' Misunderstanding of Vietnam Undercuts its Vision of Racism," Viet Thanh Nguyen faults the show for failing to represent US imperialism's "entwinement with white supremacy."[26] *Watchmen*'s depiction of Vietnam is underdeveloped and confused, but in episode 6 it does raise questions about the relationship between white supremacy and US imperialism. Recovering from an overdose of her grandfather Will Reeves's "Nostalgia" prescription, a drug that enables users to relive the past, Angela Abar vividly recalls her own childhood. In her memory we see ten-year-old Angela as she walks through a Saigon street fair celebrating "VVN Day," a holiday commemorating the US victory over Vietnam. She stops to watch a puppet show depicting a giant Dr. Manhattan shooting flames from his hands at Viet Cong soldiers, intercut with images from the Greenwood massacre of a Klansman threatening Black firemen with a torch. Dr. Manhattan's Vietnamese puppeteer gestures toward another man on a bike, who picks up a backpack and rides through the fair, his transit intercut with the image of another Klansman from the massacre scene. Finally, the bike rider leaps onto a military jeep shouting, "Death to the Invaders," and detonates a bomb.

In a subsequent memory, young Angela is questioned by Saigon police, who ask her to identify the puppet master after they remove a hood from his head. As the police pull the man out of their car, the scene cuts to an image of Angela's grandfather, Hooded Justice, the anti-Klan vigilante, putting on his own hood, and then back to the scene in Saigon, where the police rehood the Vietnamese bomber, who is then led away and shot off camera. Do these scenes suggest a moral equivalence between a Vietnamese suicide bomber and the Klan or between US white supremacy at home and abroad? The program seems to strive for a kind of modernist complexity or liberal balance that muddles sharp political antagonisms. By shooting scenes of Saigon amid Confederate monuments in Georgia, however, *Watchmen* implicitly connects US imperialism and white supremacy.[27]

And yet, by using locations in Georgia as stand-ins for Saigon, New York, and Oklahoma, *Watchmen* obscures its complicity in the conditions of white supremacy supporting its production. While there are significant differences between the Greenwood Massacre with its violent destruction of Black lives and wealth, on the one hand, and the asset stripping and upward redistribution of wealth represented by Georgia's tax credit program, on the other, the two remain connected. While in its content *Watchmen* opposes racism, in its mode of production, it participates in and benefits from the racial capitalism that calls to preserve Confederate memorials enforce. Moreover, by filming in Georgia and feeding into false narratives promoting the trickle-down benefits of corporate incentives, *Watchmen* further helps legitimate a status quo of racial inequality in the state.

Highly acclaimed for its antiracist narrative, *Watchmen* was subsidized by assets that a white nationalist state government stripped from poor people of color, which I would argue is less an irony than a mode of denial. Many appreciative accounts have been written of the show's groundbreaking narrative, yet its textual critique of racism distracts from the inequities surrounding its production. This is to say that the show's antiracist content indirectly references yet ultimately helps displace from view and critical reflection the combined race and class inequalities in its filming locations.

After white nationalist protests in Charlottesville, Virginia, in 2017 over the proposed removal of a statue of Robert E. Lee, members of the Beacon Hill Black Alliance for Human Rights (BHAHR) in Macon began calling for the removal of the local courthouse monument near the *Watchmen* location. A DeKalb County judge ruled in June 2020 that it should be taken down, so it was removed near midnight on the day before Juneteenth. Hundreds of people gathered to watch, chanting "Take it Down!" as they drank champagne from red plastic cups.[28] BHAHR's monument committee, according to the organization's website, had worked to connect the monument to "current manifestations of white supremacy in Decatur and surrounding communities." The group also organizes for educational and economic justice.[29] *Watchmen* has been credited with publicizing the Greenwood Massacre for (especially non-Black) TV audiences, but such praise makes it harder to see how Hollywood benefits from racial capitalism while obscuring Black activism against white supremacy in its Georgia locations. But as the example of the Beacon Hill Black Alliance for Human Rights reminds us, studying TV filming locations can also open critical perspectives on how poor people of color oppose dominant constructions of precarious places.

NOTES

1. "Coronavirus: Armed Protesters Enter Michigan Statehouse," *BBC News*, May 1, 2020, https://www.bbc.com/news/world-us-canada-52496514.

2. Ashley Lee, "'A Crime upon a Crime': Trump's Tulsa Rally Gives 'Watchmen' Episode New Resonance," *Los Angeles Times*, June 19, 2020, https://www.latimes.com/entertainment-arts/tv/story/2020-06-19/watchmen-tulsa-1921-massacre-trump-juneteenth-rally; Meghan O'Keefe, "HBO's 'Watchmen' was Ahead of its Time—By Nine Months," *Decider*, June 4, 2020, https://decider.com/2020/06/04/watchmen-on-hbo-2020-relevance-tulsa-massacres/?fbclid=IwAR3SibnNSJINHfGQ9jK4JL5pqdei6ZKIghDr_cnJODaJ31e3EK4kCtZYlIg; Ray Flook, "Watchmen: Damon Lindelof Knows What His Episode 10 Title Would Be," *Bleeding Cool*, June 5, 2020, https://bleedingcool.com/tv/watchmen-damon-lindelof-know-what-his-episode-10-title-would-be/.

3. For the concept of racial capitalism, see Cedric J. Robinson's *Black Marxism: The Making of the Black Radical Tradition* (Chapel Hill: University of North Carolina Press, 1983). See also Jodi Malamed, "Racial Capitalism," *Critical Ethnic Studies* 1, no. 1 (Spring 2015): 76–85.

4. For a similar account of shows shot in New Mexico, see Curtis Marez, "From Mr. Chips to Scarface, or Racial Capitalism in *Breaking Bad*," *Critical Inquiry: In the Moment*, September 2013, https://critinq.wordpress.com/2013/09/25/breaking-bad/. The series ended in 2013, but it has inspired three spin-offs—the AMC TV series *Better Call Saul* (2015) and *The Broken and the Bad* (2020), and the Netflix feature film *El Camino: A Breaking Bad Movie* (2019), which were all shot in New Mexico, to take advantage of state subsidies in one of the poorest states in the union and with large Chicanx and Indigenous populations.

5. Paul Tasi, "The Walking Dead's First Six Episodes Will Be Unique Due to Covid." *Forbes*, September 28, 2020, https://www.forbes.com/sites/paultassi/2020/09/28/the-walking-deads-first-six-season-11-episodes-will-be-unique-due-to-covid/#d2697b78551e.

6. J. A. Gold, K. K. Wong, C. M. Szablewski, et al., "Characteristics and Clinical Outcomes of Adult Patients Hospitalized with COVID-19—Georgia, March 2020," *Center for Disease Control Morbidity and Mortality Weekly Report* 69, no. 1 (May 8, 2020): 545–50, https://www.cdc.gov/mmwr/volumes/69/wr/mm6918e1.htm; Moore JT, Ricaldi JN, Rose CE, et al. "Disparities in Incidence of COVID-19 among Underrepresented Racial/Ethnic Groups in Counties Identified as Hotspots During June 5–18, 2020–22 States, February–June 2020," *Center for Disease Control Morbidity and Mortality Weekly Report* 69, no. 33 (August 21, 2020): 1122–26, https://www.cdc.gov/mmwr/volumes/69/wr/mm6933e1.htm.

7. Golden, "Coronavirus"; Marshall, "Coronavirus Infection"; "Public Welfare Expenditures," Urban Institute, https://www.urban.org/policy-centers/cross-center-initiatives/state-and-local-finance-initiative/state-and-local-backgrounders/state-and-local-expenditures.

8. *Film LA Inc. 2016 Feature Film Study.* Hollywood: Film L.A. Inc., 2016. According to the study, Georgia "hosted primary production for 17 of the top 100 domestic films released in 2016" (3). The state placed well above California and attracted nearly three times as many feature films as fifth-place New York and Louisiana (5).

9. *Film LA Inc. 2016 Feature Film Study*, 5.

10. *Film LA Inc. 2016 Feature Film Study*, 16.

11. John Charles Bradbury, "Do Movie Production Incentives Generate Economic Development?" *Contemporary Economic Policy* 38, no. 2 (August 2019), 327–42.

12. Rebecca Wanzo in Michael Boyce Gillespie, Michael Boyce, Jonathan W. Gray, Rebecca A. Wanzo, and Kristen J. Warner, "Thinking about *Watchmen*: A Roundtable," *Film Quarterly* 73, no. 4 (Summer 2020), https://filmquarterly.org/2020/06/26/thinking-about-watchmen-with-jonathan-w-gray-rebecca-a-wanzo-and-kristen-j-warner/.

13. Kevin Myrick, "No Plans to Remove Polk County's Monument to Confederate Soldiers," *The Polk County Standard Journal*, August 17, 2017, https://www.northwestgeorgianews.com/polk_standard_journal/news/local/no-plans-to-remove-polk-countys-monument-for-confederate-soldiers/article_7d822454-8361-11e7-b636-0f54981c180e.html; Ra Moon, "Filming Locations: Where was *Watchmen* Filmed?" *Atlas of Wonders*, October 2019, https://www.atlasofwonders.com/2019/10/watchmen-series-filming-location-tulsa-castle.html.

14. According to the 2000 US Census, Cedartown's population is 20.20% Black and 22.4% Latinx.

15. "Cedartown," *West Georgia Textile Heritage Trail* (Carrollton, Georgia: Center for Public History, University of West Georgia), https://westgatextiletrail.com/cedartown/.

16. Myrick.

17. Kirk Savage, *Standing Soldiers, Kneeling Slaves: Race, War, and Monument in Nineteenth-Century America* (Princeton: Princeton University Press, 2018).

18. Dell Upton, *What Can and Can't Be Said: Race, Uplift, and Monument Building in the Contemporary South* (New Haven: Yale University Press, 2015), Kindle Location 598.

19. Upton, *What Can and Can't Be Said*, Kindle Location 493. See also Savage, *Standing Soldiers, Kneeling Slaves*. On confederate monuments in Georgia, see David N. Wiggins, "Confederate Monuments," *New Georgia Encyclopedia*, October 31, 2018, https://www.georgia encyclopedia.org/articles/history-archaeology/confederate-monuments. For Confederate graves in the Cedartown area, see "Polk County GaArchives Cemeteries," *USGenWeb Archives*, October 6, 2009, http://files.usgwarchives.net/ga/polk/cemeteries/confederates.txt. Finally, I am indebted to the crowdsourced syllabus "All Monuments Must Fall," https://monuments mustfall.wordpress.com/.

20. "Character Areas and Landmarks," *Historic Oakland Foundation* (Atlanta, GA: Historic Oakland Foundation), https://oaklandcemetery.com/character-areas-and-landmarks/.

21. "Lives That Made Our City: Decatur Cemetery Walking Tour" (City of Decatur: Decatur, no date or page numbers), https://issuu.com/decaturga/docs/decatur-cemetery-walking-tour-2017.

22. Sarah Fay Campbell, "Confederate Monuments: Are They 'History,'" *The Newnan Times-Herald*, June 16, 2020, https://times-herald.com/news/2020/06/confederate-monuments-are-they-history.

23. Chris Joyner, "Georgia Capitol Heavy with Confederate Symbols," *The Atlanta-Journal Constitution*, September 5, 2015, https://www.ajc.com/news/state--regional-govt--politics/georgia-capitol-heavy-with-confederate-symbols/z051suE0a7bqO5cWhXlZnJ/.

24. In April 2019, Georgia governor Brian Kemp signed SB 77, which amended existing law to expressly protect Confederate memorials (Georgia State Senate, *State Flag, Seal, and Other Symbols*). One of the bill's co-sponsors was Republican representative Bill Heath of the 31st district, which includes Cedartown. The Trump White House followed suit with a June 26, 2020, Executive Order "Combatting Violence and Protecting Monuments, Memorials, and Statues" (Executive Order 13933).

25. Raphael Sassaki, "Moore on Jerusalem, Eternalism, Anarchy and Herbie!" *Alan Moore World*, November 18, 2019, https://alanmooreworld.blogspot.com/2019/11/moore-on-jerusalem-eternalism-anarchy.html; Chris Gavaler, "The Ku Klux Klan and the Birth of the Superhero," *Journal of Graphic Novels and Comics* 4, no. 2 (2013): 191–208.

26. Viet Thanh Nguyen, "How 'Watchmen's' Misunderstanding of Vietnam Undercuts Its Vision of Racism," *Washington Post*, December 18, 2019, https://www.washingtonpost.com/outlook/2019/12/18/how-watchmens-misunderstanding-vietnam-undercuts-its-vision-racism/.

27. See Jonathan W. Gray, "*Watchmen* after the End of History: Race, Redemption, and the End of the Word," *ASAP Journal*, Feb. 3, 2020, http://asapjournal.com/watchmen-after-the-end-of-history-race-redemption-and-the-end-of-the-world-jonathan-w-gray/.

28. Faith Karimi, "A Controversial Confederate Monument Goes Down in the Atlanta Suburb of Decatur," *CNN News*, June 19, 2020, https://www.cnn.com/2020/06/19/us/decatur-square-confederate-monument-removed/index.html.

29. Beacon Hill Alliance for Human Rights, "Our Mission: Monument Committee," https://beaconhillblackalliance.org.

Chapter 12

NOSTALGIA IS A HARD PILL TO SWALLOW

Intergenerational and Historical Racial Trauma

APRYL ALEXANDER

The *Watchmen* series opens with a depiction of the 1921 Tulsa Massacre (also known as the Tulsa Race Riot or the Black Wall Street Massacre). For context, on May 30, 1921, Dick Rowland (a nineteen-year-old Black man) was accused of assaulting seventeen-year-old white elevator operator Sarah Page, while they rode the elevator of the Drexel Building in the Greenwood District of Oklahoma. The following day, Tulsa police arrested Rowland and began an investigation. On June 1, the Greenwood district was looted and burned by white rioters, and the governor declared martial law, bringing National Guard troops into Tulsa. However, the violence continued for days, resulting in over 800 injuries, an estimated 300 deaths,[1] and over thirty city blocks destroyed in fire across thirty-six square blocks. Prior to the massacre, the Greenwood District of Tulsa was among the wealthiest Black communities in the United States. The Oklahoma Historical Society refers to the massacre as the single worst incident of racial violence in American history, and the once-thriving Black community never recovered or was compensated for the tragedy. The damage is estimated to be $200 million in current currency.

Watchmen aired days after the 99th anniversary of the Tulsa Massacre and serves as a speculative fiction of present-day Tulsa. In the *Watchmen* universe, the 1921 Tulsa Massacre ends with a young Black boy's parents arranging for him to flee the city just moments before they were murdered in the attacks. The boy, William Reeves, is given a letter by his father, which reads, "Watch over this boy." The boy then finds a baby girl, drapes her in an American flag, and carries her away. The series then fast forwards to a near-present-day Tulsa, Oklahoma. In this universe, descendants from the Tulsa Massacre are eligible to receive reparations, and white supremacists (both those involved in the massacre and those who presently engage in racist ideology) are considered terrorists.

Watchmen contextualizes historical and intergenerational trauma through its storyline of the protagonist Angela Abar, who is a descendant of those killed in the Tulsa Massacre. In the series, Angela becomes acquainted with her believed-to-be-dead grandfather and consumes a banned medication, Nostalgia, which inserts the memories of its possessor (her grandfather) into the consumer. This chapter will discuss the depiction of historical and racial trauma in the series through Angela's consumption of her grandfather's Nostalgia, as well as describe Angela's journey to radical healing.

NOSTALGIA AND INTERGENERATIONAL TRAUMA

After the series opens with the events of the Tulsa Massacre, viewers were led to believe that the series would be centered on the events following the massacre, including themes revolving around the race, racism, and state-sanctioned violence by law enforcement. The writers create a universe based in speculative fiction (i.e., a subgenre of science fiction focused on possible futures and imagined new realities) and Afrofuturism (i.e., a type of speculative fiction that depicts the contemporary realities of Black life and envisions Black futures). Viewers are introduced to a world in which the United States openly accepts responsibility for the Tulsa Massacre and reparations continue to be provided for descendants of those killed. In this universe, police officers do not have immediate access to their firearms, which limits incidents of police-involved shootings. The series opened with the incident of a Black police officer being murdered by a member of the Seventh Kavalry, a white supremacist organization, while trying to request permission to unholster his duty weapon. Given the airing of the series amid the Black Lives Matter movement, it appears that these changes in police policies are a response to prior incidents of state-sanctioned violence by law enforcement. The policy forces an officer to prove there is an imminent threat or they have established probable cause prior to a search or unholstering of an officer's weapon. Angela Abar is a Black woman who is employed as a police officer in Tulsa. Through a series of events, she meets William, her presumed dead grandfather, who was alive at the time of the Tulsa Massacre. Angela discovers her great-grandparents returned to Tulsa after her great-grandfather fought in

World War I. At the end of episode 5 ("Little Fear of Lightning"), Angela consumes her grandfather's Nostalgia, originally a dementia medication used to harvest memories but later outlawed because people were recreationally consuming it to relive their best memories, resulting in addiction. Prior to consuming the Nostalgia, Angela knew little about her familial or ancestral history since her birth parents were killed at an early age. In episode 4 ("If You Don't Like My Story, Write Your Own"), Angela delivers an acorn to plant at the Ances-Tree, a futuristic device that allows Black people to discover their family tree and whether they qualify for Redfordations (i.e., the show's version of reparations) as a descendant of the 1921 Tulsa Massacre. Angela officially confirms her relationship to William, which leads her to discovering her familial history.

Episode 6 ("This Extraordinary Being") takes the viewer into Angela's experience of consuming Nostalgia and experiencing William's memories, which are marked with incidents of racial trauma and violence. In the 1930s, William joined the New York Police Department and quickly discovered the institutional racism (i.e., racism resulting from policies, procedures of institutions that marginalize people of color) within the department and officers' connection to Cyclops, a group connected to the Ku Klux Klan, which had the mission of hypnotizing Black people to harm themselves and incite riots. After a local arson occurred and the known white male suspect was released (which suggested corruption in the police department), William experienced an attempted lynching by his police colleagues. Lynching has been a prominent form of racialized violence throughout American history. Specifically, lynchings of Black Americans comprised of around 90% of the 5,000 documented lynchings between 1882 and 1951.[2] For William, this attempted lynching was a violent form of racial trauma. William's wife initially had concerns about him pursuing a career in law enforcement. William ensured her that he would be one of the "good ones" and change the system from within. This narrative aligns with current conversations surrounding American policing and whether reform is possible. American policing was rooted in slave patrols to keep power and control over enslaved Black people and those seeking their freedom back. Discussion of reform efforts for policing in the wake of disproportionate killings of unarmed Black Americans have come into question. If these killings of unarmed Black Americans are the result of historical and institutional racism, is there room for reform? In the series, the police officers were connected to Cyclops, who were using mesmerism to violently turn Black people against each other. For William to cope and pursue justice, he took on the persona of Hooded Justice and later joins the Minutemen. In that role, he was able to address crimes in his community. However, when William asks the Minutemen for their assistance in addressing crimes against Black people through the mesmerism device, they refuse. William aligned himself with people he thought were allies in the pursuit of justice. However, when the pursuit of racial justice was part of the mission, the Minutemen did not want to get involved. Again, there were striking parallels to various civil rights movements, like the early waves of feminism, which fought for some civil liberties and rights, but not from an intersectional and racially inclusive approach. Ultimately, Hooded Justice becomes a vigilante superhero to stop Cyclops. This speculative narrative suggests that dismantling racism from within organizations became impossible for William, forcing him to find another way to pursue justice.

"You're not supposed to take someone else's Nostalgia," FBI Agent Laurie Blake says at the beginning of episode 6 ("This Extraordinary Being"). Many of the memories elicited by William's Nostalgia were marked by a series of potentially traumatic incidents. In the Diagnostic and Statistical Manual (DSM-5), the American Psychiatric Association describes *trauma* as when a person was exposed to death, threatened death, actual or threatened serious injury, or actual or threatened sexual violence through direct exposure, witnessing the trauma, or through indirect exposure to aversive details of a trauma.[3] Typically, people think of events like car accidents, childhood abuse, sexual assaults, and exposure to war as traumatic incidents, as those are often the ones that are highlighted the most. Posttraumatic stress disorder (PTSD) is a constellation of symptoms consisting of intrusion symptoms (i.e., upsetting and recurring memories, nightmares, or flashbacks); avoidance of trauma-related thoughts, feelings, or reminders; and negative alterations in cognitions and mood (i.e., negative emotions, loss of interest in activities, feeling isolated), and alterations in arousal (i.e., irritability, risky behavior, hypervigilance) which last more than six months. William's experiences witnessing his family killed and community destroyed during the Tulsa massacre, an attempted lynching, and institutional betrayal by his colleagues in policing and the Minutemen are each potentially traumatic or traumatic incidents. William copes with these incidents by becoming Hooded Justice (including wearing a noose as a part of his attire) and seeking justice for his community on his own.

Angela's experience of William's trauma through the Nostalgia provides viewers a glimpse into how she vicariously experiences William's life. In a scene where Wade attends his support group, someone discusses taking Nostalgia and remarks, "It's like I inherited her pain." Nostalgia, if consumed by someone else, can ultimately result in historical and intergenerational trauma. Increasingly, racial discrimination and stressors are being categorized as traumatic incidents. Racism-related stress is defined as "race-related transactions between individuals or groups and their environment that emerge from the dynamics of racism and that are perceived to tax or exceed existing individual and collective resources or threaten well-being."[4] "Racial trauma" refers to traumatic events related to real or perceived experiences of racial discrimination, which can include threats of harm or injury, humiliation, or witnessing harm to other Black, Indigenous, and People of Color (BIPOC).[5] "Historical trauma" refers to the collective trauma experienced over time and across generations for groups with shared identities or circumstances involving oppression, marginalization, and trauma exposure.[6] The trauma can be a single or recurring event, such as colonialism, war, genocide, enslavement, mass incarceration, police brutality, natural disaster, and disease.[7] Over the past few decades, the term has been applied to colonized Indigenous groups across the world, as well as descendants of Holocaust survivors, Black Americans, Japanese American survivors of internment camps, and Armenian genocide survivors, to name a few. Black people are a heterogenous group, comprising individuals from a variety of cultural backgrounds—descendants from American slavery, Africans residing in the United States, Caribbean Americans, etc. Black Americans have faced numerous types of historical traumas, including American slavery, Jim Crow laws, mass incarceration, medical abuse and healthcare disparities (e.g., Tuskegee syphilis study, Black maternal mortality, etc.), mass incarceration, and state-sanctioned violence by law enforcement. In fact, historical trauma may be a misnomer, as the types of historical trauma that Black Americans experienced still exist. Angela is warned that Nostalgia is "more tolerable in small doses," a nod to the number of memories she will have to vicariously experience. "Intergenerational transmission of trauma" references when the offspring of an individual who experienced trauma displays adverse outcomes.[8] Transmission of historical or intergenerational trauma can occur consciously or unconsciously, through learned behavior, through biology or epigenetics, or through disrupted familial attachment.[9] As previously noted, William's history was marked by incidents of violence and racial trauma. After Angela takes the Nostalgia, she goes through a series of events throughout her own history, as well as William's. In essence, Nostalgia serves as a chemical form of intergenerational trauma.

Not only does Angela relive the traumatic incidents from her grandfather's life, but she also has her own traumas that the Nostalgia revives. One of the symptoms of Nostalgia is experiencing memories vividly without warning, which is similar to how trauma survivors often reprocess or re-experience traumatic events. In episode 7 ("An Almost Religious Awe"),

Angela is recovering from the Nostalgia in Trieu's home, where she is now re-experiencing her own childhood memories. Young Angela (played by Faithe Herman) was being raised in Vietnam by her mother and military father, who were murdered in front of her by a bomber. She was then placed in an orphanage where she was the only Black child. The Vietnamese police find the bomber, and Angela positively identifies him as the bomber. Following this, the police immediately take the bomber away and murder him with Angela within earshot. Soon thereafter, Angela's grandmother arrives, whom she has never met, and tells her she's taking her back "home" to Tulsa. However, her grandmother dies of a heart attack on the way to the car. Viewers now discover that Angela has experienced a series of adverse childhood experiences. Adverse Childhood Experience (ACE) survey research was initiated by Kaiser Permanente and the US Centers for Disease Control and Prevention (CDC) to examine the long-term impact of early traumatic experiences on adult health and behavior. Adverse childhood experiences, such as physical abuse, neglect, parental mental health difficulty, and/or parental separation, have been known to contribute to poor mental health and physical health consequences, such as heart failure, sleep disturbance, diabetes, depression, anxiety, alcohol misuse, suicidality, and decreased life expectancy.[10] Nostalgia highlighted the many ways in which Angela experienced not only intergenerational trauma, but personal traumatic incidents. As previously stated, intergenerational trauma carries negative affects to the descendants of those of experienced traumatic events, and now Angela has her own compounded incidents of trauma. The question remains: How do we disrupt these intergenerational patterns? How do generations of Black people cope with and/or heal from intergenerational and ongoing white supremacy?

RADICAL HEALING AND REPARATIONS

What did Nostalgia do for Angela? Nostalgia forced Angela to confront her own traumas, as well as those experienced by her ancestors. As stated previously, Nostalgia was banned because it resulted in people becoming addicted to their positive memories. Radical healing involves learning about the history of racism, particularly racism in United States. The United States was created and founded because of colonialization and the genocide of Indigenous people and nations and the labor of Black people through enslavement. As the United States continues to explore ways to dismantle racism, people must acknowledge and learn from these first incidents of marginalization and oppression and the residual effects, as well as ongoing oppression and marginalization. Radical healing is defined as "the policies, actions, and practices, which aid individuals and their groups to live out their full potential in societies with a history of racial oppression."[11] Nostalgia took Angela through a journey of radical healing through revisiting the harms caused to her, her parents, and her grandfather. Angela was able to see how white supremacy continued to manifest itself through the members of Cyclops, who held positions of power in various institutions of government. The series ends with the massacre of the members of Cyclops, which may put an end to the institutional structure of racism within that group. By no means is the series suggesting violence—the series challenges the viewer to examine how institutional and structural racism perpetuates in various systems across time and evolves. With Cyclops eliminated, it is possible that Angela and her grandfather can live to their full potential—hopefully in a new Tulsa that is not governed by Cyclops.

Reparations have been long suggested as a way to acknowledge the violence and harms done to BIPOC communities to make amends. In the *Watchmen* universe, the 2008 Victims of Racial Violence Act was passed, which acknowledged the Tulsa Massacre and allowed for reparations in the form of tax exemptions for victims of the Tulsa Massacre and their descendants. Contrarians or those opposed to these settlements referred to the reparations from the Victims of Racial Violence Act as "Redfordations." This draws parallels to how individuals refer to the Affordable Care Act (ACA) as "Obamacare." Over the years, truth and reconciliation commissions (TRCs) have developed in over thirty countries to investigate human rights violations and make recommendations on how to address those abuses.[12] The most well-known TRC is South Africa's Truth and Reconciliation Commission, which convened after the end of apartheid. In the United States, Greensboro, North Carolina's TRC was created in 2004, during the 20th anniversary of a violent incident that took place in 1979 in which Ku Klux Klan (KKK) members shot and killed five members of the multiracial Communist Workers Party (CWP) and wounded 10 others.[13] State and federal trials were held for the murderers; however, all-white juries reached not guilty verdicts in each of the trials. In May 2006, the commission released its report: Greensboro should take meaningful steps in acknowledging the event, including educating school children about what occurred on November 3, 1979; the Greensboro Police Department should issue a public apology (for not taking information about the KKK disrupting the protest of the CWP seriously), issue compensation, and/or erect public exhibits educating the public about the incident, and pay city workers fair wages.

In August 2020, 105-year-old Lessie Benningfield Randle (one of two known survivors who is still living) and a group of Oklahomans filed a lawsuit demanding reparations for the 1921 Tulsa Massacre. In 2001, the Oklahoma Commission to Study the Tulsa Race Riot of 1921 was formed by the Oklahoma state legislature to conduct a thorough investigation into the massacre. The commission determined the city of Tulsa had conspired with white citizens against Black residents. The commission issued the following statement:

> We believe strongly in reparations. Our focus is on the larger scope of reparations, which means repairing past damages and making amends through acknowledgment, apology, and atonement. This process is central to racial reconciliation in Tulsa.
>
> Survivors and descendants deserve remedy and reparation for the atrocities of 1921. The Centennial Commission's work toward reparations falls in restitution through advocacy for investment in education, infrastructure and economic development in North Tulsa. While far from comprehensive, Greenwood Rising and subsequent programming and initiatives will serve to hold space for visitors to learn about our past and present in order to work for a future in which these horrific events never occur again.

Increasingly, cities and institutions throughout the United States are considering various models for reparations. The conversation reignited in 2020 after the racial injustices that occurred following the murders of Breonna Taylor, George Floyd, and other Black Americans. Current discourse surrounding reparations and restitution in the United States considers monetary payments, land reparations, landmarks or monuments with acknowledgments of harm, grants for businesses or homeownership, and/or student loan forgiveness, to name a few, for Indigenous and Black Americans. For instance, churches throughout the United States whose histories have ties to enslavement or racial discrimination are considering how to issue reparations to Black Americans.[14] In December 2020, the Amherst, Massachusetts, city council passed a resolution remarking the city is "committed to engaging in a path of remedy for Black Amherst residents who have been injured or harmed by discrimination and racial justice." In episode 3 ("She Was Killed by Space Junk"), it is mentioned that many Black Tulsa Massacre descendants had purchased land or started businesses with their Redfordations. Duke professor William Darity, one of the leading experts on reparations, has estimated that in order to shrink the racial wealth gap in the United States, it would cost up to $12 trillion.[15] In February 2021, President Joe Biden issued his support of Democratic efforts to create a commission to study reparations for Black Americans. The committee would be tasked with suggesting appropriate remedies for descendants of enslaved Black Americans. In 2021, the Austin, Texas city council approved a resolution that would acquire city funding for restitution payments. In March 2021, the Evanston, Illinois, City Council approved the distribution of $400,000 to eligible Black families for down payments or home repairs—becoming the first city in the United States to formally approve of reparations. Qualifying families must have lived in or been a direct descendant of a Black person who lived in Evanston between 1919 to 1969 and who experienced discrimination in housing because of city ordinances or policies that contributed to redlining. Families can apply for payments of $25,000, and the city council pledged to distribute $10 million over ten years. Similar to those who despised Redfordations, the public is still largely opposed to reparations. According to a 2019 Associated Press-NORC Center for Public Affairs poll, only 29% of Americans stated the government should pay cash reparations. However, 74% of Black Americans were in favor of reparations compared to 15% of white Americans. For Black Americans, reparations may still be an aspiration. *Watchmen* provided speculative fiction into what the process would be. For Angela, it was unclear if she had Redfordations before she went to the Ances-Tree. In the first episode, she was guest lecturing at a career day in her son's class. One of his peers asked if she had received her money from Redfordations in order to build her restaurant. However, given her short time with her grandmother, it is unclear if she qualified until she met William and took his DNA to the Ances-Tree and learned about her grandparents and great-grandparents. In sum, in order for communities of color to heal the intergenerational trauma and violence that has occurred, their histories must be acknowledged, and communities should engage in various forms of repair, including reparations.

CONCLUSION

Black Americans have encountered and continue to encounter the adverse effects of interpersonal, structural, institutional, historical, and intergenerational racism in the United States. The HBO series *Watchmen* served as an allegory for the historical and intergenerational trauma caused by the events of the 1921 Tulsa Massacre, as well as a speculative fiction into how the United States can repair the harms caused by racism. Scholar Shawn Ginwright notes, "Healing involves reconciling the past to change the present while imagining a new future."[16] Although concepts like reparations and reconciliation have not been fully realized, the show presents each in a way that challenges the viewer to imagine a nation in which white supremacy can be eradicated and repair and healing can occur.

NOTES

1. The Oklahoma Bureau of Vital Statistics officially recorded 36 deaths; however, historians believe as many as 300 people died.

2. See Stewart Emory Tolney and Elwood M. Beck, *A Festival of Violence: An Analysis of Southern Lynchings, 1882–1930* (Champaign: University of Illinois Press, 1995).

3. American Psychiatric Association, *Diagnostic and Statistical Manual of Mental Disorders*, 5th ed. (Washington, DC, 2015).

4. Shelly P. Harrell "A Multidimensional Conceptualization of Racism-Related Stress: Implications for the Well-Being of People of Color," *American Journal of Orthopsychiatry* 70, no. 1 (2000): 44.

5. See Lillian Comas- Díaz, Gordon Nagayama Hall, and Helen A. Neville, "Racial Trauma: Theory, Research, and Healing: Introduction to the Special Issue," *American Psychologist* 74, no. 1 (2019); and Robert T. Carter, "Racism and Psychological Emotional Injury: Recognizing and Assessing Race-based Traumatic Stress," *The Counseling Psychologist* 35, no. 1 (2007): 13–105.

6. See Maria Yellow Horse Brave Heart and Lemyra M. DeBruyn, "The American Indian Holocaust: Healing Historical Unresolved Grief," *American Indian and Alaska Native Mental Health Research* 8, no. 2 (1998): 56–78 and Nathaniel Vincent Mohatt, Azure B. Thompson, Nghi D. Thai, and Jacob Kraemer Tebes, "Historical Trauma as Public Narrative: A Conceptual Review of How History Impacts Present-Day Health," *Social Science & Medicine* 106 (2014): 128–36.

7. See Jennifer A. Coleman, "Racial Differences in Posttraumatic Stress Disorder in Military Personnel: Intergenerational Transmission of Trauma as a Theoretical Lens," *Journal of Aggression, Maltreatment, & Trauma* 25, no. 6 (2016): 561–79.

8. See Mallory E. Bowers and Rachel Yehuda, "Intergenerational Transmission of Stress in Humans," *Neuropsychopharmacology* 41, no. 1 (2016): 232–44; and Rachel Yehuda and Amy Lehrner, "Intergenerational Transmission of Trauma Effects: Putative Role of Epigenetic Mechanisms," *World Psychiatry* 17 (2018): 243–57; and Rachel Yehuda, Amy Lehrner, and Linda M. Bierer, "The Public Reception of Putative Epigenetic Mechanisms in the Transgenerational Effects of Trauma," *Environmental Epigenetics* (2018): 1–7.

9. Yehuda, Lehrner, and Bierer, 6.

10. See Vincent J. Felitti, Robert F. Anda, Dale Nordenberg, David F. Williamson, Alison M. Spitz, Valerie Edwards, and James S. Marks, "Relationship of Childhood Abuse and Household Dysfunction to Many of the Leading Causes of Death in Adults: The Adverse Childhood Experiences (ACE) Study," *American Journal of Preventive Medicine* 14, no. 4 (1998): 245–58.

11. Bryana H. French, Jioni A. Lewis, Della V. Mosley, Hector Y. Adames, Nayeli Y. Chavez-Dueñas, Grace A. Chen, and Helen A. Neville, "Toward a Psychological Framework of Radical Healing in Communities of Color," *The Counseling Psychologist* 48, no. 1 (2020): 20.

12. See Susan M. Glisson, "The Sum of Its Parts: The Importance of Deconstructing Truth Commissions," *Race and Justice* 5, no. 2 (2015): 192–202.

13. Raj Ghoshal, "What Does Remembering Racial Violence Do? Greensboro's Truth Commission, Mnemonic Overlap, and Attitudes toward Racial Redress," *Race and Justice* 5, no. 2 (2015): 168–91.

14. David Crary, "More U.S. Churches Are Committing to Racism-Linked Reparations," *PBS News Hour Weekend*, December 13, 2020. Retrieved from https://www.pbs.org/newshour/nation/more-us-churches-are-committing-to-racism-linked-reparations.

15. Rodney Brooks, "A New Book Discusses Not Just Why, But How the U.S. Should Pay Reparations to Black Americans," *Washington Post*, December 10, 2020, retrieved from https://www.washingtonpost.com/nation/2020/12/11/new-book-discusses-not-just-why-how-us-government-should-pay-reparations-black-americans/.

16. Shawn A. Ginwright, "Peace Out to Revolution! Activism among African American Youth: An Argument for Radical Healing," *Young: Nordic Journal of Youth Research* 18, no. 1 (2010): 86.

Chapter 13

"THIS EXTRAORDINARY BEING"

Alternative Archives of Black Life in HBO's *Watchmen*

BRANDY MONK-PAYTON

Loss gives rise to longing, and in these circumstances, it would not be far-fetched to consider stories as a form of compensation or even as reparations, perhaps the only kind we will ever receive.[1]

—SAIDIYA HARTMAN, "VENUS IN TWO ACTS"

The final shot of HBO's limited series *Watchmen* (2019) is of a foot; a Black foot, hovering over a pool of water. The mysterious foot belongs to Angela Abar, a.k.a. Sister Night, played by Emmy-winner Regina King, who is testing out a theory: Can she walk on water? She has just eaten a raw egg that might allow her to inherit the superpowers of her now-deceased love, Dr. Manhattan. The scene and last shot do not provide any closure; in fact, they contain a profound amount of speculation and conjecture about Black female potentiality.

The character of Angela Abar should not exist. Her grandfather miraculously survived the Tulsa Race Massacre of 1921 in Tulsa, Oklahoma, in which white mobs violently invaded what was known as Black Wall Street. The first sequence of the pilot episode dramatizes the horrific attack on the Black community, beginning with a scene of spectatorship at the local movie theater, Dreamland, in which a very young Will Williams (Danny Boyd Jr.) eagerly watches *Trust in the Law!*, a film about the heroic Black marshal of Oklahoma, Bass Reeves. His viewing is cut short due to gunfire and explosions outside. Though Will's family attempts to escape the destruction on a wagon, his mother and father are slaughtered, leaving him with a note in his pocket ("Watch over this boy") and a small infant girl in a blanket who is also still alive. The ruination of a Black utopia thus inaugurates the rise of an African American superhero and what will become his legacy.

When showrunner Damon Lindelof decided to create *Watchmen*, he notes that he took inspiration from journalist and cultural critic Ta-Nehisi Coates's oft-cited 2014 essay "The Case for Reparations."[2] The award-winning *Atlantic* piece describes in great detail the white plundering of and from Black folk so central to the fabric of the United States that continues, both in explicit and insidious ways, in the afterlives of slavery. Specifically, he makes mention of the decimation of the Greenwood district of Tulsa, a site of black entrepreneurial success terrorized by racist white residents with the assistance of the local government. In conceiving of the TV version of the Alan Moore classic comic book series published in 1986, the showrunner comments: "To not tell a story about race in the context of a political text in 2019 almost felt borderline irresponsible."[3] In the wake of the Black Lives Matter movement and Donald Trump's ascendancy to president of the United States, *Watchmen* becomes a dystopian text that confronts white supremacy by way of rendering past violence visible, making it present, and allowing it to inform the future through the science fiction/fantasy genre.

The television series is set thirty-four years after the events of the comic book and in the city of Tulsa. While the original story (and the 2009 film adaptation directed by Zack Snyder) deals with national anxieties around the threat of nuclear war with Russia during the late 1980s, the new installment narrates the domestic terrorism of a white supremacist group known as the Seventh Kavalry. The masked Sister Night is introduced to the *Watchmen* diegetic universe as a detective investigating the murder of the Tulsa police chief, which might be linked to Seventh Kavalry activity. At the same time, she finds herself confronting her own secret vigilante family genealogy.

This chapter analyzes the HBO limited series as a discrete television text and argues that it brings into view an alternative archive of Black life within and beyond the status of the human. I suggest that *Watchmen* generates such an archive through an emphasis on fabulation and, as Saidiya Hartman imagines, "the capacities of the subjunctive . . . in fashioning a narrative."[4] While attentive to the aesthetics and politics of the source material, I am interested in what the TV program in particular makes televisually possible by way of Blackness through the language of reparations. By reparations, I mean not only the material repayment of debt to the descendants of racial injustice that the series fictionalizes, I also refer to how *Watchmen* attempts to compensate, in both televisual form and content, for loss associated with anti-Black trauma. On the one hand, as Lindelof obviously states, "Superheroes cannot defeat racism."[5] On the other hand, the nine-episode series is preoccupied with issues of what W. James Booth conceptualizes as "memory-justice" that are exemplified by its African American characters and, specifically, in the psychic journeys of Angela and Will combatting racism across time and space.[6]

In the pages that follow, I assert the TV program's distinctiveness from the comic and film in the attention paid to Blackness and Black womanhood. I examine the logics of reparations at play through the show's narrative and stylistic engagement with race, history, and memory. Finally, I provide an analysis of Angela Abar and her familial relations as a provocation to think about the creation of another expression of human(ity).

THIS IS THE REMIX: RISK, RACE, AND THE TELEVISUAL *WATCHMEN*

On May 22, 2018, TV writer/producer Damon Lindelof published a letter on Instagram stating his intentions to develop the groundbreaking comic book series *Watchmen* for premium cable network HBO.[7] In the detailed five-page statement to fans of the beloved text, he relays his first encounter with the source material and his deep reverence for it. Lindelof is also extremely cognizant of the backlash he would inevitably receive from the *Watchmen* fandom and creator himself, Alan Moore. The very act of adaptation goes against the wishes of Moore, who firmly believes that his classic work is untranslatable. The showrunner instructively uses the language of remix and not adaptation to describe the new iteration of the comic created for the small screen. In this way, the program samples elements of the comic and transforms them in the service of an entirely new product. The TV show could also be considered more simply as an update in its modernizing of the time and place in which it is set (thirty-four years after the events of the comic in Tulsa as opposed to New York City) and by extension, its themes.[8] Whether the *Watchmen* television series is labeled as a remix or an update, the revisioning is committed to not only tackling issues of race, but also to putting them at the forefront of the deconstructed superhero tale.

Indeed, Lindelof writes that the *Watchmen* TV program "must ask new questions and explore the world through a fresh lens. Most importantly, it must be *contemporary*."[9] The showrunner's emphasis on present-day relevance emerges through the show's focus on African American characters who navigate US legacies of white supremacy. "Risk is imperative," Lindelof comments, in order to successfully resonate with audiences in the current social and political climate of anti-Black violence.[10] As a premium cable channel, HBO promotes itself as a risk-taking network. Kristen Warner writes that in the television industry, "risk is a way to draw an audience and earn critical attention."[11] HBO's programming embraces racial inclusion as a strategic kind of risk by branding its content as diverse. Such diversity in representation, which can be seen both in front of and behind the camera, is then lauded by TV critics and viewers. *Watchmen* contributes to this brand through its specificity at the level of race. In his letter, Lindelof comments on the demographic of the program's twelve-person writers' room:

> I have the pleasure of sitting in a Writers Room each and every day that is as diverse and combative as any I've ever been a part of. In that room, Hetero White Men like myself are in the minority and as *Watchmen* is (incorrectly) assumed to be solely our domain, understanding its potential through the perspectives of women, people of color and the LGBTQ community has been as eye-opening as it has been exhilarating.[12]

Here, the showrunner tries to shift the perception of the comic book's address as dominated by straight white male readers at the same time as he expands its audience reach by prioritizing marginalized voices in his remix. Attentiveness to issues of identity infuses the labor of producing the series. For instance, none of the first six episodes is directed by white men, and two of these episodes are cowritten by Black writers. In the dynamically inclusive creative process, Lindelof had to build consensus about ideas on making the show as he encountered "hard truths" in which his assumptions about race, gender, and sexuality were challenged.[13] Therefore, he highlights how a diversity of folks with different experiences and values from which to explore *Watchmen*'s social and political themes working off-screen infuses the on-screen storytelling in terms of narrative and characterization. Lindelof's embrace of risk by creating an equitable and charitable work environment allows for a collective re-vision of the text to come to fruition.

This emphasis on collaboration arguably sets the limited series apart from the Snyder film adaptation of *Watchmen*, which can be considered an auteurist project as well as "fan-centric" enterprise in its fidelity to the original text and cultivation of a posttheatrical viewer experience.[14] The TV show seems to seek a different kind of niche and loyal audience—that of the HBO viewer. HBO is known for prestige programming that pushes aesthetic boundaries, so much so that the premium network's tagline ("It's Not TV. It's HBO") attempts to distinguish it from regular television in its bid to be approximate that which is considered cinematic. In form and content, *Watchmen* fits right in with fare like *The Sopranos* (1999–2007), *The Wire* (2002–2008), *Game of Thrones* (2011–2019), *Westworld* (2016–present), and the Lindelof cocreated series *The Leftovers* (2014–2017). The ideal spectator of these programs that

HBO assumes is its target demographic are white liberals that solidify the channel's claims to "quality."

As the rewards for taking risks in programming can often be tied to practices of promoting diversity, equity, and inclusion in the TV industry, *Watchmen*'s centering of race relations is lucrative. The series is timely and resonant in the era of Black Lives Matter activism. Lindelof comments that the national anxiety undergirding the current cultural moment in the United States is because of an overdue "reckoning" with white liberal complicity in the machinations of white supremacy.[15] Part of this complicity manifests as the basic refusal to see, and engage with, the violent history of America. To attempt to rectify such a looking away, Ta-Nehisi Coates' understanding of reparations in his *Atlantic* essay renders it as a public mandate to look at the spectacular and quotidian horrors of anti-Blackness. For his part, Lindelof reveals that he could no longer ignore the deeply ingrained racial division (and outright antagonism) in the United States after reading "The Case for Reparations": "As a white man and a beneficiary of this system, do I approach this with guilt and shame or can I approach it from a vantage point of service?" Interestingly, the self-described progressive showrunner resists the language of debt and instead discusses the series as a project that he was "compelled" to do.[16] Thus, the creation of the *Watchmen* television series can be understood as a kind of civic duty at the level of media representation to depict, and contend with, the country's anti-Black racist environment.

Such a creative compulsion has the effect of integrating Blackness into the sci-fi/fantasy (super)hero genre in an unprecedented way. The TV series insists on upending the mythology of the comic book by conjecturing: *What if* Blackness became the organizing principle of the *Watchmen* story? Conjectural narrative form is central to comic books as well as contemporary cult television.[17] The televisual remix presents the print source material as canon but hypothesizes about key elements of *Watchmen*'s world-building in an act of what Toni Morrison would call "playing in the dark."[18] An emphasis on self-reflexivity is still apparent within this speculative storytelling mode. For example, while *Tales of the Black Freighter* is the comic book inside the comic book, *American Hero Story* is the show-within-the-show of the TV series. *American Hero Story* airs with an extensive content warning, seeming to start a conversation with *Watchmen* fans on the comic's treatment of women, people of color, and the LGBTQ community. The tales of Hooded Justice and the original Minutemen from the comic are remediated through this stylized faux-program about costumed adventuring. Characters retained from the comic book for the TV series are Adrian Veidt, Laurie Blake (whose parents are Minutemen icons the Comedian and Silk Spectre), and the glowing blue-hued god, Dr. Manhattan. In keeping with the practice of conjecture, the remix's Seventh Kavalry white supremacist group dons the mask of original comic book character Rorschach; in this diegetic universe, the reactionary social conservative Walter Joseph Kovacs (or Rorschach as he is popularly known) is reinterpreted as the arbiter of right-wing extremism.

Perhaps the most pernicious distinction between the two texts is their contrasting approaches to the portrayal of authoritative arms of the state as embodied by the police. On the show, members of law enforcement are forced to conceal their identities by wearing masks after a wave of antipolice violence perpetrated by the Seventh Kavalry culminated in what is called the "White Night." Amidst current widespread police brutality against Black folks and criticisms of TV police procedurals as "copaganda," *Watchmen* does not wade into "Blue Lives Matter" discursive territory of police victimization. Instead, it complicates the means and ends of law enforcement to ensure justice is served. The comic book was already a deconstruction of the figure of the superhero, and the television series extends such deconstruction to the police.

With a narrative focus on race, policing, corruption, and white supremacy, the shift to Oklahoma as the primary setting for *Watchmen* proves to be most integral. Lindelof comments: "Tulsa just felt like Krypton to me."[19] Both showrunner and some audience members on social media noted the parallel between the real-world city of Tulsa and the fictional home planet of Superman. And like Clark Kent, who becomes the Man of Steel, the young Black boy who survives the looting and burning of the once-thriving mecca for Black Americans initiates the creation of a new vigilante superhero who will come to be known as Hooded Justice.[20]

THE TULSA RACE MASSACRE AND THE CASE FOR COMPENSATION

The first episode of *Watchmen*, "It's Summer and We're Running Out of Ice," begins with an act of televisual risk: representing the historical Tulsa Race Massacre of 1921 in Tulsa, Oklahoma, in which a violent white mob invaded the prosperous Greenwood District of the city known as Black Wall Street. The mob killed as many as 300 African American residents, while thousands more lost their homes and businesses. The horrific decimation of a place and its people between May 31, 1921, and June 1, 1921, seemed excised from historical record and thus lost to national public memory. An account of the deadly two-day attack, which the Oklahoma Historical Society believes to be the single worst incident of racial violence in American history, is documented in *The Burning: Massacre, Destruction, and the Tulsa Race Riot of 1921* by journalist Tim Madigan. The *Watchmen* production team did extensive research by consulting Madigan's book as well as the Greenwood Cultural Center, and they also used various primary source materials like photographs to depict the event with a sense of authenticity.[21] Indeed, bringing such horror into view required visual redress at the level of the image. Lindelof makes explicit the educational goal in discussing the decision to focus on Tulsa, remarking: "My responsibility was to make sure that I didn't just use this for entertainment" and that, with the proper retelling of actual history, the series could "be an emissary of and advocate for this knowledge."[22]

Despite Lindelof's pedagogical intentions for the show, some critical and audience response to the gruesome opening sequence speaks to the continued trend of sensationalizing anti-Black violence as a form of televisual amusement. Leslie Lee suggests that the entire series, starting with the first scenes, exploits "real black trauma" and "real black pain" for the purposes of character and story development.[23] A descendant of a Tulsa Massacre survivor, Marilyn Christopher, describes how she encountered the graphic violence committed against her family through its dramatization on screen. She comments: "Once I saw dead Black bodies, I said, 'I don't want to watch this . . . I know I should appreciate this, but I guess I didn't.'"[24] Here, Christopher's viewing experience is mired by the proximity of the on-screen brutality to what her ancestors actually endured off-screen. At the same time, she is keenly aware of her estrangement from how her family's legacy has been used for the purposes of the TV series. *Watchmen* producers did not communicate with descendants of prominent Greenwood residents and families like the Williamses about their backstories serving as vehicles for the program's narrative. The question of appropriation, then, becomes another kind of violence at the intersection of race and property ownership.[25] Within such an ethical conundrum, Christopher refuses to be compensated by representation that would reproduce intergenerational trauma through her act of spectatorship.

The series delicately balances the pressure of "historical reenactment" with "speculative world-making."[26] In episode 2, "Martial Feats of Comanche Horsemanship," Angela Abar visits the pseudofictional Greenwood Center for Cultural Heritage armed with a DNA sample of an elderly Black man named William Reeves, who is a prime suspect in the mysterious hanging of Tulsa police chief Judd Crawford (Don Johnson). Angela goes to a kiosk at the museum, which is primarily dedicated to the memory of the events of 1921 and is greeted by an interactive video recording of African American scholar and public intellectual Henry Louis "Skip" Gates Jr. is the United States treasury secretary in this alternate universe in which Robert Redford is president (the Hollywood actor's candidacy was implied at the end of the original comics run). The treasury secretary virtually assists visitors in providing their DNA to be processed for potential eligibility to apply for a lifetime tax exemption. In his eighth term as president, Redford has distributed what are colloquially called "Redfordations," which are effectively payments to the survivors and direct descendants of racial violence like that of the Tulsa Race Massacre. The appearance of Skip Gates as a figure who assists individuals in locating and understanding their ancestry operates as an intertextual reference as he is also the host of the acclaimed *Finding Your Roots* (PBS, 2012–present) genealogical program. Actual photographic footage of Greenwood before and after its ruination plays for Angela—and, by extension, *Watchmen* viewers—as Secretary Gates relays that President Redford "offers his sincerest condolences for the trauma you or your family may have suffered." The liberal policy of material reparations called the Victims of Racial Violence Act is ridiculed by some white Tulsa residents as an undeserved and racist handout. They protest outside of the heritage center shouting, "Redfordations are abominations!" because the reparations provide Black Tulsans with economic relief.

It should be noted that on September 1, 2020, actual Greenwood residents—as opposed to the fictional ones portrayed in the limited series—did file a lawsuit for reparations. At 105 years old, Lessie Benningfield Randle, one of two known survivors of the massacre still alive, became lead plaintiff in the case. In an op-ed for the *Los Angeles Times*, attorney for the survivors and current residents affected by the event Damario Solomon-Simmons wrote, "For a long time, the word 'reparations' was a non-starter, but it is finally losing its taboo."[27] The lawsuit describes the enduring damage to the Greenwood community and how the massacre is felt to this day in terms of continued racial disparities in the city that dictate the quality of life for Black Tulsans. Indeed, many families were never able to economically recover from the devastating event and are still living in poverty. As Solomon-Simmons states: "Instead of inheriting Black Wall Street's wealth, survivors like Mother Randle and their descendants inherited neglect, indifference and decades of obstruction from the city of Tulsa."[28] Thus, financial compensation is necessary to abate the entrenched racism that continues to stymie the historically Black neighborhood.

The rhetoric of reparations circulates increasingly and less controversially within 21st-century popular and public culture. In addition to the demand for monetary redress, Salamishah Tillet argues that "mnemonic restitution" is a post-civil-rights-era reparative gesture that revises the historical record so as to "fully recognize past and present African Americans in the civic myth and culture of the nation."[29] *Watchmen* constructs a robust alternative history of the United States that includes the introduction and passing of the Victims of Racial Violence Act in the televisual diegesis. In the words of Secretary Gates, the legislation begins the difficult work of "righting the wrongs of a dark past so that we might share a bright future." But, more importantly, the series inserts into the American superhero archive and US imaginary a black-masked crusader as a form of reparation for past discrimination and oppression.

At the end of episode 2, the Greenwood Center for Cultural Heritage calls Angela to tell her the results of the DNA test; indeed, Will is eligible to be a beneficiary of the Victims of Racial Violence Act, but the test also confirms her kinship to him—he is her grandfather. After this revelation, Will communicates to Angela: "I wanted to meet you and show you what you came from." Before she can officially arrest and gather additional information from the old man, he is whisked away in her car by a flying space vehicle, leaving his wheelchair and a bewildered Angela behind. As the narrative progresses across the next seven episodes, Angela comes to learn more about her family roots and identity as a Black woman grappling with the status of justice through the mask that she hides behind.

THE AESTHETICS OF MEMORY JUSTICE

Reparations are fundamentally tied to questions of memory: the demand to remember and commemorate can be a potent way to begin healing the chronic wounds spurred by racial subjugation. Memory justice can come in many forms, but it is dedicated to uncovering the truth of the past through processes of bringing loss and those lost into full view.[30] The *Watchmen* TV program is preoccupied not only with memorialization but also with the status and function of memory. The sixth episode, entitled "This Extraordinary Being," is a tour-de-force in engaging with memory justice through flashback. The acclaimed episode reveals the origin story of Hooded Justice to Angela in a kind of fever dream that is induced by Nostalgia—a pill that, if taken, affects one's memory and allows its consumers to re-experience the past. While its name reflects a sentimental longing to go back in time to encounter people, places, and things with happy associations, Angela's journey under the influence tackles feelings of injury, grief, and anger under conditions of anti-Blackness.

Outlawed by the Redford administration, Nostalgia is a drug (instead of a brand of cologne in the original comic) that functions to harvest memories so that those who become addicted are able to live perpetually in the past. Angela takes a lethal dose of the pills prescribed to her grandfather and, as TV critic Emily Nussbaum comments in her review of the series, "drops down a tunnel of inherited trauma, and what she finds there rewrites not just her own history but the mythology she's inside."[31] Indeed, Angela begins to assume the identity of an adult Will (Jovan Adepo) and his journey through becoming a police officer and, subsequently, a masked vigilante. In the largely black-and-white episode, apparitions appear in color, and doors become portals to different spaces. The hour of surreal television makes use of a roving camera with tracking shots weaving in and out of Will's memories seamlessly. Will's perspective becomes Angela's as they meld into one during key scenes such as his graduation from the New York police academy. She and the TV viewer bear witness to his most painful past experiences, and Angela even feels his pain acutely as it comes to reside in both of their bodies.

One such torturous scene is Will's near lynching by his so-called colleagues on the police force. His white counterparts threaten him by covering his head with a burlap bag and using a rope to string him up to a tree. Will is elevated and then promptly crashes to the ground where the audience sees Angela gasping for air. Just like the KKK terrorist attack in Tulsa, the memory serves as another pivotal moment in Will's development as an African American man who will go on to become the famed Hooded Justice. Indeed, after the incident, a bloodied and traumatized Will channels his rage by saving a white couple from assailants in an alley while wearing the burlap bag as a hood. His wife, June (Danielle Deadwyler)—who is revealed to be the infant whom he protected in 1921—tells him that he will get justice when he wears the hood and not the badge. Indeed, she has also been a witness to Will's pent-up wrath all her life ("You're an angry, angry man") and believes that catharsis can come from masking himself.

"This Extraordinary Being" is an hour of television that is indebted to the revolutionary thought of postcolonial theorist Frantz Fanon, from *Black Skin, White Masks* to *The Wretched of the Earth*. The former book's fifth chapter "The Lived Experience of the Black" (formerly translated as "The Fact of Blackness") ruminates on the objectification of the Black subject by the white gaze in a process of epidermalization. The chapter provides an account of an encounter on a train in French Algeria in which the Martinique-born Fanon becomes an object of fixation for a young white child, a fixation that fixes him within an "epidermal racial schema."[32] Accompanied by his mother, the child utters the deictic "Look, a Negro!" that spurs a crisis of visibility for Fanon. This moment is often cited for its material and psychic ramifications for the Black "object among other objects." Will experiences a Fanonian crisis of recognition as an African American cadet in the overwhelmingly white New York City police force in 1938, which ultimately manifests explicitly through his creation of Hooded Justice. As badges are placed on the new recruits, Will is skipped over and thus rendered invisible; he is acknowledged by the sole Black lieutenant whom he admits inspired him to become an officer. Lieutenant Battle chuckles ("Sorry to hear that") and whispers for him to "Beware of the Cyclops." Once he assumes the character of Hooded Justice, pivotal sequences depict Will's transformation into the vigilante hero. His reflection can be seen in a mirror as he paints the area of his face around his eyes white, exemplifying Fanon's conceptualization of the psychoanalytic split subject. Indeed, the true racial identity of Hooded Justice—who wears a noose around his neck reminiscent of the lynching of Black folk across history—must remain hidden in the service of preserving the whiteness of costumed adventuring.[33]

Will's drive to vigilantism in the name of justice stems from his experience coming-of-age filled with anguish and suffering. The originary violence of the Tulsa Massacre from which he barely escapes begins at the Dreamland Theater and functions as a kind of primal scene for the character. The child-version of Will is watching a silent Western film in which he comes to identify with the courageous Bass Reeves on screen. Will returns to this memory of spectatorship when prompted by June to work through his trauma. He will also stumble upon a secret operation called the Cyclops connected to both law enforcement and white supremacist terrorism, which is brainwashing Black moviegoing audiences into committing violence through mesmerism by film projection. The site of the movie theater also figures prominently in Fanon's rumination on Black subject formation. At the end of the fifth chapter, Fanon describes being at a movie theater in the interval: "I wait for myself. Just before the film starts, I wait for myself."[34] The mass medium of film is foundational to his explication of representation and its impact under colonialism.

Fanon's emphasis on Black subjectivity routed through masculinity is indicative of his exclusion of Black women to his theoretical formation. The woman of color is unknowable to him and thus "marks" an "epistemological limit."[35] *Watchmen* also renders its women of color and their motivations opaque at the same time that it highlights the function of the figure of the Black woman to initiate psychic relief for trauma. The Black women in Will's life, from his mother to his granddaughter, are critical to the character's narrative trajectory. Will's mother, Ruth Williams (Alexis Louder), plays the piano at an empty and ransacked Dreamland Theater during the massacre as destructive blasts can be heard outside. She appears this way at the piano sporadically in "This Extraordinary Being" as an ectoplasmic figure—a specter who haunts the frame and Will through time and space. Though she leaves Will and returns to Tulsa to raise their son, Marcus, an elderly June (Valeri Ross) connects with her young granddaughter, Angela (Faithe Herman), in Vietnam decades later before her untimely death. These three women underscore the importance of the Black maternal in *Watchmen*. I read Angela in particular as example of a "future text" whose iconography opens up representational possibility in popular culture for Black women.[36]

SISTER NIGHT'S MASKED BLACK WOMANHOOD

Regina King says she never read the original *Watchmen* comic series or watched the film adaptation, which gave her the opportunity to generate the character of Angela Abar from a blank slate, save for a provocative artist's drawing of King-as-Angela/Sister Night provided to her by Lindelof when he gave her the script.[37] Cloaked in a white turtleneck under a black hooded pantsuit with a black knit face mask and spray-on black eye mask, Angela's alter ego, Sister Night, is an homage to the faux blaxploitation film called *Sister Night* and its heroine whom a young version of herself idolizes. Like her grandfather, Angela experiences trauma at a young age, beginning with the murder of her parents in a freedom fighter terrorist attack in Vietnam.[38] In the aftermath, she is placed in an orphanage and develops a strong desire to be a police officer when she grows up.

Watchmen viewers first meet Angela as an adult in an elementary school classroom far removed from Vietnam on Career Day as she teaches students how to make mooncakes. She owns a store, the Milk and Hanoi Bakery, and seems to be living a quaint suburban life in Tulsa with her husband and three kids after retiring from the police force. However, looks are deceiving. Angela relies on masquerade, seemingly passed down from generation to generation, to protect herself from the pains of the past that are both individual and systemic. Sister Night becomes her iconic identity who has "a nose for white supremacy" much like Hooded Justice. Yet Angela's personal heritage evades her. Thus, she breaks into the Greenwood Center for Cultural Heritage in episode 4, "If You Don't Like My Story, Write Your Own," which begins to write the story of her own family tree. Visiting the Ances-Tree at the center, she watches as a hologram tree takes root and grows branches on her paternal side. Angela comes face-to-face with her great grandparents who died in the 1921 massacre, Obie Williams and Ruth Robeson, in a single archival photo. The photographic image fills a void in her background and attachment to where she came from: Tulsa.

Watchmen is invested in uncovering genealogical relations and also examining alternative forms of kinship. Angela was thrust into an unexpected maternal role in the aftermath of the "White Night" killing spree. She and her husband, Calvin (Yahya Abdul-Mateen II), adopted the three white children of her slain police partner, Doyle, and his wife. Thus, she became a mother to nonbiological children. The series makes a point to highlight her blended domestic life and role as a parent; for example, the mug she uses to obtain Will's DNA reads "Officially the World's Greatest Mom." While Angela comforts her son, Cal is a doting father who plays games with his daughters and reads them bedtime stories. Yet, the family unit is not only multiracial but also multispecies—Cal is actually the omnipotent superbeing Dr. Manhattan.

Angela's romantic relationship with the famed Jon "Dr. Manhattan" Osterman is revealed in the penultimate episode, "A God Walks into Abar." Dr. Manhattan strikes up a conversation with a lonely Angela at Mr. Eddy's Bar in Saigon on the 22nd anniversary of her parents' death. The two drink and banter while sitting across the table from each other; they fall in love across the years, and all at once (Dr. Manhattan experiences time differently, he reminds Angela). In order to keep who he is a secret, Dr. Manhattan takes on the human physiognomy of a deceased Black male named Calvin Jelani and allows a device to be implanted in his head that gives him amnesia so that he cannot remember his true god status. Angela and Calvin are in a relationship for ten years before it ends in tragedy when, despite Angela's attempt at protecting her love, Dr. Manhattan's identity is exposed, and he is subsequently killed.

The conclusion to the series shows audiences that Angela has potentially inherited Dr. Manhattan's superpowers. With the promise of a new family unit being created after bonding with her absentee grandfather over Jon's death, she recalls previous conversations with the god about the chance that he could transfer his otherworldly abilities to someone else. In the final shot of her foot tentatively placed on the surface of the pool water, *Watchmen* produces a televisual interval in which another reality can emerge. Indeed, perhaps Jon has passed down to her "the power . . . to reconsider the impossible as a possibility, the kind of speculation needed to bring new futures."[39] Such futures cannot be verified, but they might not be doomed to repeat the past by offering transformative ways of being human and cultivating human connection.

CONCLUSION

Watchmen was the most nominated television program at the 72nd Emmy Awards with 26 nods combined in acting, directing, writing, and other technical categories. King won her fourth Emmy for the program (Lead Actress in a Limited Series) at the virtual awards ceremony that aired on September 20, 2020. She gave her acceptance speech via video wearing a hot pink suit over a black t-shirt with the words "Say Her Name" emblazoned above an artistic rendering of the face of Breonna Taylor, a Black woman killed in her home by law enforcement in Louisville, Kentucky, on March 13, 2020. Taylor's death and the lack of charges brought against police officers sparked outrage during the summer of 2020 in the aftermath of the murder of another unarmed Black individual, George Floyd, which was caught on tape at the hands of those purported to be "the law." Multiple campaigns to "Arrest the cops who killed Breonna Taylor" emerged on social media to raise public awareness and demand accountability from the justice system. In a *New York Magazine* article, writer Zak Cheney-Rice comments, "For all that is extraordinary about how she's been commemorated, the one thing Taylor is not is a beneficiary of justice under the law, because the law is not for people like Breonna Taylor."[40] Such a statement is a stark reminder that *Watchmen*'s "clarity remains an insufficient remedy" to the racial injustices that ail this country.[41] As an extraordinary television series, it broaches questions regarding the police, authority, law, and the elusiveness of justice from a safe remove on the small screen.

Despite this distance, when *Watchmen* won Best Limited Series, Lindelof accepted the award while wearing a "Remember Tulsa '21" shirt to highlight the 100th anniversary commemoration in Summer 2021. In the Black Lives Matter era, the TV program enacts memory justice at a narrative level between its fictional characters who navigate the traumas of anti-Black racism, but also in its broader refusal to forget what actually happened in Greenwood. Indeed, *Watchmen* begins to uncover this violent history for TV viewers. A month after the entertainment industry recognized the program with awards, news emerged of human remains found in Tulsa while searching for victims of the race massacre.[42] The alignment of these two events speaks to *Watchmen*'s uncanny resonances with the social and political climate.

Ultimately, as one critic suggests, "Very little about HBO's *Watchmen* is safe . . . the entire undertaking is a risk."[43] The series is a risk due to its very existence as remix that goes against the wishes of creator Alan Moore. However, it is also a risk because race—and Blackness in particular—is at the center of the story that it tells. With risk also comes possibility, and the series confronts white supremacy with the potential of activating a social and political consciousness in its address to both an imagined and real audience. While survivors and descendants of the Tulsa Race Massacre demand reparations for the heinous crime, *Watchmen* engages in fabulation as a means of televisual compensation. The program provides "speculative joy" for viewers by commenting on the intersection of Blackness and the fantastic.[44] In its experimental historiography, *Watchmen* produces a poignant archive of Black life that fosters a legacy that will endure.

NOTES

1. Saidiya Hartman, "Venus in Two Acts," *Small Axe* 12, no. 2 (2008): 4.

2. Jeremy Egner, "Who Will Watch *Watchmen*?," *New York Times*, last modified October 16, 2019, https://www.nytimes.com/2019/10/16/arts/television/watchmen-hbo-damon-lindelof-regina-king.html.

3. Noel King, "*Watchmen* Creator Damon Lindelof: Not Talking about Race Felt 'Irresponsible,'" *NPR*, last modified October 22, 2019, https://www.npr.org/2019/10/22/771998690/watchmen-creator-damon-lindelof-not-talking-about-race-felt-irresponsible.

4. Hartman, 11.

5. Ethan Sacks, "Who Watches the Watchmen? That's the Question for the TV Sequel," *NBC News*, last modified October 19, 2019, https://www.nbcnews.com/pop-culture/tv/who-watches-watchmen-s-question-tv-sequel-n1065701.

6. W. James Booth, "The Unforgotten: Memories of Justice," *American Political Science Review* 95, no. 4 (2001): 777.

7. Graeme McMillan, "Damon Lindelof Explains His Vision for HBO's 'Watchmen' in Heartfelt Letter to Fans," *Hollywood Reporter*, last modified May 22, 2018, https://www.hollywoodreporter.com/live-feed/damon-lindelof-posts-open-watchmen-letter-instagram-1114216.

8. Thomas Johnson, "Appropriation Anxiety: *Watchmen* (2019)," *Adaptation* 13, no. 3 (2020): 398.

9. Damon Lindelof, "Day 140", *Instagram*, May 22, 2018, https://www.instagram.com/p/BjFsj6JHEdq/?igshid=um11wcqxcybo.

10. Lindelof. "Day 140." *Instagram*, May 22, 2018.

11. Kristen Warner, "[Home] Girls: *Insecure* and HBO's Risky Racial Politics," *Los Angeles Review of Books*, last modified October 21, 2016, https://lareviewofbooks.org/article/home-girls-insecure-and-hbos-risky-racial-politics/.

12. Lindelof, "Day 140", *Instagram*, May 22, 2018.

13. Tirhakah Love, "'Hard Truths' in the 'Watchmen' Writer's Room," *Medium*, last modified October 23, 2019, https://gen.medium.com/damon-lindelof-heard-some-hard-truths-in-the-watchmen-writer-s-room-24101b6c11b7.

14. Aaron Taylor, "The Continuing Adventures of the 'Inherently Unfilmable' Book: Zack Snyder's *Watchmen*," *Cinema Journal* 56, no. 2 (Winter 2017): 127.

15. Jeremy Egner, "Who Will Watch *Watchmen*?," *New York Times*, last modified October 16, 2019, https://www.nytimes.com/2019/10/16/arts/television/watchmen-hbo-damon-lindelof-regina-king.html.

16. Love.

17. Jeffrey Sconce, "What If: Charting Television's New Textual Boundaries," in *Television After TV: Essays on a Medium in Transition*, ed. Lynn Spigel and Jeffrey Sconce (Durham: Duke University Press, 2004), 109.

18. Michael Boyce Gillespie, "Thinking about *Watchmen*: With Jonathan W. Gray, Rebecca A. Wanzo, and Kristen J. Warner, *Film Quarterly* 73, no. 4 (2020): 52. In this important conversation about the television series, Rebecca Wanzo references Toni Morrison's idea of "playing in the dark" to discuss how *Watchmen* infuses Blackness into the core of its mythology, stating, "A racialized nationalism is important to the foundations of vigilantism, heroism, and alienated citizenship."

19. Egner.

20. It should be noted that Hooded Justice's race is not explicitly stated in the comic book, though he expresses sympathy for the Nazi Party.

21. Mike Pesca, "How *Watchmen*'s Director Staged One of the Worst Race Massacres in American History," *Slate*, last modified October 18, 2019, https://slate.com/culture/2019/10/watchmen-interview-nicole-kassell-director.html.

22. Victor Luckerson, "Watching *Watchmen* as a Descendant of the Tulsa Race Massacre," *New Yorker*, last modified September 20, 2020, https://www.newyorker.com/news/news-desk/watching-watchmen-as-a-descendant-of-the-tulsa-race-massacre.

23. Leslie Lee, "Whitewashing 'Watchmen,'" *Truth Dig*, December 21, 2019, https://www.truthdig.com/articles/whitewashing-watchmen/.

24. Luckerson.

25. Luckerson. The Christopher family attests that "Many of the family's most prized personal effects have already wound their way into commercial products like *Watchmen*." Rebecca Wanzo has discussed the commodification of the Tulsa Race Massacre in her talk, "How Should We Theorize Injury in Fan Studies?" *Fandom + Piracy Mini-Series*, Berkeley Center for New Media, February 25, 2021.

26. Nicole Simek, "Speculative Futures: Race in *Watchmen*'s Worlds," *symploke* 28, nos. 1–2 (2020): 392.

27. Damario Solomon Simmons, "Reparations Are the Answer to Protestors' Demands for Racial Justice," *Los Angeles Times*, last modified June 8, 2020, https://www.latimes.com/opinion/story/2020-06-08/racial-protest-tulsa-massacre-reparations. In 2005, the United States Supreme Court rejected an appeal to hear a case that also sought reparations.

28. Simmons.

29. Salamishah Tillet, *Sites of Slavery: Citizenship and Racial Democracy in the Post–Civil Rights Imagination* (Durham, NC: Duke University Press, 2012), 137–38.

30. Booth, "The Unforgotten: Memories of Justice."

31. Emily Nussbaum, "The Incendiary Aims of HBO's *Watchmen*," *New Yorker*, last modified December 9, 2019, https://www.newyorker.com/magazine/2019/12/09/the-incendiary-aims-of-hbos-watchmen.

32. Frantz Fanon, *Black Skin, White Masks*, trans. Richard Philcox (New York: Grove Press, 2008), 92.

33. Will's Blackness is not the only thing hidden about the character. The revelation that he is in an interracial homosexual relationship with Captain Metropolis is beyond the scope of this chapter.

34. Fanon, 119.

35. Kara Keeling, "'In the Interval': Frantz Fanon and the 'Problems' of Visual Representation," *Qui Parle* 13, no. 2 (Spring/Summer 2003): 95. See also Gwen Bergner, "Who Is That Masked Woman? Or, the Role of Gender in Fanon's *Black Skin, White Masks*," *PMLA* 110, no. 1 (January 1995).

36. Nina Cartier, "Black Women On-Screen as Future Texts: A New Look at Black Pop Culture Representations," *Cinema Journal* 53, no. 4 (Summer 2014): 150–57. Cartier expands on Alondra Nelson's notion of "Future Texts" (inspired by Ishmael Reed) connected to new formations in race and technology in *Social Text* 20, no. 2 (2002): 1–15.

37. Josh Wigler, "*Watchmen* Star Regina King on Bringing a 'Wonderful Story of Legacy' to Life," *The Hollywood Reporter*, last modified October 21, 2019, https://www.hollywoodreporter.com/live-feed/watchmen-series-premiere-regina-king-sister-night-1249099.

38. It is outside the scope of this chapter to engage critiques of state violence and empire, as epitomized by how *Watchmen* represents Vietnam and the character arc of Lady Trieu, another important woman of color on the series. For more, see Aaron Bady, "Dr. Manhattan is a Cop: *Watchmen* and Frantz Fanon," *Los Angeles Review of Books*, December 31, 2019, https://lareviewofbooks.org/article/dr-manhattan-cop-watchmen-frantz-fanon/.

39. Simek, 402.

40. Zak Cheney-Rice, "The Law Is Not Made for Breonna Taylor," *New York Magazine*, last modified September 27, 2020, https://nymag.com/intelligencer/2020/09/the-law-is-not-made-for-breonna-taylor.html#:~:text=Breonna%20Taylor%20has%201ed%20a,became%20a%20national%20cause%20c%C3%A91%C3%A8bre.

41. Jonathan W. Gray, "*Watchmen* after the End of History: Race, Redemption, and the End of the World," *ASAP/Journal*, February 3, 2020, http://asapjournal.com/watchmen-after-the-end-of-history-race-redemption-and-the-end-of-the-world-jonathan-w-gray/.

42. "1921 Tulsa Race Massacre: Human Remains Found during Excavation—CNN," accessed December 24, 2020, https://www.cnn.com/2020/10/20/us/tulsa-massacre-remains-found/index.html.

43. Adam Epstein, "HBO's 'Watchmen' Is Weird and Dangerous, Just Like It Needs to Be," *QZ*, last modified October 17, 2019, https://qz.com/1729339/hbos-big-watchmen-risk-totally-pays-off/.

44. Michael Boyce Gillespie, "Thinking about *Watchmen*: With Jonathan W. Gray, Rebecca A. Wanzo, and Kristen J. Warner," *Film Quarterly* 73, no. 4 (2020): 51.

Part Three

NOSTALGIA AND TRAUMA

While the theme of section 2—race and American history—offers the greatest deviation from Alan Moore and Dave Gibbons's original maxiseries, the focus of the third and final section of *After Midnight: "Watchmen" after "Watchmen"* brings us back to one of the themes of the original book: nostalgia and trauma. While the entirety of the book could be considered an antinostalgic reflection on the nearly fifty-year-old superhero genre that foregrounds the immense psychological baggage that comes with crime fighting, the theme becomes most pronounced in the triad relationship between Sally Jupiter, Edward Blake, and their daughter Laurie Juspeczyk. In the ninth chapter of the series, Laurie's revelation that her birth was the result of Edward raping her mother—a repressed memory—is punctuated by her destroying the crystalline world that her estranged partner, Dr. Manhattan, has created on Mars with a bottle of Adrian Veidt's perfume, Nostalgia. The act brings Manhattan to forgo his apathy and become involved in solving the central mystery of the book, teeing up the final act. In short, Moore and Gibbons seem to be saying to us that nostalgia is a refuge of willful ignorance that distracts us from coping with our trauma and confronting the reality in front of us.

As hinted at in the previous section, particularly in the chapters by Apryl Alexander and Brandy Monk-Payton, the HBO series builds upon these two intertwined themes and adds the theme of intergenerational trauma within the African American experience. While Nostalgia—the fragrance and concept—in the original series plays to the public craving for a utopian ideal for a past that never really existed during the Cold War, Damon Lindelof's version partially subverts this representation of the concept. In the HBO series, Nostalgia is a pharmaceutical drug that allows users to turn their favorite memories into pill form so they can relieve anxiety, dementia, and trauma by allowing them to re-experience them. This brings users to abuse the drug and overdose, resulting in the pill being banned. However, Angela's use of the pills brings the realization that Will Reeves, her grandfather, is Hooded Justice and permits her to inhabit his subjectivity as he tries to fight systemic racism. In short, in Angela Abar's case, Nostalgia becomes a positive instrument that allows her to confront the roots of intergenerational trauma and focus her energy in the present.

The final four chapters focus on the double-edged nature of nostalgia throughout the *Watchmen* sequels. In chapter 14, Jeffrey SJ Kirchoff explores how—in the case of *Doomsday Clock*—we can consider it a positive rhetorical tool, capable of unifying two disparate narrative universes of Moore and Gibbons's "stronger loving world, to die in" (their quotation of John Cale's "Sanctus" ends the series) and the hope and optimism of the New 52. In the next chapter, James Denis McGlynn analyzes how the HBO series continues Moore and Gibbons's original citation and adaptation of pre-existing music to "enable audiences' vivid entry into its troubled protagonists' subjective experiences." In chapter 16, Tracy E. Moran Vozar applies the psychological concept of attachment theory to round out our understanding of how the role of family can help us better understand the heroes and villains at the center of the HBO series. Next, Lindsay Hallam analyzes how the television series—like the original series—challenges nostalgia by providing an alternate history and present that both deconstruct the superhero narrative and reveal masked trauma. Finally, in her afterword, Suzanne Scott brings us full circle, back to considerations of adaptation, in her consideration of the "unadaptable" totem of the original series' narrative MacGuffin—Ozymandias's squid—and how the plot point can fruitfully open a discussion about transmediation and media specificity.

Chapter 14

THE EPIDEICTIC USE OF RESTORATIVE NOSTALGIA IN *DOOMSDAY CLOCK*

JEFFREY SJ KIRCHOFF

Nostalgia, broadly speaking, is often viewed with great skepticism, which is perhaps unsurprising when considering its origins. "Nostalgia" was first coined by Johannes Hofer in 1688 to describe a curable disease whose symptoms included a longing for home and feelings of loss and displacement.[1] While scholars seemed to have (mostly) moved on from the position that nostalgia is a "disease," it is still largely viewed as a naïve, unproductive activity. William Kurlinkus posits that "the majority of research on nostalgic making [. . .] has focused on critiquing (and occasionally deploying) nostalgia as an uncritical longing, a state recycling, or a nefariously propagandistic weapon."[2] Despite that scathing take on nostalgia, there are still some who find nostalgia to be a productive practice. Michael Chabon, an author who unabashedly and unapologetically crafts stories rooted in nostalgia, argues that "Nostalgia [. . .] is the emotional experience—always momentary, always fragile—of having what you lost or never had, of seeing what you missed seeing, of meeting the people you missed knowing, of sipping coffee in the storied cafes that are now hot-yoga studios. It's the feeling that overcomes you when some minor vanished beauty of the world is momentarily restored."[3] Though Kurlinkus and Chabon offer seemingly competing notions, these views suggest one commonality: that nostalgia can be employed in powerful, rhetorical ways. And, as Nancy Jolma points out, nostalgia can be mapped onto works of literature in a variety of ways to help illuminate an author's theme.[4] This chapter explores that possibility within the *Watchmen* comic franchise, paying particular attention to Geoff Johns and Gary Frank's

Doomsday Clock (originally released in 2017 and concluded in 2019); specifically, I show how this text uses restorative nostalgia as epideictic rhetoric in an effort to revitalize and unify their reading community.

RESTORATIVE NOSTALGIA AND EPIDEICTIC RHETORIC

Like many others, my understanding and use of restorative nostalgia is principally informed by Svetlana Boym, though other thinkers have refined my application of this concept to *Doomsday Clock*. For Boym, restorative nostalgia sees nostalgics intent on re-creating a past home (broadly defined).[5] Building on the ideas of Boym, Simon Eckstein argues that restorative nostalgia is more interested in reconstructing "monuments of the past," including "literature, art, architecture, or mythology";[6] this mirrors Frederic Jameson's description of nostalgia as a "desperate attempt to appropriate a missing past."[7] Due to restorative nostalgics' goal of reconstruction, Boym, as well as other scholars, have positioned this brand of nostalgia as associated with "national and nationalist revivals all over the world" as these nostalgics "believe their project is about truth."[8] Thus, many scholars point to propaganda as the best example of (and most frequent use of) restorative nostalgia, citing Donald Trump's catch-phrase of "Make America Great Again" as a modern example of this form. This understanding of restorative nostalgia characterizes it as an uncritical look back that simultaneously aims to blithely romanticize and preserve the past. Using this understanding, one could see nostalgics trying to surround themselves with re-created artifacts that serve as reminders of the past in an effort to block out the present and ignore reality. This is a melancholy outlook, of course—one tinged with a pessimistic view of the present. In this understanding, the re-creation of the past can be used to blot out reality (block out the present) or rewrite the present with the past.

However, this is not the only way one can understand restorative nostalgia. I would posit that we could also view restorative nostalgia as a critical examination of the present and past. That is, the anxieties created by the present could facilitate an examination of both the present and the past to determine what caused the problems that are causing the present anxiety and how/whether rebuilding an aspect of the past could solve the present issue. In this way, restorative nostalgia could mark a thoughtful, critical analysis of both past and present, and the rebuilding of monuments is done deliberately to work through present-day issues. In this way, I draw some from Michael Pickering and Emily Keightly, who seek to reclaim nostalgia (broadly speaking); they believe that solely positioning nostalgia as naïve or pessimistic is far too limiting. Rather, they believe that nostalgia can be used to "recognize aspects of the past as the basis for renewal and satisfaction in the future."[9] As they later note, nostalgia is "a means of taking one's bearings for the road ahead in the uncertainties of the present. This opens up a positive dimension in nostalgia, one associated with desire for engagement with difference, with aspiration and critique."[10] Thus, one *might* see restorative nostalgia as a critical look at the present and determine which aspects of the past can be rebuilt to quell the anxieties, shortcomings, or concerns of the present. The difference, then, is that the former understanding of restorative nostalgia aims to rebuild the past to forget the present, while the latter rebuilds to improve the present. Just as there is no objective gaze into the past, there is no objective analysis of the present. In this way, I would argue that a present moment might prompt a restorative nostalgic gaze in some, while others would resist any gaze into the past, content to live in the present. The difference may be minimal, but one suggests that the present needs to be replaced, while the other is hopeful that the present can be adjusted and improved. It is this latter understanding of restorative nostalgia that is present in *Doomsday Clock*.

Nostalgia, and particularly restorative nostalgia, is often a device used to achieve impactful epideictic rhetoric, one of three genres that Aristotle outlines in his treatise, *On Rhetoric*. Epideictic rhetoric is thought of as ceremonial rhetoric rooted in praise and blame; specifically, in book I, chapter III, Aristotle describes "the ceremonial oratory of display" as praising or censuring somebody with the epideictic orator specifically concerned with the present day, as "all speakers praise and blame in regard to *existing* qualities, but they often also make use of other things, both reminding [the audience] of the past and projecting the course of the future."[11] In this short passage, we find two core tenets that have shaped years of scholarship: the focus of epideictic is on praise and/or blame and the rhetor is concentrated on the present (though events from the past and speculation about future—as it relates to the present—can be appropriate).

While the topic and temporal nature of epideictic are integral to understanding Aristotle's conception of the epideictic, it is equally important to understand the extended exigency for this genre. In his translation of Aristotle's treatise, George Kennedy notes that for Aristotle "praise corrects, modifies, or strengthens an audience's belief about the civic virtues or the reputation of an individual."[12] Thus, for Aristotle, the goal is not necessarily to argue for something new, but rather to uphold something previously established. Cynthia Miecznikowski Sheard summarizes this notion adroitly:

"Epideictic has been seen as a rhetoric of identification and conformity whose function is to confirm and promote adherence to the commonly held values of a community."[13] Sheard continues by noting that epideictic rhetoric reminds us "of the shared values and needs, interests and goals, that hold us together as members of groups."[14] Here, then, Sheard suggests that for many epideictic rhetors, the purpose is to *unify* groups or communities—bring them together—by reinforcing commonly held virtues and commonplace ideals. It is here that we can see the relationship between nostalgia and epideictic; as William Kurlinkus notes, the content of epideictic rhetoric is often nostalgic, as rhetors may choose to review "who we were so that we can maintain [or re-establish] that identity into the future."[15] He goes on to note that nostalgic rhetoric, within a community, answers the question "Who are we?" and because epideictic "reaffirms and intensifies community values," nostalgia can support the goals of epideictic rhetoric.[16] We will see how these two work together in our examination of *Doomsday Clock*.

UNDERSTANDING THE GENESIS OF *DOOMSDAY CLOCK*

In order to effectively position *Doomsday Clock* as epideictic rhetoric, it is important to at least briefly outline two key moments in DC Comics' publishing history that this text speaks to overtly. These moments, which would be well-known by fans of DC Comics (ostensibly at least a significant portion of *Doomsday Clock*'s audience), will illuminate how restorative nostalgia is used to fulfill an epideictic function. The first of these moments is the publication of *Watchmen* in 1986 and the second is the DC's 2011 decision to reboot their comic line in the short-lived "New 52." Though the two publishing moments may seem unrelated, *Doomsday Clock* actively invokes both and needs to in order to adroitly speak to the impassioned DC reader.

Perhaps no graphic text has been written about quite as much as Alan Moore and Dave Gibbons's 1986–1987 superhero epic, *Watchmen*. Amidst the impressive and diverse scholarship published on this complex text, there is one prevalent, recurring conclusion: Moore and Gibbons innovatively and effectively deconstruct the notion of a superhero and in doing so, subvert and alter readers' understanding of the concept. Tired of comics waxing nostalgic for golden- and silver-age superhero stories, Moore and Gibbons strive to break free of status quo superhero narratives by building a fictional world devoid of hope and inserting flawed, apathetic, and disturbing superheroes at its center. The result, as comic fans and scholars know, was acclaimed by fans and critics alike. *Watchmen* scored a host of awards, including three Jack

Kirby Awards in 1987 (Best New Series, Best Writer, and Best Writer/Artist), four Eisner Awards in 1988 (including Best Finite Series, Best Graphic Album, Best Writer, and Best Writer/Artist), and a Hugo Award in 1988. Most prominently—and most cited—was its inclusion on *TIME* magazine's 2010 Top 100 English-language novels since 1923, the only graphic novel to receive such an honor. Of course, it is imperative to note that the accolades stemmed not only from their darker take on superheroes, as individuals also pointed to its innovative use of the comic book form to tell the story and its ability to effectively layer and connect a number of genres (including science fiction, memoir, medical reports, pirate stories, and of course, the superhero story) seamlessly. However, despite the many interesting facets of *Watchmen*, it was the "grim and gritty" superhero story that seemed to influence the comic world the most. As David Hughes writes, "Although intended to be the last word on comic book superheroes, ironically *Watchmen* breathed new life in the genre, establishing the cynical comic book hero as a staple of the superhero fiction, and leading to a succession of mostly inferior imitations which continue to this day";[17] to that point, Sara J. Van Ness observes that several "copycat works" followed, all boasting similarly dark, brooding superheroes.[18]

Creators Moore and Gibbons were fairly dismayed with this turn. Moore harshly opines that comic writers gravitated towards the violent Rorschach and determined that, moving forward, all superheroes had to be "violent psychopaths."[19] To that end, Moore maintains in several interviews that their intention was not to call for the rise of deconstructive superhero tales. Rather, he instead hoped that *Watchmen* would inspire creative and different takes on what he saw as a stale medium, saying, "I was hoping naively for a great rash of individual comic books that were exploring different storytelling ideas and trying to break new ground."[20] That is, Moore thought the takeaway from *Watchmen* should not be his deconstruction and overall criticism of superheroes, but rather his efforts to breathe life in a potentially stale genre. Ironically, rather than inspire new, original superhero stories, *Watchmen* instead ushered in a new era of superhero narrative: one that continually strives to deconstruct the superhero in worlds that are progressively darker and darker.

In many ways, DC's "New 52" initiative cemented *Watchmen's* "legacy" of inspiring brooding, grim, pessimistic stories. Launched in 2011, DC's "New 52" refers to its company-wide "reboot" of their superhero titles. Such a move wiped out years of superhero continuity; the heroes would be starting with a clean slate—new stories, new histories, new origins, and (of course) new costumes. DC Comics crafted the New 52 with two primary goals in mind:

first, provide a new launching point for readers, as they were concerned that their stories were becoming overly reliant on what some perceived to be a convoluted and confusing continuity and, second, as an opportunity to integrate more diversity—including more female superheroes and ethnically and racially diverse superheroes—into their line.

Unfortunately for DC Comics, the New 52 by and large alienated its readers by wiping out its heroes' histories and also failed to realize its goal of injecting more diversity. As Geoff Johns pointed out, when wiping out the substantial history of superheroes, there may be a clean slate (which can be exciting as a creator), but there are also a lot of important relationships removed from the equation; Johns specifically cites Superman and Lois Lane and Green Arrow and Black Canary as two "powerhouse" couples that were no longer couples in the New 52 paradigm, resulting in heroes who were somehow less joyful, optimistic, and full of love.[21] Not only were many of these comics devoid of joy, but DC also ramped up the violence in an attempt to appeal to the adult reader. As Jason Serafino notes, DC promised readers a "harder edge" and it delivered with a "Wonder Woman [. . .] always scowling [. . . and] Cyborg [looking] like a walking aircraft carrier."[22] He goes on to observe that the New 52 was "needlessly violent and 'gritty' but without enough depth or substance to make people actually want to read the book."[23] Moreover, the goal to integrate more diversity was largely problematic, as the initial slate of titles featured scantily clad heroines posing sexually on covers and splash pages (see Catwoman and Starfire as two of the more egregious examples of this oversexualization).

The New 52 struggled enough that after five short years, DC Comics pulled the plug and launched a soft reboot with its 2016 "Rebirth" initiative that looked to merge the best elements of the New 52 with previous, beloved elements from stories that had been erased from continuity with the New 52. As then copublisher Dan Didio notes, "REBIRTH is designed to bring back the best of DC's past, embrace the stories we currently love, and move the entire epic universe into the future."[24] Many have viewed Rebirth as a kind of public apology for the New 52, and that apology begins with a one-shot special that Johns produced. In this special, it is revealed that ten years of history had been stolen from the world of DC and that this manipulation came at the hands of Dr. Manhattan, officially merging the dark and gritty world that Alan Moore and Dave Gibbons created with the legacy characters of DC Comics. This is where *Doomsday Clock* comes in. Johns notes that the point of the story is to see if the grime of *Watchmen* can infect the hope of the Rebirth initiative—or if hope can ultimately win out. He also opines that he didn't "like the DC Universe where it was [with the New 52] and wanted a story that put back what I missed as a fan."[25] That, in large part, is the goal of *Doomsday Clock*—to see if hope can defeat pessimism and to restore legacy to the DC Universe. Given that this is a direct plea to galvanize and bring back the community of readers, it will become apparent how this text serves as epideictic rhetoric—and as we will see, this rhetoric is largely accomplished through the use of restorative nostalgia.

DOOMSDAY CLOCK, RESTORATIVE NOSTALGIA AND EPIDEICTIC RHETORIC

Doomsday Clock begins by striving to paint just as troubling, dark, and "grimy" a world that graces the pages of *Watchmen*. The narrative of *Doomsday Clock* features two worlds—the world from the original *Watchmen* and the world featuring DC's legacy characters (Superman, Batman, Wonder Woman, etc.). Both worlds are in a state of disarray that blatantly reflects the crises of the time Johns and Frank crafted this text. The political climate of the *Watchmen* world is bleak—there is the collapse of the European Union, Russia is threatening to enter Poland, North Korea is set to invade Texas, hundreds have broken through "the wall" and flooded into Mexico. News media outlets are forcibly being shut down with the installment of the National News Network being the sole source of news. Meanwhile, the president of the United States cannot be bothered by this as he is more interested in golfing. All of this has led to a rally cry of "Make America Safe Again." The narrative world featuring DC's legacy characters isn't in much better shape. Superheroes are no longer a symbol of hope (perhaps a not-so-subtle reference to the dark, violent heroes of the New 52) but have instead become a "disease" that public doesn't trust. This is perpetuated in part because of the so-called Superman Theory, which accuses the US government of creating superheroes. Just as Moore and Gibbons's *Watchmen* was written to reflect on the crises of its time—principally the Cold War and threat of nuclear destruction—Johns and Frank are setting up a narrative that is steeped in the crises of their time: questioning what news is "real" and what news is "fake," distrust of government, and tenuous global relations. Simply put, there is plenty of "grime" found in *Doomsday Clock*—both worlds seem to be on the brink of war thanks in part to poorly run governments and any peace is tenuous at best. However, where *Watchmen* ultimately succumbs to the grime, thanks to Ozymandias's insane plan to bring peace that results in the deaths of millions, *Doomsday Clock* looks to erase the grime and instill hope through epideictic rhetoric and restorative nostalgia.

Just as photographs and mementoes are artifacts facilitating nostalgia in *Watchmen* (e.g., Hollis Mason's framed photos from the past in his flat; Edward Blake's secret closet with mementoes; Sally Jupiter's retirement home featuring posters and framed photos), so are they employed in *Doomsday Clock*. While photographs and mementoes are not quite as prominently displayed in the sequel, one photograph in particular plays an important role in the restorative nostalgia found within the text. Ironically, this photograph is one that also appears in *Watchmen* and was decidedly not a facilitator of nostalgia then. The photo I refer to is of Jon Osterman, before the accident that turns him into Dr. Manhattan, and Janey Slater, the one-time girlfriend of Osterman. Taken in 1959 at an amusement park, it shows Osterman with his arm around Janey, who is eating popcorn. In *Watchmen*, the events of that particular day are recounted in Manhattan's usual stilted patter. When the photograph is taken, the two are not "young lovers," as the carney describes them, but colleagues sharing a road trip. However, by the end of the evening they have made love, and this becomes the first step in a relationship that ends badly, which is perhaps mirrored in the poor physical condition of this photograph in *Watchmen*. Simply put, this photograph is callously disregarded—Manhattan found it "in a derelict bar," and while he looks at it briefly on Mars after leaving Earth to start chapter 4, he drops it before the end of the first page of said chapter, noting, "I'm tired of looking at the photograph now."[26] The photo itself is in awful shape—the top left- and right-hand corners are missing, the bottom of the photo is curled up, and you can see some mold settling in around the border. This should come as no surprise—Manhattan, as introduced in *Watchmen*, is not a nostalgic character. He is the only character, in fact, who does not seem to engage in any nostalgia and, as the Comedian points out, is quickly losing touch with humanity. In the original *Watchmen*, the photograph seems to symbolize Manhattan's inability to cherish memories and his desire (inability?) to not be attached to memories.

Thus, it is surprising to see this photograph play such an integral role in *Doomsday Clock*; it is our first clue as readers that "hope" might emerge victorious over the "grime" of *Watchmen*. The photograph first makes an appearance at the end of issue 7—an issue that sees Adrian Veidt making a nostalgic plea of his own for Mantattan to help save their world, which has predictably crumbled after the events Veidt engineered in *Watchmen*. Manhattan is not interested in the problems of the world he left, though; rather, he is beginning to feel curiosity for the first time in a long time due to his inability to see the future past a certain moment. Specifically, Manhattan muses on Mars that "One month in my future, I see Superman. He's yelling at me, though I'm deafened by the thunder from the world falling apart around us. His eyes burn with anger as he throws his fist forward. Then I see nothing. A year. A century. A millennium. Still nothing [. . .] And I wonder . . . one month from now . . . does Superman destroy me? Or do I destroy everything?"[27] As Manhattan considers this, readers see the photograph of Jon and Janey settle on the surface of Mars. It is unclear where this photograph comes from initially, but as readers continue on in the series, it becomes apparent that Manhattan is leaving a replica of this picture behind everywhere he goes. In issue 11, for instance, Lex Luthor reveals that he has found several images all over America—each one identical in every way. He observes that these photographs have been left behind throughout time and that they "seem to be . . . left behind by someone. Like a trail of bread crumbs dropped across most of the last century and into this one."[28] That Manhattan is producing replicas of this image wherever he goes certainly suggests that the photograph carries some kind of significance—at least a greater significance than it ever did during the narrative of *Watchmen*. But Luthor surmises that Manhattan is unaware that he is leaving behind this trail, which would suggest that the production of this image is on a subconscious level and that Manhattan is not even cognizant of what this image truly means to him.

The photograph makes a more meaningful appearance when Superman is in the midst of his climactic fight with other superheroes in issue 12. While Superman is simultaneously fending off warring superheroes and protecting endangered innocent citizens, Dr. Manhattan detachedly looks on. Yet as Superman fights, the photograph mysteriously appears in four consecutive panels, and when we return to the fight five pages later, it appears again in three more panels.[29] Superman realizes what Luthor did—that Manhattan is producing these images with each step he takes. In an effort to get Manhattan to do *something*, Superman makes an appeal steeped in pathos by asking who the woman is in the photo, surmising that she—and the photograph—must be important to him. Curiously—in a moment that seems wholly inconsistent with the character of Dr. Manhattan—Manhattan is moved by this. In a three-panel sequence, Manhattan flashes back to the past to the moments immediately preceding the accident that changed Osterman to Manhattan—the first image focuses on Janey, the second on Janey's watch, and the third on a terrified Jon. Though a short panel sequence, it undeniably changes the course of the story. The fourth panel shows a calmer, relaxed Dr. Manhattan—his face suggests he is at peace, which is a stark contrast to the tense, dour expressions Manhattan sports throughout much of *Watchmen* and *Doomsday Clock*. It is at this moment that Manhattan admits that Janey meant something to him; though he does not wax nostalgic in a dramatic monologue, he simply says "She did [mean something to me]" in a moment of stark clarity. Superman suggests, then, that "the darkness you see . . . maybe it takes everything you have to save your world. Maybe you make that choice."[30] Superman seems to be inferring that the people in the photograph—perhaps not realizing that Manhattan is one of those individuals—would want Manhattan to save the world.

In yet another moment that seems completely out of character—and thus, I suppose, surprising—Manhattan literally uses the past to rewrite and modify the present; that is, he undoes the changes he had made within the DC Universe (as chronicled in *DC Rebirth* #1) and in doing so, saves the present from all their troubles. After moving the lantern that saved Alan Scott, the first Green Lantern, out of Scott's reach, Manhattan moves it back within Scott's grasp, allowing Alan Scott to become Green Lantern.[31] This creates a domino effect that sees the (re)formation of the Justice Society (omitted from the New 52), Clark Kent's adventures as Superboy, and the creation of the Legion of Super-Heroes (missing from DC publication since 2013, other than a guest appearance in a miniseries in 2015). In this way, Manhattan could arguably be seen as engaging in restorative nostalgia, which possibly was facilitated by his own mininostalgic awakening when looking at the photograph with fresh eyes. For the first time since becoming Dr. Manhattan, he was unable to see into the future, and with Superman's encouragement, looked to the past for answers. By gazing into and analyzing the past, Manhattan determines that Superman is the heart of the metaverse and that the multiverse actually responds to changes made within the metaverse. It's important to recognize that it is the act of looking into the past—and past timelines—that allows Manhattan to determine that every era of Superman needs to be preserved.[32] For the readers of DC Comics, this serves an epideictic function as well. Fans had long lamented the exclusion of the storied superhero team of the Justice Society of America (who have graced DC Comics since 1940)—this nostalgic recall of this team could be a way to galvanize the readership of DC and further move away from the direction of the New 52.

On a narrative level, it is challenging to believe that one brief exchange with Superman inspired Manhattan's first feelings of nostalgia since 1959. However, it is this feeling of nostalgia that subsequently facilitates the past merging with the present and thus serves as a very obvious instance of restorative nostalgia. Geoff Johns realizes that this is a pretty stark change for Manhattan; he observes in an interview that "Manhattan goes from one truth where we're all puppets on a string to another truth whereas maybe there are no strings and that maybe we have more control over this than he previously thought and that's a really important evolution for his character."[33] Johns goes on to note that he purposefully changes the way Manhattan talks after his exchange with Superman in an effort to show just how important Superman is within the DC Comics universe; Johns exalts in the same interview that Superman is "something to aspire to and be inspired by, what and who he is; that's what the whole series is talking about."[34] In this way, then, Manhattan becomes a mouthpiece for Geoff Johns, as Manhattan's rhetoric throughout the rest of the text following his exchange with Superman is nothing short of proselytizing Superman. As Manhattan alters the present, he glowingly refers to Superman in messianic terms. One might say that Manhattan has an awakening when he exults "I now understand Superman's true purpose. He will show them the way [. . .] He is the bridge stretching across generations that will lead everyone to peace."[35] In this way, Manhattan turns from self-proclaimed villain of Earth Prime[36] to epideictic orator composing a love letter to Superman and the rest of the DC Universe in an effort to inspire hope and unite the heroes. This is quite the shift for Dr. Manhattan. Throughout this series, he had been adamant that hope was a foolish endeavor. He tells Firestorm that "hope decays,"[37] and he later opines that hope does not last.[38] But by the end of *Doomsday Clock*, he believes that "hope is the north star of the metaverse."[39] Readers can trace Manhattan's conversion to his exchange with Superman; in this exchange, Superman clearly calls attention to the photograph Manhattan was repeatedly producing. It is this look into the past that opens Manhattan up to the possibility that past timelines were needed to preserve and support Superman. That is, Manhattan looks to the so-called truth of the past—the truth being that the JSA and Legion of Super-Heroes were integral to the development of Superman—to modify the troubling present and, in doing so, bring back hope to the world and strengthen the community of superheroes to take on the evils of the day. Moreover, the optimism that ends *Doomsday Clock* is exactly the kind of optimism that was missing in the New 52; given the strong aversion many DC fans had to the New 52, this serves as a powerful call for DC Comics to move in a more hopeful direction and thus reunite the DC Comics reader base.

CONCLUSION

In *Doomsday Clock*, we see restorative nostalgia at play when Dr. Manhattan literally re-examines the past to discover the "truth" that Superman is at the center of the metaverse because he is such a beacon of hope. This truth comes to light when Superman not only "saves" Manhattan's life, but he encourages Manhattan to reflect on how people from Osterman's past were important to him. While this seemingly creates an uneven narrative—this moment is brief, seemingly out of the blue, and entirely out of character for Dr. Manhattan—the unexpectedness only adds to the overall impact. Johns and Frank choose to have Manhattan be the creator of the New 52—at least in the narrative universe—and his cold, unfeeling imprint is felt by the loss of hope that largely marked the New 52. After all, how can Manhattan be expected to craft a world that is hopeful when he doesn't understand humanity anymore? Having Manhattan serve as the creator of the New 52 becomes a sharp rebuke of the entire line and an open acknowledgment that the tone of the reboot was more in line with the way Manhattan sees the world. This all changes when Manhattan unexpectedly feels hope from Superman, as he sees the importance of hope in the world and sets out to completely do away with the New 52; put differently, a now humanized Manhattan is able to (re)create the DC universe with Superman's ideology at the center. This humanity is seen not only as Manhattan restores the universe but also in the aftermath, as he takes to raising a child (the son of two villains introduced in *Doomsday Clock*) and dreams of what could have been with Janey (he notes that "it is a nice daydream to live in").[40] It's a complete character reversal. If we are to buy into the idea that Manhattan symbolizes the New 52, this character reversal ostensibly reverberates throughout the entire line of DC Comics, removing pessimism and replacing it with hope. Manhattan's narrative restoration of the past facilitates the epideictic rhetoric. Not only do Johns and Frank literally inject hope, they also bring back two beloved teams that were either untouched in the New 52 (JSA) or failed in the New 52 (Legion of Super-Heroes). Put together, these moments serve as epideictic rhetoric, as the text strives to bring together a fractured, jaded (reader) community.

NOTES

1. Svletlana Boym, "Nostalgia and Its Discontents," *The Hedgehog Review* (Summer 2007): 7.

2. William Kurlinkus, *Nostalgic Design: Rhetoric, Memory, and Democratizing Technology* (University of Pittsburgh Press, 2018), 28.

3. Michael Chabon, "The True Meaning of Nostalgia," *New Yorker*, March 25, 2017.

4. Nancy Jolma, "'As If There Was No Fear': Exploring Nostalgic Narrative in Bo Carpelan's Novel *Berg*," *Humanities* 7, no. 106 (2018): 3.

5. Svletlana Boym, "Nostalgia and Its Discontents," *The Hedgehog Review* (Summer 2007): 13.

6. Simon Eckstein, "'There's No Place Like Home': Reflective Nostalgia in *Titus Groan* and *Gormenghast*," in *Miracle Enough*, ed. G. Peter Winnington (Cambridge Scholars, 2012), 95.

7. Fredric Jameson, "Postmodernism, or, the Cultural Logic of Late Capitalism," Stanford University, Accessed October 1, 2020, https://prelectur.stanford.edu/lecturers/jameson/excerpts/postmod.html.

8. Svletlana Boym, "Nostalgia and Its Discontents," *The Hedgehog Review* (Summer 2007): 13.

9. Michael Pickering and Emily Keightly, "The Modalities of Nostalgia," *Current Sociology* 54, no. 919 (2006): 921.

10. Pickering and Keightly, 921.

11. Aristotle, *On Rhetoric*, translated by George Kennedy (Oxford University Press, 2006), 48–49.

12. Aristotle, 47.

13. Cynthia Miecznikowski Sheard, "The Public Value of Epideictic Rhetoric," *College English* 58, no. 7 (1996): 766.

14. Sheard, 765.

15. William Kurlinkus, *Nostalgic Design: Rhetoric, Memory, and Democratizing Technology* (University of Pittsburgh Press, 2018), 84.

16. Kurlinkus, 84.

17. David Hughes quoted in Sara J. Van Ness, *Watchmen as Literature* (McFarland, 2010), 13.

18. Sara J. Van Ness, 14.

19. Nicholas Barber, "*Watchmen*: The Moment Comic Books Grew Up," *BBC*, August 9, 2016, accessed November 10, 2020.

20. Alan Moore, "On Superheroes" interview by *Wired* staff, *Wired*, February 23, 2009, accessed November 10, 2020.

21. Aaron Sager, "Exclusive: DC Comics' Geoff Johns Reveals Teaser, Details on *Watchmen/Rebirth* Title *Doomsday Clock*," *SyFy*, January 8, 2019 (updated), accessed November 10, 2020.

22. Jason Serafino, "Where DC's New 52 Went So Wrong," *Tech Times*, May 24, 2016, accessed November 10, 2020.

23. Serafino.

24. DC Comics, "DC Entertainment Reveals First Details of 'REBIRTH' to Retailers at Comics Pro 2016," Press Release, February 18, 2016, DC Comics, accessed November 12, 2020.

25. Aaron Sager, "Exclusive: DC Comics' Geoff Johns Reveals Teaser, Details on *Watchmen/Rebirth* Title *Doomsday Clock*," *SyFy*, January 8, 2019 (updated), accessed November 10, 2020.

26. Geoff Johns and Gary Frank, *Doomsday Clock* No. 7 (2018): 28.

27. Geoff Johns and Gary Frank, *Doomsday Clock* No. 11 (2019): 12.

28. Geoff Johns and Gary Frank, *Doomsday Clock* No. 12 (2020): 13.

29. Johns and Frank, 19.

30. Johns and Frank, 19.

31. Johns and Frank, 33.

32. Geoff Johns, "Doomsday Clock," interview by Sam Stone, *CBR*, December 19, 2019, https://www.cbr.com/doomsday-clock-postgame-geoff-johns/.

33. Johns, "Doomsday Clock" interview.

34. Geoff Johns and Gary Frank, *Doomsday Clock* No. 12 (2020): 35.

35. Geoff Johns and Gary Frank, *Doomsday Clock* No. 10 (2019): 28.

36. Geoff Johns and Gary Frank, *Doomsday Clock* No. 9 (2019): 26.
37. Geoff Johns and Gary Frank, *Doomsday Clock* No. 12 (2020): 1.
38. Johns and Frank, 34.
39. Johns and Frank, 34.
40. Johns and Frank, 43–44.

Chapter 15

THE ADAPTATION OF NARRATIVE AND MUSICAL SOURCE MATERIAL IN HBO'S *WATCHMEN*

JAMES DENIS McGLYNN

Alan Moore's assessment of his original *Watchmen* narrative as being "beyond adaptation" is a stance that has regularly been reiterated in both scholarship and popular media, having been "uncritically echoed by uncountable online pundits, both academic and amateur alike."[1] It is perhaps unsurprising then that Damon Lindelof's deft navigation of this apparent obstacle was to be praised as one of the greatest achievements of his 2019 *Watchmen* series, which is often referred to as a "remix"—rather than a sequel or adaptation—of Moore and Gibbons's original narrative.[2] Lindelof's *Watchmen* decidedly avoids any direct adaptation of the original *Watchmen* narrative, yet, intriguingly, the resulting project remains prominently characterized by a complex adaptive logic that seems to inform almost every facet, if not every shot, of Lindelof's nine-part series, whether in the symbolism it pulls from Moore and Gibbons's comic, prominent stylistic parallels, or even certain shared narrative devices.[3]

However, one of the more surreptitious processes of adaptation that characterizes Lindelof's series is its soundtrack's notable adaptation of pre-existing music. Lindelof's *Watchmen* continually reworks and rearranges pre-existing musical material in all manner of eclectic ways, often facilitating important narrative, stylistic, and structural functions. In this sense, the series' soundtrack forms yet another strand of the seemingly all-encompassing aspirations for adaptation that underpinned Lindelof's vision for

Watchmen. Quite often, the *Watchmen* soundtrack seems to consciously adapt the functions served by depictions of music in graphic novels, with certain prominent soundtrack inclusions channeling specific musical moments from Moore and Gibbons's original comic. Furthermore, pre-existing music is frequently adapted and reworked throughout *Watchmen* in ways that appear to directly mirror the series' complex adaptation of its source text, whether in the playful rearrangements of pre-existing music that permeate Atticus Ross and Trent Reznor's original compositions, the many atypical and adventurous cover recordings that populate its eclectic compilation score, or the manner in which pre-existing music is prominently adapted by way of postproduction editing and digital effects. These are the qualities that sparked my most formative investigation into the centrality of music in Lindelof's series, leading me to further explore how *Watchmen*'s conscious resolve to adapt music's role from the comic appears to intentionally reinforce the series' wider aesthetic of adaptation.

This chapter is an examination of the role of music in HBO's *Watchmen*, in which I frame the series' soundtrack as an essential facet of Lindelof's seemingly all-encompassing aspirations for comic-to-screen adaptation. It illustrates how representations of music from the original *Watchmen* comic are adapted to function in the series, as well as exploring how the series' recurrent use of musical rearrangement constitutes and reinforces its prominent aesthetic of adaptation. Lindelof's *Watchmen* thus affords us a new entry point into several fertile areas of inquiry, inviting us to revisit (i) the musicality of the graphic novel, (ii) adaptations from comic to screen, and (iii) how music can form a narratively important constituent of such adaptations. It is around these three qualities that this chapter it structured. Above all, I hope to highlight one of the most impressive functions of the *Watchmen* soundtrack: how, by deftly adopting music as a central facet of its aesthetic of adaptation, the series enables audiences' vivid entry into its troubled protagonists' subjective experiences.

EXISTING SCHOLARSHIP ON MUSIC IN *WATCHMEN*

While descriptions of a supposed field of "*Watchmen* studies" may seem hyperbolic,[4] Moore and Gibbons's original graphic novel has indeed been represented in a substantial body of scholarship. The role of music in *Watchmen*'s various screen and print iterations has received less critical attention, yet some scholarship does exist. For example, a 2011 postgraduate study explores the soundtrack for Zack Snyder's 2009 adaptation.[5] Elsewhere, a chapter by Mary Borsellino examines the representation of music in the graphic novel. Borsellino's chapter essentially comprises a survey of references, impressively itemizing the many extratextual musical allusions that populate the original text and offering some cursory commentary on their narrative impact.[6] With specific reference to *Watchmen*, Tim Summers offers the only account that approaches a theorization of music's role in comics. Summers argues that, given the extent to which music's interaction with other forms of media has been explored, the study of music and comics comes as a timely and important undertaking: "With the emergence of 'comics studies' and the now well-established fields of research into both music and literature, and music and visual art, it is appropriate that music in comics may now be given consideration in an academic context."[7]

Although Summers claims that "no attempts have been made to interrogate the aesthetic effects that are created when comics involve themselves with music," it is important to note that several such studies do exist. Keiron Brown's assessment of music's representation in comics approaches a similarly novel mode of study to that of Summers.[8] Brown also cites several other publications that examine comics' relationship with music.[9] However, because Summers is the only other musicologist to have approached *Watchmen* in such depth (and given his ambitious defense of graphic novels as an inherently musical medium), his article remains an unavoidable point of reference for examinations of both *Watchmen* and music in graphic novels.

DEPICTIONS OF MUSIC IN GRAPHIC NOVELS

Before turning to Lindelof's *Watchmen*, it is also essential to take note of how musical idioms are employed in graphic novels more generally. At least some awareness of the forms that music can take in comics is imperative to understanding the role of music in Lindelof's series, especially given this chapter's central focus on the parallels between Lindelof's comic-to-screen adaptation of *Watchmen* and the adaptations of pre-existing music found therein.

Uses of music in comics have often been viewed as attempts to elevate or "literaturize" a graphic novel, or to otherwise signal more symbolic or artful aspirations to readers. Similarly, music's capacity to temporalize the graphic novel medium has received significant scholarly attention. Brown describes how the lion's share of "critical attention paid to the media of music and comics has historically focused on parallels between the temporal rhythm and pacing of music and the implied rhythm and temporality of comics."[10] In *Comics and Sequential Art*, the American cartoonist Will Eisner similarly defines comic books' graphical "reality" by way of analogy with music: "A comic becomes 'real' when time and timing is factored into creation. In music or other forms of auditory communication where rhythm or 'beat' is achieved, this is done with actual lengths of time. In graphics the experience is conveyed by the use of illusions and symbols and their arrangement."[11]

Consonant with Eisner's account, so much writing on temporality in comics has examined examples that incorporate visual representations of music.[12] The "Kitty Kat Keller" song in Moore's *V For Vendetta* (1988) and its conspicuous use of staff notation is undoubtedly the most frequently cited example, with Summers even describing its containing chapter as being "underscored."[13] Here, Summers highlights the widely accepted capacity of the graphic novel to *score* itself,[14] transcending the silence of the medium and generating an effect "loosely comparable to a film's soundtrack."[15]

However, perhaps the most important function aligned with music in comics (and one Lindelof prominently adapts, as this chapter explores) is its contribution to the hermeneutic engagement that graphic novels cultivate in their readership. Hillary Chute vividly describes the position of constant inquiry that audiences are placed in, whereby "a reader of comics not only fills in the gaps between panels but also works with the often disjunctive back-and-forth of reading and looking for meaning."[16] Summers similarly aligns this quality with comics' unique mode of literary consumption, arguing that the "significance of music in comics is that it serves as a prompt to musical hermeneutics."[17] This is visible in comics' use of songs, musical excerpts and lyrical material to create complex networks of underlying metaphorical significance, "[constructing their] readership as literate and proficient in interpreting such recontextualizations of musical meaning."[18] Such musical juxtapositions are typically either consonant with a narrative, forging the same "allusive authorial commentary often provided by the lyrics of pre-existing pop songs heard in film"[19] or, by contrast, "exhibit conspicuous indifference," or what Michel Chion would characterize in film as "anempathetic" music.[20] As I will later examine, the original *Watchmen* comic's use of musical material for ironic or anempathetic effect is especially adapted in the soundtrack for Lindelof's series.

Even for those who maintain "sound is not really a strong element in graphic novels," it is widely conceded that "*Watchmen*, in particular, makes extensive connections to songs which are meaningful to the plot."[21] Summers, Brown, Eisner, and Xavier Xerexes all draw on terminology from film music studies in their assessments of music in comics; moreover, they all acknowledge the shared capacity of music in both graphic novels and screen scoring to facilitate (i) the communication of symbolic or literary aspirations,

(ii) extratextual commentary, or (iii) shifts in temporality. While there are doubtless other forms that music takes in comics, these three functions are those most prominently adapted in HBO's *Watchmen*, recapturing the central reflexivity of the original graphic novel that Lindelof so visibly strove to retain.

WATCHMEN (2019) AND ITS ADAPTATION OF THE GRAPHIC NOVEL

Lindelof's *Watchmen* flaunts its status as an adaptation as a central facet of its style and narration. The series adapts countless aspects of the original comic's symbolic, stylistic, and reflexive gestures to function televisually. This can be seen in the near-continuous stream of visual cues from the comic (i.e., the "Hiroshima Lovers" graffiti tag), retained stylistic motifs (the episode titles which, mirroring the graphic novel, are introduced without fanfare some way into each instalment, using the same emboldened typeface), and other more elaborate narrative adaptations (the fictional "series-within-a-series" *American Hero Story*, which co-opts the same extranarrative framework served by the graphic novel's "comic-within-a-comic" *Tales of the Black Freighter*). Such citations are potent, amplified by their recurrence and encouraging audiences' investigative, hermeneutic engagement with the series—what Jenkins might call "cultural activator[s], setting in motion its decipherment, speculation and elaboration."[22] One memorable example of such a citation is the blood that we see dripping onto police chief Judd Crawford's badge in the first episode's final shot, mirroring the graphic novel's opening and linking the central murder mysteries that initiate the plots of both narratives. These numerous debts to the original *Watchmen* might be regarded as the series' primary means of establishing its prominent aesthetic of adaptation, facilitating its communication of a rich sense of density and its evocation of a complex, infinite world beyond what is depicted onscreen: the "vast suggested histories of wonder" that *Watchmen* co-creator Dave Gibbons cites as one of the comic medium's defining features.[23]

Where then does music figure in *Watchmen*'s aesthetic of adaptation, and how does it contribute to communicating this profound density that Lindelof transposes from Moore and Gibbons's original comic? Even the most surface-level examination of the series reveals the centrality of music in *Watchmen*. Like many of the other qualities that Lindelof adapts from the graphic novel, the series' soundtrack seems to be carefully structured to reinforce this profound sense of density, suggesting the existence of a rich history and storied society beyond the confines of the series' nine-episode narrative arc. Furthermore, given how often we have said that music is used to narrative, stylistic, and structural effect in the comic medium, as well as Lindelof's concerted efforts to adapt so many other aspects of the original *Watchmen*, it seems logical that music was to be approached with the same degree of considered stylization in his HBO series. Crucially, music also contributes to the investigative audience engagement that *Watchmen* strives to cultivate in viewers, directly adapting the hermeneutic engagement with which Summers and Chute characterize the experience of consuming comics. Numerous elements of the soundtrack are employed to this effect. By sonically adapting this potent kernel of the graphic novel, Lindelof's series encourages the same active audience interpretation and "looking for meaning" in its soundtrack: whether through conspicuous repetition of certain music, the fragmentation, reordering and processing of the soundtrack's constituent elements, or the series' notable incorporation of musical rearrangements, such that rearranged variations of the soundtrack's pre-existing music garner important leitmotivic significance across the narrative.

This phenomenon persists throughout the *Watchmen* soundtrack and is especially evident in the many ways the series adapts music's functionality from the comic. For example, the soundtrack often sits in ironic counterpoint to *Watchmen*'s narrative, just as Borsellino and Summers describe uses of music in the graphic novel: "Poor Jud Is Dead" from *Oklahoma!* prefigures Judd Crawford's hanging in Tulsa, Oklahoma; "The Blue Danube," "Rhapsody in Blue," and "Mr. Blue" all accompany scenes involving the blue-skinned Dr. Manhattan; songs by the Ink Spots evoke the Seventh Kavalry's Rorschach masks. Other musical cues serve anempathetic functions similar to those in the comic (Eartha Kitt's languid delivery of "Santa Baby" accompanies a frenzied home attack sequence), while the series' "ostentatiously 'literary' use [of lyrics] as titles"[24] facilitates the same "literaturizing" function as in many of the comic's chapter titles. The series even adapts some of the most minor musical details from the comic: Pirate Jenny derives her name from Brecht and Weill's *Die Dreigroschenoper*, the play that inspired the comic's *Black Freighter* sections;[25] Devo's song "Mongoloid" and the episode title "She Was Killed by Space Junk" (a Devo lyric) harken to Laurie Blake's allusions to the idiosyncratic rock band in the comic; "You're My Thrill," heard diegetically in the comic, accompanies Angela Abar's conversation with Blake, as the latter discusses the "yahoos [she] used to run around with" during the events of the original *Watchmen*.[26]

Other more complex musical structures are also forged in the *Watchmen* soundtrack, the most memorable being the series' adoption of *Oklahoma!* as a central extratextual narrative frame. At its simplest, this reinforces Lindelof's resituation of *Watchmen* from Manhattan to Tulsa, Oklahoma, beginning with the first episode's title (the lyric "It's Summer and We're Running Out of Ice"), along with a diegetic performance of the musical's title song and Judd Crawford's drunken rendition of "People Will Say We're in Love." As the series progresses, *Watchmen* continually develops this *Oklahoma!* analogy, anticipating both Judd's death (the similarly named Jud dies in the musical) and the posthumous revelation concerning his criminal history (Jud is the antagonist in *Oklahoma!*). This extratextual analogy continues to the series' finale, in which the *Oklahoma!* opening number "Oh, What a Beautiful Morning" is inversely used at the series' conclusion. The song's original associations (introducing Oklahoma's peaceful and pastoral scenery) anempathetically juxtapose with the bodies that now line the Tulsa streets. Angela Abar even returns to the theater in which *Oklahoma!* was performed in the first episode, the stage now silent and bare. While an initial reading of *Watchmen* might view its "ostentatiously literary" use of song lyrics as titles as the extent of its musical significance,[27] the lengths to which Lindelof goes to incorporate music as part of his series' broader symbolism and structure speaks to the far greater weight placed on musically adapting the comic.

Of course, it would be impossible to suggest that *Watchmen*'s soundtrack does not conform to other more standard or clichéd scoring tropes. Western art music is used as a time-tested signifier of "high culture,"[28] while the classical era's Germanic associations are continually aligned with the series' white supremacist antagonists (in particular, Mozart's "Lacrimosa").[29] Yet, while not all aspects of the soundtrack conform so closely to the series' aesthetic of adaptation, there is enough evidence to make a compelling case that musical adaptation constituted a central facet of Lindelof's vision for *Watchmen*. The series employs music to adapt the comic book medium's characteristic density, invite audiences' hermeneutic engagement, adapt music's functions from the comic, imbue the narrative with stylized "literary" qualities, and establish the series' reflexivity and sardonic self-referentiality—qualities that are frequently aligned with music's role in the original *Watchmen* comic.

However, there is one further musical idiom in *Watchmen* that neatly mirrors the series' adaptation of the graphic novel; that is, the series' recurrent adaptation of pre-existing music throughout its soundtrack, rendering musical rearrangement a central component of *Watchmen*'s overall adaptive aesthetic. The final section of this chapter thus explores *Watchmen*'s rearrangement of pre-existing music as further evidence of the apparently all-encompassing aspirations for adaptation that informed Lindelof's series.

MUSICAL REARRANGEMENT IN THE *WATCHMEN* (2019) SOUNDTRACK

Just as *Watchmen* flaunts its status as an adaptation, the soundtrack for Lindelof's series similarly foregrounds its own adaptive logic by establishing musical rearrangement as a central stylistic trait. In lieu of any consistent definition for rearrangement, I ordain the term to describe any artistically motivated adaptation or reinterpretation of all or part of an existing musical composition, with all its associative "baggage." Of course, this departs from other, more prevalent understandings of the term, which typically view rearrangement as synonymous with more straightforward processes of reinstrumentation. Yet, given the diversity of ways in which pre-existing music is reworked in *Watchmen*, I believe that my use of the term to denote this far broader set of "musical remakes" seems appropriate. Rearrangement is established as a part of *Watchmen*'s audiovisual identity from the outset, with pre-existing music being adapted in a wide variety of ways: whether digital effects are used to rework pre-existing recordings, or postproduction editing is deftly employed to reinvent the series' pre-existing music, affording *Watchmen*'s music editors a more explicitly compositional role (for example, in the episode "A God Walks into Abar," we hear Strauss's "Blue Danube" interwoven with Offenbach's "Belle nuit, ô nuit d'amour," such that both compositions are perceived as one continuous whole: Figure 1). However, the most convincing evidence of this idiom is undoubtedly the selection of musical rearrangements and extratextual citations that populate the *Watchmen* soundtrack and intricately interact with its narrative.

FIGURE 1. COMPOSITIONAL MUSIC EDITING IN *WATCHMEN*

(Episode 8, "A God Walks Into Abar")

Cue	Title	Time	Bar #	Scene
1	"An der schönen, blauen Donau," Op. 314 Johann Strauss II (1867)	07:25–9:18	1–52	"The manor is a special place, a place I'm connected to from my childhood"
2	-	9:18–9:36	61–76	'This is the first time I know love"
3	"Belle nuit, ô nuit d'amour" ("Barcarolle") Jacques Offenbach (1881)	9:46–11:23	18–52	"Now here are some new faces . . ."
4	-	11:23–13:12	53–91	Jon opens package (shifts to nondiegetic) "Make it your purpose to make something beautiful"

Many of these rearrangements are facilitated through so-called *hyper-orchestration* techniques: contemporary scoring methods which adopt digital edits, miking techniques, and other production processes to elicit musical variation and narrative signification.[30] It is perhaps unsurprising that Trent Reznor and Atticus Ross's original music for the series should incorporate such techniques: in his definition for hyperorchestration, Sergi Casanelles makes specific reference to Reznor and Ross's score for *The Social Network* (2010), in which mic positionings are used to generate variations of the soundtrack's prerecorded piano music. Alongside the synth pulses, jarring modal chord progressions (e.g., "WATCH OVER THIS BOY"),[31] and harshly distorted guitar grinds that are now synonymous with their scoring collaborations (e.g., "NUN WITH A MOTHERF*&*ING GUN"), Reznor and Ross' *Watchmen* score demonstrates an acute awareness of hyperorchestration techniques' potential to generate such variation. One memorable example is their nonvocalized rearrangement of David Bowie's "Life on Mars?" which accompanies the series' long-anticipated return of Dr. Manhattan (who, contrary to the protagonists' assertions and Bowie's sung inquiries, was not on Mars). The rearrangement begins as a faithful piano reduction of Bowie's original arrangement. However, prominent synthesized bass pulses soon transform our perceived meter of the music and, at the song's climax (Bowie's sustained lyric " . . . Mars"), the original accompaniment is cut short, replaced with several looped iterations of the chorus. The music becomes increasingly submerged in a constant crescendo of reverberated hyperorchestral sonorities until the cue's sudden end.

For the remainder of this chapter, I will explore what is undoubtedly the series' most structured use of rearrangement, in the episode "Little Fear of Lightning," which is an hour-long character study of Wade Tillman. The way that musical rearrangement is used to communicate Tillman's experience as an adult PTSD sufferer serves as the series' most complete textual study of musical rearrangement's explicitly narrative function. The episode's title is derived from a well-known aphorism about fear from *20,000 Leagues Under the Sea*, yet this harkening to Verne's famous nautical adventure might similarly be intended to evoke the giant squid creatures shared by the plots of both *20,000 Leagues* and *Watchmen*. This raises an interesting point regarding Lindelof's adaptation of the "alien squid" from the original *Watchmen*, through which the superhero-turned-antagonist Adrian Veidt engineers the catastrophic "11/2" event in New York. While this plot point serves as the denouement of the original *Watchmen* narrative, Lindelof's *Watchmen* instead adopts this supernatural event as the starting point for a much more human narrative, examining the psychological and sociological impact that this hypothetical catastrophe could have borne for the next generation of New Yorkers. In Lindelof's words:

> Obviously, there's a silliness to saying a giant transdimensional cephalopod with one eye basically drops into the middle of Manhattan and the resulting psychic shock wave kills three million people. . . . But when you want to really ground the absurdity into something that's tangible and people will feel, I think the idea of PTSD . . . the idea that the squid was literally genetically engineered to cause people emotional trauma so that many years after this event, they would still fear it. We needed to palpably relate that to the audience.[32]

In this respect, Lindelof treats 11/2 as a prompt for this episode's three-dimensional psychological profile of Tillman, exploring the impact that a disaster of this magnitude could have hypothetically borne for another generation of Americans, in the intermittent years between Moore and Gibbons's original narrative and the events of the HBO series. Crucially, this is achieved through a complex network of musical rearrangements that unite the episode's recurrent harkening to the disaster.

In the cold opening, Tillman is revealed to have been visiting the nearby Hoboken during 11/2, as a young Jehovah's Witness. The episode consequently follows Tillman in the present (now the masked detective "Looking Glass"), depicting the impact of his 11/2 survival on his day-to-day life and debilitating paranoia. The episode's various vignettes ultimately culminate in Tillman's discovery of the true conspiracy behind 11/2: that it was a hoax engineered by one culpable individual. In this way, the challenging focal point of "Little Fear . . . " is its stark portrayal of a man who discovers that his entire adult perception of the world is founded in lies, as we watch him uncover the vast conspiracy that precipitated his traumatic past.[33]

Pre-existing music is the most important vehicle through which Lindelof's *Watchmen* establishes and reinforces Tillman's experience of trauma. The soundtrack for "Little Fear . . . " is quite distinct from that of other episodes, largely because of the highly structured and narratively motivated way pre-existing music is incorporated, restated, and rearranged. Diegetic source music heard during 11/2 recurs throughout the episode, garnering a leitmotivic association with trauma, mirroring music's real-world capacity to enmesh itself with traumatic memories,[34] and convincingly reinforcing Kathryn Kalinak's view of the score as "one of the most potent . . . textual operators for conveying altered states of consciousness."[35] The music in question is George Michael's "Careless Whisper," which is heard on no less than

FIGURE 2. REARRANGEMENTS OF GEORGE MICHAEL'S "CARELESS WHISPER" (1982)
(Episode 5, "Little Fear of Lightning")

	Rearrangement	Time	Scene
1	Original 1982 recording - George Michael Reworked through hyperorchestration techniques	05:11	Roxy tempts young Wade in the Hall of Mirrors Association with traumatic memory established
2	"Careless Whisper" - Alexandr Misko Solo acoustic guitar rearrangement	21:49	Cynthia: ". . . and for seven years I tried to convince you I wasn't going to run off with your clothes and leave you naked."
3	"NO RHYTHM" - Trent Reznor and Atticus Ross Solo piano rearrangement	25:12	Tillman: "I thought about that one-eyed fucker all the time and it terrified me, but I am no longer afraid."
4	"NO RHYTHM" variation - Trent Reznor and Atticus Ross Block chords only, no melody	30:16	Renee: ". . . and the girl's stumbling around Herald Square, walking under the tentacles, through all the dead bodies . . ."
5	"Careless Whisper" - Nataly Dawn	51:31	Montage, featuring present-day Tillman at Tulsa PD and young Tillman during 11/2

five occasions throughout the episode: whether in its original arrangement, pre-existing cover renditions, furtively rearranged in the original score or reworked through hyperorchestration techniques (Figure 2).

The first use of "Careless Whisper" (during the introductory 11/2 flashback) is the only time we hear its original recording. Although seemingly diegetic, the song's recognizable saxophone hook is playfully synched to the moment a distressed Wade reluctantly accepts the sexual advances of a local teenager, Roxy. This metadiegetic status of the music cue is further reaffirmed when the 11/2 disaster occurs, at which point "Careless Whisper" begins to mutate. The song is slowed to half speed, resulting in hauntingly distorted vocal qualities. What's more, loud sustained sonorities, initially perceived to represent the diegetic "ringing" in Tillman's ears after the explosion, soon become distinctly musical and are audibly pitched at the same E–D descent of the famous "Careless Whisper" saxophone hook. At this point, we can thus discern that the music of George Michael is being adapted and intermeshed with sound design that is discernibly musical, reinforcing the compositionally motivated decisions informing its adaptation. We might consequently regard this instance as the first thematic statement (and variation) of "Careless Whisper," setting the precedent for its recurrence to signify Tillman's tarnished memories of the song as an adult PTSD sufferer. Four subsequent reworkings of "Careless Whisper" further reinforce this association with Tillman's traumatic experience of 11/2, such that the song's recurrence garners a semiotic potency and continually harkens to the memories precipitating Tillman's lifelong struggle with trauma.

What is notable about the recurrence of "Careless Whisper" is its capacity to communicate incredibly specific aspects of Tillman's relationship with his trauma. The second "Careless Whisper" is a pre-existing guitar cover by Alexandr Misko, first popularized in a 2017 YouTube video. This sparse, melancholic rendition nondiegetically accompanies a scene where Tillman meets his ex-wife, Cynthia. The narrative rationale behind the song's recurrence is quickly revealed, as Cynthia implies the reasons for their divorce was Tillman's failure to process his trauma. Interestingly, she implies that Tillman's PTSD is just as entangled in his teenage humiliation by Roxy as his experience of 11/2 (we hear her say "For seven years I tried to convince you I wasn't going to run off with your clothes and leave you naked").

The third time we hear "Careless Whisper" is particularly significant, as it is the first time the song is newly rearranged in Reznor and Ross's original score. The cue, whimsically titled "NO RHYTHM," is heard during Tillman's chairing of his "Extra-Dimensional Anxiety" support group. Before "NO RHYTHM" is introduced, one of the group's young contributors provides explicit dialogic reinforcement of the themes of trauma already aligned with the song: "There's this thing, genetic trauma . . . Basically if something really bad happens to your parents, it gets locked into their DNA. So, when my mom got hit by the blast, even though I wasn't born until ten years after 11/2, it's like I inherited her pain." In the moments that ensue, Tillman's reaction comprises a complex trajectory of well-realized emotions, exposing fears that Tillman conceals from his fellow attendees (the scene cuts to the concealed EMR-blocking lining of Tillman's baseball cap, as the speaker unwittingly says, "I don't want to end up one of those fucking nutters with my head wrapped in that magic tin foil"). As Tillman responds, the scene effectively charts his genuine confrontation of his traumatic memories and rejection of "genetic trauma" (epitomized in the candor of his incantation, "I am no longer afraid"). The accompanying solo piano rearrangement of "Careless Whisper" during Tillman's candid monologue is significant, especially considering piano music's long-established associations with Romanticism, emotivity, and even touch-sensitivity (from which the instrument derives its name, *pianoforte*). Yet, along with the sincerity and emotional development this piano music seems to empathetically reinforce, the fact that "NO RHYTHM" is a new rearrangement of "Careless Whisper" for *Watchmen* is vitally important, implying a leitmotivic intentionality that the episode's other "Careless Whisper" covers cannot. This third iteration also provides evidence of other facets of Reznor and Ross' compositional input: I have already described how their rearrangement of Bowie's "Life on Mars?" departs from that song's original arrangement, omitting a prominent chord progression at the song's climax. In an intriguing parallel, "NO RHYTHM" transplants the missing progression from "Life on Mars?" as the basis of its "Careless Whisper" reharmonization. In the first four bars of "NO RHYTHM," the same descending chromatic bassline omitted from "LIFE ON MARS" accompanies the piano's non-vocalized "Careless Whisper" melody, varied only by its downward major 4th transposition (the G-E descent thus becomes D-B).

A further two iterations of "Careless Whisper" reappropriate the song to represent other facets of the protagonist's ongoing relationship with trauma. After meeting another of the support group's attendees, Renee, a rearrangement based on "NO RHYTHM" accompanies Renee's spoken account of her own post-11/2 trauma. This time, the "Careless Whisper" melody is removed, yet the reharmonized chord progression of "NO RHYTHM" is used to the same leitmotivic ends. The final rearrangement of "Careless Whisper," Nataly Dawn's bossa nova-infused cover, accompanies a montage of Tillman's daily goings-on after his discovery of Veidt's 11/2 conspiracy. Here, the rearranged "Careless Whisper" is closely aligned with Tillman's discovery of the carefully planned events that precipitated 11/2. We witness a short montage, incorporating shots of the vulnerable teenage Tillman, bodies lining Hoboken in 1985, the adult Tillman arriving at Tulsa PD, and his newly redundant EMR-blocking mask, idle on its stand. This montage, accompanied by Dawn's understated reworking of "Careless Whisper," seems to consciously reinforce the transformed narrative that Tillman's revelation has imposed on his life. Although he ambles through the same routine, his perception of the world and his trauma are altogether transformed.

This episode offers convincing evidence of music's key role in Lindelof's adaptation of *Watchmen*. In "Little Fear . . . ," the rearrangement of preexisting music is effectively employed to garner narrative functions inspired by real-world psychological connections between musical and traumatic experiences. Furthermore, the soundtrack's diverse musical sources (diegetic, nondiegetic, metadiegetic) and eclectic modes of rearrangement (whether through hyperorchestration techniques, pre-existing cover renditions, reharmonizations, or instrumental variation) enable our vivid entry into Tillman's subjective experiences.

Interestingly, this stylized and narratively engaged approach to music and trauma is not unique to this episode of *Watchmen* and was a clearly a central consideration in creating some of the series' other vivid character

Figure 3. Metadiegetic visions of William Reeves's piano accompanist mother.

studies. In a later episode for example, the exact same method elucidates another protagonist's relationship with their traumatic past. The episode "This Extraordinary Being" focusses on William Reeves (Jovan Adepo) and charts the events that would later inspire his masked vigilantism as Hooded Justice. Just as "Careless Whisper" is aligned with Tillman's memory of 11/2, so too is Reeves's childhood memory of his parents' murder in the 1921 Tulsa Massacre associated with music he heard during the atrocity: his mother's piano accompaniment for his favorite silent film, *Trust in the Law!* This original composition ("TRUST IN THE LAW") recurs throughout the episode, linking scenes concerning Reeves's future with the tragic events that would eventually inspire his crime-fighting vocation. Crucially, this piano music is always performed by a spectral vision of Reeves's deceased mother, metadietically audiovisualizing Reeves's experience of trauma (Figure 3).

CONCLUSION

Having explored the diverse ways in which pre-existing music is adapted in *Watchmen* (whether through hyperorchestration techniques, compositionally conceived music editing, atypical cover renditions, or original rearrangements), it is impossible to ignore the aesthetic and narrative consequences of musical rearrangement in the series. Besides forming a recognizable facet of the series' stylized adaptation, the structured incorporation of rearrangement throughout *Watchmen* implies a great degree of consideration and compositional intentionality behind even the most innocuous musical decisions.

This impression is compounded when we examine the eclectic functionality that the adaptation of pre-existing music serves in the series: whether enabling our vivid perception of subjective points of audition, structurally buttressing the series' complex narrative arcs, adapting music's function from the comics, or facilitating the series' nuanced psychological explorations of its protagonists.

This chapter frames musical rearrangement as a central thread of *Watchmen*'s wider aesthetic of adaptation. Lindelof's series does not merely adapt Moore and Gibbons's original narrative, but the very medium in which it was conceived and first came to life, simulating graphic novels' allusive density and encouraging the same sense of hermeneutic engagement that comics demand of their readers. Given the "underscored" quality so often attributed to graphic novels in scholarship, it may seem inevitable that music was to form such a central aspect of Lindelof's *Watchmen* adaptation. However, I believe the real innovation of the series' adaptation can be found in the curious parallels between Moore and Gibbons's "graphic-novelization" of music, Lindelof's adaptation of their graphic novel, and *Watchmen*'s adaptation of the pre-existing music contained therein. Based on these conspicuously shared processes, I believe *Watchmen* stands out as not only an important example of innovation in comics-to-screen adaptation, but also as an intriguing exemplar of rearrangement's eclectic narrative potential in current scoring practices more generally.

NOTES

1. Aaron Taylor, "The Continuing Adventures of the 'Inherently Unfilmable' Book: Zack Snyder's *Watchmen*," *The Journal of Cinema and Media Studies* 56, no. 2 (2017): 126.

2. Megan Farokhmanesh, "Damon Lindelof's *Watchmen* Will Be a 'Remix' with Original Characters, Not a Remake," *The Verge*. November 18, 2020, https://www.theverge.com/2018/5/23/17383826/damon-lindelof-watchmen-remix-original-characters-remake; Joshua Meyer, "HBO's *Watchmen* Demonstrates the Right Way to 'Remix' a Classic," */Film*, October 19, 2019, https://www.slashfilm.com/why-watchmen-works.

3. These many narrative, visual, and symbolic debts to Moore and Gibbons's *Watchmen* comic will undoubtedly be confronted in more detail by other scholars in this collection (e.g., the recognizable *Watchmen* "smiley" is formed by egg yolks when Angela Abar is baking; the series' episode titles mirror those of the graphic novel; an equivalent newsstand vendor character provides the same expositional role as in the graphic novel, reminding viewers of the peripheral city dwellers whose lives are being affected by the protagonists' actions).

4. Jason S. Polley, "Watching the Watchmen, Mediating the Mediators," *Literature Compass* 10, no. 8 (August 1, 2013): 594.

5. Andreana Marchi et al., "Who Listens to the Watchmen? A Sound Study on the Filmic Adaptation *Watchmen*," *Estação Literária* 7 (2011): 162–75.

6. Mary Borsellino, "The Ghost of You: *Watchmen* and Music," in *Minutes to Midnight: Twelve Essays on Watchmen*, ed. Richard Bensam (Edwardsville: Sequart Research & Literacy Organization, 2011), 24–37.

7. Tim Summers, "'Sparks of Meaning': Comics, Music and Alan Moore," *Journal of the Royal Musical Association* 140, no. 1 (2015): 3, https://doi.org/10.1080/02690403.2015.1008865.

8. Kieron Brown, "Musical Sequences in Comics," *The Comics Grid: Journal of Comics Scholarship* 3, no. 1 (2013): 1–6, https://doi.org/10.5334/cg.aj.

9. Will Eisner, *Comics and Sequential Art: Principles and Practices from the Legendary Cartoonist* (New York: W. W. Norton, 2008); Qiana Whitted, "Blues Comics," *The Hooded Utilitarian*, August 24, 2011, http://comixtalk.com/music_and_comics_two_great_tastes_taste_great_together/; Lian W. Peters, "Music in Eric Drooker's *Flood!*," *Journal of Graphic Novels and Comics* 4, no. 2 (December 1, 2013): 332–45, https://doi.org/10.1080/21504857.2012.758164.

10. Brown, 352.

11. Eisner, 24.

12. Brown cites the use of handwritten staff notation to represent jazz improvisation in Dave McKean's *Cages* and chord diagrams to depict garage rock performances in Bryan Lee O'Malley's *Scott Pilgrim*. See Brown, 1.

13. Summers, 6; Brown, 3.

14. This analogy excludes audiovisual webcomics that are indeed scored by composers, along with comics that include accompanying soundtracks: Xaviar Xerexes cites several such examples, including Kean Soo's *Exit Music*, Jonathan Altschuler and Colleen Macisaac's *Music Comics* and Cat Garza's *Those Were the Salad Days*. See Xerexes, "Music and Comics: Two Great Tastes That Taste Great Together?," *Comix Talk*, March 19, 2006, http://comixtalk.com/music_and_comics_two_great_tastes_taste_great_together/.

15. Brown, 1.

16. Hillary Chute, "Comics as Literature? Reading Graphic Narrative," *PMLA* 123, no. 2 (2008): 452.

17. Tim Summers, *Understanding Video Game Music* (Cambridge: Cambridge University Press, 2016), 140.

18. Summers, "Sparks of Meaning," 7.

19. Summers, "Sparks of Meaning," 6.

20. Michel Chion, *Audio-Vision: Sound on Screen*, trans. Claudia Gorbman (New York: Columbia University Press, 1994), 8.

21. Marchi et al., 164.

22. Henry Jenkins, *Convergence Culture: Where Old and New Media Collide* (New York: New York University Press, 2006), 97.

23. Alan Moore and Dave Gibbons, *Watchmen: The Deluxe Edition* (New York: DC Comics, 2013), 7.

24. Summers, "Sparks of Meaning," 8.

25. Borsellino.

26. Later, Laurie discusses her mother's rape by Eddie Blake (who, in the original *Watchmen*, is revealed to be her father), all the while accompanied by "You're My Thrill." In Freudian terms, this musical-narrative juxtaposition might be convincingly read as an attempt to musically convey oedipal desire, especially given (i) her reminiscing to 1940 and Blake's rape of her mother, (ii) Laurie's attempted sexual advance on Blake in 1966, being unaware that he was her father, and (iii) the indelible link forged in the graphic novel between "You're My Thrill" and Laurie's first successful sexual encounter with Dan Dreiberg.

27. Summers, "Sparks of Meaning," 8.

28. Anahid Kassabian, *Hearing Film: Tracking Identifications in Contemporary Hollywood Film Music* (New York: Routledge, 2001), 32.

29. It is interesting to note the similar associations forged between Mozart's "Lacrimosa" and traditions of institutional racism in the second series of *The Crown* (2016–). In the episode "Imbroglio," we hear the piece during a flashback to 1937, in which the young Prince Philip is seen among the funeral procession for his sister, Princess Cecile of Greece and Denmark. In this scene, the young prince is dwarfed among the swastika-emblazoned streets of Darmstadt under Nazi rule. While the equivalent associations lent to "Lacrimosa" in *The Crown* present us with an intriguing parallel, the funereal origins of the Mozart's *Requiem* mass (originally commissioned by Count Franz von Walsegg for his late wife in 1791) renders this use of the piece more conventional (if not clichéd) in recent soundtracks, in which "Lacrimosa" is often heard accompanying similarly morbid narrative events.

30. Sergi Casanelles, "Mixing as a Hyperorchestration Tool," in *The Palgrave Handbook of Sound Design and Music in Screen Media*, ed. Liz Greene and Danijela Kulezic-Wilson (London: Palgrave Macmillan, 2016), 57.

31. All track titles are capitalized in the official *Watchmen* soundtrack release. This is undoubtedly an attempt to conjure imagery of the original comic's canary yellow typeface, imbuing the soundtrack with the same "transmedia logic that drives the economic structure of the entertainment industry" in which comic book culture has long gestated. See Angela Ndalianis, "Why Comics Studies?," *Cinema Journal* 50, no. 3 (Spring 2011), 114.

32. Damon Lindelof, "*Watchmen*: Damon Lindelof Explains the Whole Squid Thing," interview by Adam Chitwood, Collider, November 17, 2019, https://collider.com/watchmen-squid-explained-damon-lindelof/.

33. Given the centrality of this revelation, this episode's title might also be said to evoke the similarly fallacious revelation concerning *20,000 Leagues*'s own squid, which, in Verne's novel, is revealed to be Captain Nemo's *Nautilus* submarine. Nemo also features in another of Moore's graphic novels, *The League of Extraordinary Gentlemen*. Given the characteristic extratextual density of the comic medium and the extent to which we have said *Watchmen* adapts this density, the significance of these allusions seems quite intentional.

34. James McDonald, "Rock and Memory: A Search for Meaning," *Popular Music and Society* 17, no. 3 (1993): 1.

35. Kathryn Marie Kalinak, *Settling the Score: Music and the Classical Hollywood Film* (Madison: University of Wisconsin Press, 1992), 178.

Chapter 16

DIVERSE FAMILY STRUCTURES IN *WATCHMEN*

Who's in This Family Tree Anyway?

TRACY E. MORAN VOZAR

The sins of the father are to be laid upon the children.

—WILLIAM SHAKESPEARE, *THE MERCHANT OF VENICE*

People who wear masks are driven by trauma. They're obsessed with justice because of some injustice they suffered, usually when they were kids.

—LAURIE BLAKE (NÉE JUSPECZYK)

Family dynamics might not be the first theme you think of when you reflect on HBO's 2019 *Watchmen* series. For a caregiver and child psychologist, however, the strong themes pertaining to diverse family structures and family systems theory are front and center. Notable themes that permeate the current series and tie it to its preceding comics and film include intergenerational attachment and trauma, separation, grief, and loss of loved ones. Throughout the narrative, an overarching question of "Who makes a family?" along with metaphors of chickens and eggs and striking family tree imagery link the series' episodes. Attachment styles, or the ways in which children relate to their caregivers that later influence their adult relationships, are showcased in the interactions among family members. In particular, a looming, at times protective, at times absent, and at times menacing image of the roles of parents weaves throughout *Watchmen*—the seemingly contradictory roles of Lady Trieu as loving, devoted daughter and harsh, uncaring mother and dynamic of Judd to Angela as benevolent father figure and prime betrayer. These are fascinating story lines and notable examples of attachment styles playing out on screen. Another theme of good versus evil or heroes versus villains—or, more accurately put, empaths versus narcissists—unfolds within families and across characters' relationships. Angela as trustworthy, caring matriarch juxtaposed with the harsh cruelty and psychopathy of Ozymandias provides a dialectic of caregiving styles that is enthralling.

WHAT IS A FAMILY?

As a viewer as well as a psychologist who studies and works clinically with children and their families, many of *Watchmen*'s scenes, episodes, connections to prior comics and films, as well as the overall arc of the series' narrative kept harkening back to themes of family dynamics. At the heart of this thematic thread are questions of "What is a family?" and "Who is a caregiver?" The narrow, Westernized, and largely Caucasian view of the nuclear family with the mother as the central caregiver was the hallmark of the era the *Watchmen* comic so vividly depicts. The nuclear family archetype certainly does not fit with the diverse family structures the *Watchmen* series highlights in its alternate 2019 reality. Instead, "family" in *Watchmen* is now a much broader, more nuanced, and likely more realistic depiction of the numerous ways in which people come together to care for each other as family. "Kinship or true kinship" is a historical term used in anthropology and ethnography to connote familial relationships of blood and marital origins. The troubled intergenerational kinship family of Ozymandias, mother Bian, Lady Trieu, and daughter Bian in *Watchmen* depicts anything but the nuclear family stereotype of the *Watchmen* comics. In contrast, the term "fictive kinship" was used to connote close social relationships akin to familial ones, but without the blood or marital ties. The Abar family as an adoptive multiracial family developed out of the trauma and loss of the Abar childrens' birth parents, an exemplar of a fictive kinship family, and is notably more loving, close, and connected than the juxtaposed "true" kinship Ozymandias family. In fact, ethnically diverse "families" abound in the series, with the additional examples of the white and Vietnamese Ozymandias/Trieu/Bian family and the Angela and Judd paternal figure dynamic. Angela and Judd's relationship is a prime example of a newer, more modern concept of "chosen kinship," which recognizes that social ties and "families" are often created from bonds of social support, mutual caring, and other mutual reciprocal relationships. The *Watchmen* officers are a type of chosen kinship support network with complicated and unique dynamics in each cohort depicted. Chosen kinship networks feature prominently both in modern American society and in

Watchmen's 2019 alternate universe and highlight the myriad and complex manners in which one can be considered part of a family.

ATTACHMENT THEORY

Attachment theory is a useful approach for considering relationship dynamics and the manners in which relationships develop and change over time, developing initially between infants and their caregivers. The theory originates from the work of Caucasian, Western psychologists of the 20th century, including Bowlby, Ainsworth, and others who discovered that separations from or intense difficulties with a primary caregiver, such as those that occurred for European infants and children during World War II, can have lasting impacts on caregiver-child relationships.[1] The concept of *attachment* refers to the infant and young child's tendency to seek closeness, comfort, protection, and support from a few primary caregivers.[2] The health or security of a child's developing relationships to primary caregivers (e.g., parents, childcare providers, grandparents, and others who typically care for the child) is linked to healthy social emotional development. The theory suggests that these early life relationships are also relevant to adult relationship health and overall well-being as the security of childhood relationships sets the stage for how individuals behave in and think about their future relationships.[3] Findings from the adult literature suggest that there is generally stability in attachment security over time, therefore we can make some reasonable assumptions regarding how adults will behave in relationships based on their style(s) of attachment in childhood.[4]

Attachment experts use classifications or categories of attachment to describe the general health and security of a particular caregiver-child relationship. Based on numerous observations of primary caregivers and young children interacting, attachment theorists decided upon four attachment styles: secure, insecure-avoidant, insecure-ambivalent, and disorganized.[5] A secure attachment style is one in which we observe the child to express distress upon separation, seek comfort from caregivers upon reunion, and to be comforted easily. A child developing in the context of a secure attachment believes they can trust the caregiver to both support them in exploring the world and to provide them with comfort when care and closeness are needed. Secure relationships seldom last long in *Watchmen*. A prominent exception is Angela and Cal's marriage, which is characterized by trust, warmth, and overall security, as are their relationships with their children. The loving and supportive exchange between the two in the moments leading up to the White Night attack gives us a glimpse into the security of their partnership. This warmth and trust permeate their relationships with their children, demonstrating how a secure adult relationship can prove to be healing and can even positively impact the security of attachment with their children.

The remaining nonsecure attachment styles are, according to the theory, more indicative of clinical concern and convey broad risks for relationship difficulties and emotional development. Perhaps not surprisingly, they also show up more commonly and more prominently in the many flawed characters of *Watchmen*. In an insecure-avoidant attachment style, the child shows little distress in response to a separation from the caregiver and demonstrates little need for closeness or comfort from the caregiver upon reunion. In perhaps one of the clearest examples of an insecure-avoidant attachment style on screen, Ozymandias appears to need nothing or no one, unless they meet his physical needs at the time. His relationships with his own children (both biological and adopted), described below, as well as his known romantic relationships, consistently indicate his narcissism and avoidant nature. Notably, Rorschach, one of our "heroes" in the *Watchmen* comic, also demonstrates an insecure-avoidant attachment style. Having experienced a troubled childhood with a lack of secure relationships with his absent father and abusive mother, Rorschach develops a narcissistic and avoidant nature. Arguably, his involvement with the chosen kinship network of superheroes contributes to his heroism versus Ozymandias's villainy, though the gray area between right and wrong in the *Watchmen* universe is vast.

Other forms of insecure attachment result in similarly pained but different relationship dynamics. In an insecure-ambivalent attachment style, the child experiences a high degree of distress in response to separation from their caregiver and difficulty in receiving comfort from the caregiver upon reunion. Lady Trieu's cloning of her mother in the form of her daughter, Bian, to keep her close and present for her planned world takeover is an extreme and science-fictional example of insecure-ambivalent attachment. Trieu cannot cope with the loss of her mother, Bian, and uses cloning and nostalgia to try to recreate her mother in her biological daughter, aptly also named, Bian. Trieu's lack of understanding of secure parent-child relationships is clear when she uses an infant as a bartering tool with the couple on the farm.

Mary Main and colleagues later added the disorganized attachment style in response to their observations of children who demonstrate a heterogeneous, disorganized pattern of relating to primary caregivers.[6] Disorganized attachment behaviors from the child include mixed strategies of approaching and avoiding the caregiver as well as acting out (e.g., aggression, self-harm, swearing). Notably, disorganized attachment style is most predictive of current and longer-term psychopathology as well as a warning sign of potential child maltreatment and/or neglect.[7] The Comedian initially comes to mind as an exemplary disorganized attachment figure—capable and desiring of some degree of closeness and heroics, but often demonstrative of extreme cruelty, violence, and lack of regard for others.

INTERGENERATIONAL ATTACHMENT

Considering caregiver-child relationships within an intergenerational attachment frame provides more nuanced understanding of attachment styles and how they develop. Intergenerational attachment refers to the manners in which attachment styles tend to replicate from generation to generation of parents and children within families, as the ways in which one was parented tend to influence the ways in which we parent.[8] One central thread to the dynamics among characters in *Watchmen* are separations, losses, and difficulties within relationships. The theme of families becoming and being reshaped due to trauma in an intergenerational manner permeates other primary relationships in the series. Like her own children's experience, Angela became an orphan following her own parents' violent murders by terrorism. Her grandmother, June, finds Angela living in an orphanage, though their reunification as a family is cut short by June's heart attack. Angela's grandparents, Will and June, became orphaned due to the murders by terrorism of their own parents during the Tulsa Massacre. This enormous loss is immediately followed by the deaths of the adults intended to care for the children, resulting in a young Will transitioning overnight from child to parentified caregiver for infant June. Further, stepping back from the Abars specifically, *Watchmen* opens with the depiction of the violent slaying of hundreds of Black families lost at the 1921 Tulsa Massacre, as well as the devastation of thousands of Black-owned homes and businesses, setting a historical stage for the series and for the interwoven diverse family dynamics to play out. For further discussion, Apryl Alexander explores intergenerational trauma fully in her chapter included in this volume.

The theme of biological lineage being important but obfuscated cuts across central characters in *Watchmen*. There is the relationship between Angela and Will, which unfolds over time and with the help of a phenomenal family tree graphic visible at the Greenfield Cultural Center—a museum dedicated to helping descendants of those at the Tulsa Massacre understand their heritage. From the outset of the series, Judd is introduced as a sort of father figure to Angela, and her grief at his death is striking. Later the complexities and sinister nature of that relationship are revealed, but the initial feeling that Angela, Judd, and their entire police department are a type of family, watching out for one another following the murders of so many of their own, was intense. Angela's use of Nostalgia allows her to occupy her kinship grandfather, Will's, subjective experience, which draws the two closer via Angela's investigation of her fictive father, Judd's, death. There is also the intergenerational dynamics among Lady Trieu, her "daughter" Bian, and Ozymandias. This fascinating family tree connects Lady Trieu's mother to Veidt, resulting in Trieu's birth.

OZYMANDIAS—NEGLECT AND NARCISSISM

At the extreme and injurious end of the independence promoting continuum is Ozymandias in a caregiving role. He did not raise his daughter, Trieu, but rather abandoned her and her mother, only later to rely on Trieu for his escape (i.e., "Save Me Daughter"). Further, once his daughter has successfully brought him back from exile, Ozymandias plays a central role in destroying her prior to her reaching her life's goal. Trieu seemingly inherited much of her father's narcissism, craving to rule the world through the pilfering of Dr. Manhattan's powers. She also retains a close, and likely obsessive, relationship to her mother. Desperately wanting her mother to witness her success via world domination, Trieu clones her mother in the form of her daughter, Bian. This parental narcissism playing out as a sense of children existing to fulfill the needs of their parents, not as distinct individuals to be cherished, links the generations in the Ozymandias/Trieu lineage. Trieu's lack of empathy and understanding within a caregiver/child relationship is also depicted in another adoptive family in the series. Trieu offers a couple desiring a family an infant in exchange for her father's recently crashed spaceship on her land. The seemingly tender moment of the start of a new family turns terrifying when Trieu threatens to kill the infant if the Clarks do not agree. In retrospect, knowing Trieu's propensities towards narcissism and emotional abandonment, this threat was almost certainly real as she views others as vehicles to her own greater purpose.

A similar, and somehow perhaps even more sinister and narcissistic, family dynamic plays out on Ozymandias's adopted home planet. Dr. Manhattan had created clones of Mr. Phillips and Ms. Crookshanks, in homage to the couple who had cared for him and his father and had asked that he create "something beautiful" in exchange. The beautiful creation of the pair as well as their castle is quickly corrupted by the exiled Ozymandias, who uses the clones for his own gain. Ozymandias pulls hundreds (perhaps thousands?) of cloned fetuses from the magical stream, but like his treatment of his biological daughter, only keeps those who meet his purposes. As was true for his absent fathering of Lady Trieu, he is not fit to or patient enough to parent these children, condemning the infant clones to excruciatingly painful and accelerated childhood development so that they quickly reach adulthood and can serve his every whim.

MULTICULTURAL CONSIDERATIONS OF ATTACHMENT THEORY

Despite decades of research documenting the utility of attachment theory, there are notable weaknesses to the theory, some of which may be especially salient in considering relationships depicted in *Watchmen*'s alternate 2019. Critiques of attachment theory highlight that outside of the white, Westernized nuclear family dynamics upon which attachment theory is based, the theory may not be valid, particularly when strictly and conventionally applied. Many cultures, societies, and families differ from nuclear family composition and related views in important manners for childrearing.[9] In non-Westernized societies, multiple and flexible caregiving arrangements are more commonplace. Caregiving for young children may be accomplished in more partnered or communal manners than in the traditional nuclear family and the predominantly maternal caregiving context from which attachment theory derived. For example, a central family in the series are Angela and Cal Abar and their children, a multiracial (and multispecies) adoptive family resulting from the prior murder of Angela's partner and his wife. Angela and Cal divide parenting responsibilities, with Cal likely serving a more primary caregiving role. The role of fathers was rarely examined specifically in early attachment theory work and especially not the role of fathers as primary caregivers. Cal as the father figure serving in the primary caregiving role stereotypically and historically reserved for mothers is another nod to the diverse family structures. Overall, the family trees depicted in *Watchmen* are less nuclear and more extended, diverse, and dynamic in their composition. Chosen kinships, adoptive caregivers, single parents, extended friend/family networks, and even cloned children abound in *Watchmen*.

The question of whether and/or how to apply attachment theory to families of color, chosen kinship, and other diverse family structures is thankfully gaining attention in the literature.[10] When considering attachment theory from a multicultural and chosen kinship perspective, a more nuanced understanding of attachment is useful. At the heart of the nuance is what is the primary goal of child-rearing within the cultural background(s) of the family of interest. From a collectivist cultural lens, numerous caregivers play important roles in child caregiving and development of mutual dependence and contribution to the group's well-being are developmental goals. This contrasts with Westernized white cultural perspectives which emphasize child caregiving from one or two primary caregivers and increasing independence as a child development goal. Attachment might be more comprehensively considered from a cross-cultural perspective if the culture of the family of interest is understood first. For example, in more collectivist communities, a child may be raised by multiple caregivers who value interdependence within the family and during childhood. Children may be raised by extended family members, multiple caregivers, and/or by chosen kin rather than by a primary caregiver, who in Western nuclear families and in the early attachment literature typically translated to mothers. In *Watchmen*, these contrasting caregiving goals and familial cultural values are well showcased, in the extremes, by the caregiving styles of the more interdependent and flexible Abars versus the narcissistically independent Ozymandias and Lady Trieu dynamic.

FAMILY TREE, REVISITED

The characters in *Watchmen* are wonderfully nuanced—especially when in caregiving roles. Parents are depicted as complicated, with superheroes not necessarily proving to be super parents. Will is an example—as Hooded Justice, he's the godfather of all superheroes to follow in the *Watchmen* universe, but he fails to be an effective father to his son Marcus, resulting in their eventual estrangement. Other fathers in the Abar household are also heroic yet flawed. Cal is loving and protective but hides the secret of his superhero identity from his children. Will's father, a military veteran, sacrifices himself in heroic fashion to save his son, pleading for others to "watch over this boy." The depiction of parents as flawed and complicated adults, often trying to care for and protect their children but falling short despite their efforts, is refreshingly realistic, especially for a science fiction show set in another reality.

In *Watchmen*, an overarching theme of "heroes" (e.g., Angela, Will, Cal/Dr. Manhattan) placing the needs of their families, broadly defined and diversely comprised, above their own personal interests wonderfully balances that of the villains (e.g., Judd, Keene, Trieu, Ozymandias) placing the needs of the self above those of their family. There's a spotlight placed on the importance of intergenerational transmission of identity and trauma within family systems. The imagery of family trees comes to mind in considering where each of the families starts and finishes throughout the series—some wither, some change, and some flourish despite adversity. *Watchmen* calls into question the assumptions of attachment theory's past and highlights the possibilities for the future of well-being in families. A broader continuum of family structures, caregiving roles, and goals in childrearing is not only possible, but desirable, both in *Watchmen*'s alternative 2019. and in our present.

NOTES

1. See John Bowlby, *Child Care and the Growth of Love* (Melbourne: Penguin Books, 1953); and M.D.S. Ainsworth, M. C. Blehar,. E. Waters, E and S. Wall *Patterns of Attachment: A Psychological Study of the Strange Situation* (Oxford, UK: Lawrence Erlbaum, 1970).

2. See Julianna Finelli, Charles. H. Zeanah, and Anna T. Smyke, "Attachment Disorders in Early Childhood," in Charles H. Zeanah, ed. *Handbook of Infant Mental Health* (New York: Guilford Press, 2019) and Charles H. Zeanah and Anna T. Smyke, "Attachment Disorders," in *Handbook of Infant Mental Health*, ed. Charles H. Zeanah (New York: Guilford Press, 2019).

3. See Mary Main, Nancy Kaplan, and Jude Cassidy, "Security in Infancy, Childhood and Adulthood: A Move to the Level of Representation," *Monographs of the Society for Research in Child Development* 50 (1985): 66–104.

4. Main, Kaplan, and Cassidy; see also Marinus H. van IJzendoorn, "Adult Attachment Representations, Parental Responsiveness, and Infant Attachment: A Meta-Analysis on the Predictive Validity of the Adult Attachment Interview," *Psychological Bulletin* 117, no. 3 (1995): 387–403.

5. See Mary D. Salter Ainsworth, Mary C. Blehar, Everett Waters, and Sally N. Wall, *Patterns of Attachment: A Psychological Study of the Strange Situation* (Oxford, UK: Lawrence Erlbaum, 1978).

6. See Mary Main and Erik Hesse, "Parents' unresolved traumatic experiences are related to infant disorganized attachment status: Is frightened and/or frightening parental behavior the linking mechanism?" in M. T. Greenberg, D. Cicchetti, and E. M. Cummings, eds., *Attachment in the Preschool Years: Theory, Research, and Intervention* (Chicago: University of Chicago Press (1990), 161–82; and Mary Main and Judith Solomon, "Procedures for Identifying Infants as Disorganized/Disoriented during the Ainsworth Strange Situation," in *Attachment in the Preschool Years: Theory, Research, and Intervention*, eds. M. T. Greenberg, D. Cicchetti, and E. M. Cummings (Chicago: University of Chicago Press, 1990), 121–60.

7. See Finelli, Zeanah, and Smyke; and Charles H. Zeanah and Anna T. Smyke, "Attachment Disorders," in *Handbook of Infant Mental Health*, ed. Charles H. Zeanah (New York: Guilford Press, 2009), 421–34.

8. See Main, Kaplan, and Cassidy.

9. See Heidi Keller, "Attachment and Culture," *Journal of Cross-Cultural Psychology* 44, no. 2 (2013): 175–94.

10. Donalee Brown, Yolanda Hawkins Rodgers, and Kalindi Kapadia, "Multicultural Considerations for the Application of Attachment Theory," *American Journal of Psychotherapy* 62, no. 4 (2018): 353–63.

Chapter 17

"SO, YOU'VE TAKEN SOMEONE ELSE'S NOSTALGIA"

Trauma, Nostalgia, and American Hero Stories

LINDSAY HALLAM

In episode six of *Watchmen*, titled "This Extraordinary Being," protagonist Angela Abar is transported back in time after overdosing on a medication called Nostalgia. In these pills are the memories of Angela's grandfather, Will Reeves, which she then experiences. Rather than a *Back to the Future* style trip back to the "good old days," Angela experiences American history from the perspective of a Black man whose life is marked by a series of traumatic events. Will's trauma is part of a wider, collective trauma, a direct result of having to live in a racist society that does not recognize or acknowledge its history of injustice and inequality.

I will explore how the *Watchmen*'s alternative history acts as a corrective to the nostalgic view of American history as one that is righteous and just. This narrative is reinforced by the superhero narratives that are so currently in vogue (and so often present the superhero as almost exclusively white and male). The television series, just as the comic did before it, provides an alternative history and present that deconstructs the superhero narrative, revealing the trauma that is so often (literally) masked.

While there have been some who have perceived the series as having a pro-police stance,[1] as the show progresses, this perspective becomes muddied. Kristen Warner asserts: "While I've read really persuasive analysis arguing that the show reinforces the power of the state, I would counter: it may, but I think the series finds itself much more comfortable in the space of ambivalence. It refuses to be simply about good and evil."[2] As Warner attests, the series consistently resists the reinforcement of binaries, which is central to its deconstruction of superhero tropes. Many of the conventions of the superhero genre, from its iconography (particularly the mask) to its narrative structures (such as the origin story and the superhero's inciting trauma), are perpetually broken down, continuing the original graphic novel's subversion of the boundary separating heroes from villains.

"THIS IS MY ORIGIN STORY": THE BIRTH OF A NATIONAL HERO

The opening scene of the series in many ways encapsulates the ideas and concerns to follow. We see what appears to be a very straightforward scenario, one that has played out in countless films, television series, and comic books: a hero chases a villain, defeats him, and saves the day. Yet, many of the well-worn tropes become complicated as the scene unfolds. Initially, we see a man in white on a horse being chased by a man dressed in a black hood and robes. Setting up the binary of black and white, and the connotations associated with each element of this binary, it at first appears that the one being pursued is the hero. The man in white uses a gun that he shoots at the man behind him, while the man in black wields a rope and lassoes the man in white, so he falls off his horse. As he falls to the ground the man's white hat—a symbol demarcating the goodness of a hero in the Western genre—is seen in the foreground as a priest and the rest of his congregation come out of the nearby church. A mid-shot reveals further that the man in white is wearing a sheriff's badge, another symbol of goodness and justice. However, the man in black then tells the townsfolk that their sheriff was stealing their cattle and is in fact the villain. The man in black pulls back his hood, revealing a Black man, also wearing a badge. A young boy recognizes him as Bass Reeves, "The Black Marshal of Oklahoma." The townsfolk, realizing who he is, clap in grateful appreciation.

At this point the scene shifts from the screen to show a young Black boy in the audience, watching the film in awe and wonder. We then see the rest of the film from behind the boy's head, staring up at the screen with him. Bass Reeves refuses the people's calls to lynch the thief (it is notable that even though he uses a rope, he will not use it to perform this act), and the young boy reads out the words on the title screen: "There will be no mob justice today. TRUST IN THE LAW." As he speaks this last sentence, there is a close-up of the boy, his face full of joy. There is then another cut, to behind the woman at the piano, the previously stable camerawork now shaky and handheld. The woman's piano-playing falters; the sound of a siren and other unrest outside fade in. Reality intrudes into the theater.

In the final episode of the series, this young boy, Will Reeves remembers this moment as an old man: "The last thing I saw before my world ended was Bass Reeves." The film leaves a deep and indelible mark on the boy, influencing him throughout his life, directly leading him onto the path he takes as an adult. In this case a film has a positive effect; the boy looks at the image on screen and sees someone like him achieve greatness and respect. Unfortunately, the respect that Bass Reeves receives on screen from the all-white townsfolk does not exist in the real world, as just beyond the cinema's doors the massacre of African American people by white supremacists, which actually occurred in Tulsa in 1921, is taking place. Later, as an adult, Will encounters an instance when the filmed image is used for the opposite effect, as a means to harm, which is more emblamatic of cinema's long history of harmful depictions of people of color.

Further, this opening film-within-a-show sets up the tension that exists throughout the series in its interplay between real events and those that are clearly fictional and fantastical. The film Will watches does not exist, but the film's hero, Bass Reeves, was a real person—although he did not go around hiding his face in a black hood.[3] The representation of the events in Tulsa are depicted in a way that clearly demonstrates that this was a violent racist attack, traumatizing an entire community. However, after young Will escapes by being concealed in a truck, he later finds everyone else he escaped with dead, except for a baby whom he wraps in a blanket with a red and white stripe pattern that recalls the design of the American flag. After the realism of the scene of massacre, this next moment visually references images from superhero origin stories, in particular the arrival of Superman on Earth, who as a baby is wrapped in the same blue and red that will become part of his costume (colors also referencing the American flag).

Will does indeed refer to this as "my origin story," a key element of all superhero narratives. Series creator Damon Lindelof maintains that he is "obsessed" with origin stories—a factor that led to the extensive use of flashbacks in his previous series *Lost*—with origin stories provided for several of *Watchmen*'s main characters, such as Angela Abar and Wade Tillman.[4] However, origin stories always come in two parts, as Lindelof explains, using Batman as an example: "Batman's origin comes in two parts: origin part number one is the murder of the Waynes, and part two is the moment that he decides to become Batman, you know, as an adult."[5] With this as a model, the opening of the first episode is just part 1 of Will's origin: "There's a childhood trauma that doesn't really become worked out until adulthood, and so we always knew that part two was going to involve this period when this little boy becomes Hooded Justice."[6] This model also applies to the origins of both Angela and Wade, with both sustaining childhood traumas (or in the case of Wade, in young adulthood, with the trauma coming at the same moment that he discovers his sexuality), and then an inciting incident in adulthood (the White Night) that leads them to put on a mask and assume a persona.

Thus, the mask that each of them wears becomes a visual representation of their trauma(s). Will is revealed to be Hooded Justice, a character from the original comic and the first superhero. In the graphic novel Hooded Justice is the only hero whose identity is not divulged, creating space for Lindelof and his writing team to integrate this character into the show's exploration of America's racist history. Lindelof speaks of the process of making this connection:

> Hooded Justice is a character that never gets revealed to us, why? [. . .] [W]hat if this man was hiding, under the mask, another mask, it was multileveled. What if he was hiding his race? And why would a Black man hide his race in 1938, if he was a vigilante? Well, the reason is because if a Black man was fighting crime in 1938 New York, he'd be murdered.[7]

While the first part of Will's origin story comes from a collective trauma, the second part arises from a personal, although still racially motivated, attack. Inspired by Bass Reeves to become a police officer, he is confronted with harsh realities that the movie hero never had to face as he is beaten by his fellow officers, hung by a rope, and then cut down. Hooded Justice's trademarks—a hood with a rope around his neck—are remnants, painful reminders, of this traumatic event.

Will performs his first act of vigilante justice immediately after this attack, still wearing the hood. In a moment lifted from many other superhero stories, Will hears a woman scream in an alleyway and runs to help. There is a well-dressed white couple—reminiscent of Batman's parents, Thomas and Martha Wayne—being robbed by a gang. In a moment of rage, Will beats them all, saving the couple. His identity still masked, the couple, like the townspeople in the Bass Reeves film, thank him unreservedly.

Despite achieving notoriety in the press who designate him as a hero, Will realizes that in order to continue his vigilantism he must don further masking. Underneath his hood, he puts on makeup to conceal his dark skin and pass for white. As Lindelof stated earlier, the masking is "multileveled."

Further levels are introduced through the form in which Will's traumas are displayed—his memories are experienced via his granddaughter, who takes Nostalgia pills, which contain Will's memories.

"SOMEONE ELSE'S NOSTALGIA": POP CULTURE AS WHITE SUPREMACY

We see Will's memories through his descendent, in a literal depiction of how trauma is passed through the generations. In his book *Haunting Legacies: Violent Histories and Transgenerational Trauma*, Gabriele Schwab argues: "Violent histories generate psychic deformations passed on from generation to generation . . . The damages of violent histories can hibernate in the unconscious, only to be transmitted to the next generation like an undetected disease."[8] The assumption of a persona and the donning of a mask thus become "psychic deformations." During her overdose on Nostalgia, we see Angela at different points in Will's place, most notably after the failed lynching, and then later when Angela is reflected in the mirror after Will puts the white makeup around his eyes—she, too, wears her grandfather's mask. There are further reflections of Will in Angela's costuming as Sister Night, as she also has a hood and makeup around her eyes—only now she darkens her skin rather than lightening it.

Angela's journey to the past may be aided by Nostalgia, but it is not in any way a nostalgic trip back to "the good old days." Lindelof has spoken of a desire to "weaponize nostalgia," expressing the danger of nostalgia as "a plot device rather than a theme."[9] There is also a reference here to the graphic novel, where Nostalgia is the name of a line of cosmetics sold by Veidt Enterprises. Lady Trieu has since purchased Veidt Enterprises and is later revealed as Veidt's daughter, so her appropriation of the brand not only serves to capitalize on the original product's aim to "conjure an idyllic picture of times past" (with its success "directly linked to the state of global uncertainty"), but it also sets up further intergenerational links.[10]

The creation of the drug Nostalgia, which becomes a poison when used incorrectly, was initially designed by Lady Trieu to help those with dementia and Alzheimer's. It was soon abused, as people used it to relive their traumas, rather than as a means to work through them. This again circles back to the original form of Nostalgia, which was also designed as a retreat from reality, but for Laurie Blake the breaking of a bottle of the perfume triggers a series of memories building to the realization of her father's true identity and her mother's associated trauma. This leads to the key point that both the graphic novel and the show make about the effects of nostalgia: what at first appears as a harmless trip down memory lane is another form of a mask, hiding a past that for many is traumatic. Lindelof explains: "If you were a white person, nostalgia means something much different to you than if you're a Jewish person or if you are a person of color in this country."[11] Remembering America's history is difficult for many people, as it brings up a lot of pain and anguish. To then represent the past as idyllic is to marginalize that pain.

Yet, this is often what occurs in popular culture. When asked in an interview about the current popularity of superhero films, *Watchmen* graphic novel author Alan Moore has stated his complete disdain for the genre. Recognizing not only the toxic nostalgia that keeps its mostly adult admirers in a state of arrested development, Moore also detects an underlying racism:

> Save for a smattering of non-white characters (and non-white creators) these books and these iconic characters are still very much white supremacist dreams of the master race. In fact, I think that a good argument can be made for D.W. Griffith's *Birth of a Nation* as the first American superhero movie, and the point of origin for all those capes and masks.[12]

Certainly, this is a sentiment that *Watchmen* directly extrapolates from: the origin story for superheroes on screen was one where heroes fight to maintain the supremacy of their race.[13] The supposed "heroes" in *The Birth of a Nation* (D. W. Griffith, 1915) do indeed wear masks and capes, but they are the Ku Klux Klan, who, in the context of the film, are depicted as righteous and just. In her article "How the Klan Got Its Hood," Alison Kinney explains that this film is in fact responsible for creating the standard white regalia that the KKK still wears to this day: "Among the variety of Klansman costumes in the film, there appeared a new one: the one-piece, full-face-masking, pointed white hood with eyeholes, which would come to represent the modern Klan."[14] It is well-documented that *The Birth of a Nation* not only had an effect on the appearance of the KKK, but that it also led to a revival at a time when its popularity was flagging. As historian John Hope Franklin asserts: "With an assist from Birth of a Nation, the new Ku Klux Klan, a 'High Class order of men of Intelligence and Order,' was launched. It would spread all across the South and into the North and West in the 1920's."[15] Stephen Weinberger writes that while there was an increase in lynching the year of the film's release,[16] this number declined the following year with "little evidence of an increase in overt racism."[17] However, this film did signal the beginning of a long history of racist representations on screen, supporting a larger system of white supremacy.

Contemporary superhero films continue the trope established by *The Birth of a Nation*, with the majority of heroes still portrayed as white and male. Of the twenty-three films from the Marvel Cinematic Universe released as of this writing, only one has had a Black lead (*Black Panther*, Ryan Coogler, 2018), and only one has centered on a woman (*Captain Marvel*, Anna Boden and Ryan Fleck, 2019). This lack of diversity also extends offscreen, with only two films directed by people of color (Coogler and Taika Waititi, director of *Thor: Ragnarok*, 2017) and one film codirected by a woman (Boden). The *Watchmen* series thus bucks these trends on both counts, with both its Black female lead and seven of its nine episodes directed by women and people of color.[18]

At the beginning of "This Extraordinary Being," in which Will is revealed as Hooded Justice, a clip from the television show *American Hero Story* also reveals the face of Hooded Justice: as a white man with chiseled good looks and piercing blue eyes. This whitewashing of history has links to other nostalgic revisions of the past, most famously in *Back to the Future* (Robert Zemeckis, 1985) where white teenager Marty McFly seemingly gives African American performer Chuck Berry the idea for his own song. For decades white characters on screen have appropriated the achievements of people of color while also simultaneously downplaying the systems of racism that have kept them oppressed.

In *Watchmen* the masking of police is a direct consequence of the White Night, an incident instigated by the Seventh Kavalry (an offshoot of the KKK) with this outcome in mind. Although many of the police wear masks out of fear and for protection, the idea behind it is an inherently fascistic one. Just as the KKK keep their identities secret so they can continue to terrorize Black citizens, having the police similarly masked would most certainly lead to the same result. Of course, there are countless news stories proving that in reality this is already the case without masks, just as white supremacists have also begun to take off their hoods, replacing them with MAGA hats and tiki torches. But as Jonathan W. Gray contends: "*Watchmen* makes the connections between law enforcement and white supremacy explicit in ways seldom seen in popular culture."[19]

At the beginning of the series, Angela wears a mask and participates in acts of police brutality. Under the mentorship of Judd Crawford, the chief of police later revealed as a member of the Seventh Kavalry, Angela, as Sister Night and the other masked cops, such as Looking Glass, Red Scare, and Pirate Jenny, function essentially as henchmen and women. They are helping, albeit unknowingly, to bring the Seventh Kavalry's plans to fruition. The process of uncovering not only who Judd was, but more importantly discovering who she really is by learning of her heritage, leads Angela to take off her mask—she is not seen wearing it after the events of "This Extraordinary Being." Angela is fundamentally changed, a point that Michael Boyce Gillespie believes complicates the arguments that the series presents a pro-establishment, and specifically pro-police, stance: "The cop critique suggests that Angela Abar essentially remains the same throughout. Is she really just a cop by the close of the series? How can a show that suggests that cops are historically in collusion with white supremacists be read as pro-cop?"[20] In the process of working through multiple traumas, by the end of the series, Angela has moved from henchwoman to (potentially) a superhero with actual superpowers.

"WOUNDS NEED AIR": UNMASKING TRAUMA

The change that Angela undergoes is a profoundly difficult one and not one that everyone can reach. The character of Wade Tillman, also known as Looking Glass, expresses the difficulty of moving on from trauma. At the beginning of episode five, titled "Little Fear of Lightning," the origin of Looking Glass is revealed. As a young man in 1985 Wade was a devout Christian who went to Hoboken to spread the word of God. He meets a young woman who takes him to a hall of mirrors and entices him to take off his clothes, which she then runs away with. As he stands humiliated, the event that concluded the story of the graphic novel, the giant squid attack of 11/2 occurs, and he leaves the hall of mirrors, confronted by all of the death and carnage resulting from the incident.

In 2019 Wade has assumed the persona of Looking Glass, with the ability to tell when someone is lying or telling the truth. Looking Glass wears a mask made of "reflectatine," a material that reflects like a mirror. After seeing the events of 1985, it becomes clear that his mask references the hall of mirrors, his ability stemming directly from this inciting trauma. In counterpoint to Will and Angela, whose traumas comment on America's very real history of racial violence, Wade's trauma comes from an event that is completely fictional. Lindelof recognizes the fine line that the series treads by combining these elements: "We're talking about real trauma, real pain, real America, and also the ridiculousness of, and there's a psychic squid, and there's film projectors that are involving mesmerism. So how are these two things going to play well with one another? The challenge of that was extreme . . . If you get this stuff wrong, it can be harmful."[21] While there have been many films and television shows that have represented actual traumatic events in a realistic way, there is a tradition within genre storytelling to use allegory as a way to work through trauma, both personal and collective. Adam Lowenstein remarks that there is a tendency for critics to "favor 'realist' representations over 'allegorical' ones,"[22] but he goes on to argue that there is space within a genre cinema context to disrupt established discourses surrounding historical trauma.

The rise in popularity of the superhero film began in the early 2000s, in the wake of 9/11 and the subsequent War on Terror, a fact that has been commented on in several books and articles published since.[23] These texts posit that, through allegory, these genre films are vehicles for working through the trauma associated with this real event. As Dan A. Hassler-Forest attests: "by watching films that offer an indirect representation of the 9/11 attacks, it becomes possible for viewers to give meaning to events that were too sudden and traumatic to be understood as they occurred."[24] The fantastical "ridiculousness" of the stories on screen, presented through action sequences and special effects, present an exciting spectacle that masks the underlying process of working through trauma. In the *Watchmen* series, the squid attack is referred to as "11/2," clearly referencing 9/11—an event that appears not to have happened in this alternate timeline. In a sense, 11/2 has "replaced" 9/11 as the most historically significant and traumatic event to occur on American soil within the past few decades (perhaps even preventing 9/11 from occurring). Echoing Lowenstein's contention that there is space through allegory to interrogate dominant discourse, Hassler-Forest adds that many superhero films contain subversive elements and "actually encourage a reading that runs counter to the current American administration's policies."[25]

Similarly, the alternative 2019 of *Watchmen* also includes these critiques, exploring how America's long history of racial injustice continues to traumatize subsequent generations. In her book *Trauma Cinema: Documenting Incest and the Holocaust*, Janet Walker acknowledges that in representations of traumatic events and memories there is prevalence of "non-realist" strategies employed by filmmakers, "characterized by disturbance and fragmentation of the films' narrative and stylistic regimes . . . drawing on innovative strategies for representing reality obliquely, by looking to mental processes for inspiration . . . "[26] For the experience of trauma to be more fully expressed, film and television style must reflect the shattering effects of trauma, which fragments and splinters memory and subjectivity. As mentioned previously, the motif of the mask, signaling the creation of a new identity, paradoxically visualizes the aspect of the self that the wearer wants to suppress. The nonlinear structure of the series, with frequent shifts back and forth in time, echoes the mental process of compulsively returning to the site of trauma, while also expressing the continued reverberations from this moment, which can reach across generations.

Stephen Williams, the director of "This Extraordinary Being," spoke of his process of visualizing Angela's experiences as she relives Will's traumatic memories:

> I wanted to make sure that we invested in a visual grammar that was going to allow for as immersive and intensive an experience as possible . . . How to approach depicting memory and depicting all the sensory experiences pursuant to you having that kind of experience—that's where we started. That led to a visual design that incorporated black and white, really long takes with few interrupted cuts, and also the insertion of specific splashes of color for accentuation.[27]

The techniques that Williams highlights here—long takes, black and white, splashes of color—all work together to represent events in Will's life in a way that is not realistic, but in a way that expresses how Will processed these moments mentally and emotionally. The long takes and masked edits create the feeling that all of these memories intertwine, creating a direct and seamless connection between the two parts of Will's origin story. The camera floats weightlessly, at some points seemingly taking on Will's point of view, but then at other points interchanging Angela in Will's place. Will's assumption of the persona of Hooded Justice in adulthood (playing out in black and white) is inextricably linked to his initial trauma in Tulsa, 1921, symbolized by inserts of color images in the background of scenes, showing his mother playing the piano and lynched men being dragged behind a police car. Yet, intrusions from Angela's present also appear in color. Together, the techniques used in the sequence of Angela's overdose of Nostalgia express the series' overarching idea that the aftershocks of trauma reverberate outwards across time and generations.

And so, throughout the series, the experience and aftermath of trauma is presented in a variety of ways. From its opening scene, conventions of the superhero genre are deconstructed through the interweaving of real historical events with fictional ones from the original graphic novel. The element of the origin story, vital to all superhero narratives, relies on an initial trauma, which in this series becomes inseparable from America's traumatic history of racist violence. Further tropes of the superhero genre are used to express the passing on of trauma from one generation to the next, particularly the central motif of the mask, a symbol of pain that is inescapable, tied to an unjust past that is still being worked through. Nostalgia for the past, once thought to be soothing, now becomes a poison, a compulsion to repeat previous traumas. The superhero story is thus revealed as one of popular culture's greatest lies, upholding a representation of an American ideal that is tied to patriarchal white supremacy. Just as the graphic novel did before it, the series unravels these representations and genre conventions, laying bare the traumas at the heart of American history.

NOTES

1. Aaron Bady, "Dr. Manhattan Is a Cop: *Watchmen* and Frantz Fanon," *Los Angeles Review of Books*, December 31, 2019, https://lareviewofbooks.org/article/dr-manhattan-cop-watchmen-frantz-fanon/?fbclid=IwAR28p2FsLTHK4dDx_Jf-gfnDlCJ1q-1ssShHTpiR_KMLcEjevVB74iY9koY; Noah Berlatsky, "HBO's *Watchmen* Tackles Criminal Justice and Race, But Can't See Past the Hero Black Cop Trope," *NBC News*, November 25, 2019, https://www.nbcnews.com/think/opinion/hbo-s-watchmen-tackles-criminal-justice-race-can-t-see-ncna1089716.

2. Michael Boyce Gillespie, "Thinking about *Watchmen*: A Roundtable," *Film Quarterly*, June 26, 2020, https://filmquarterly.org/2020/06/26/thinking-about-watchmen-with-jonathan-w-gray-rebecca-a-wanzo-and-kristen-j-warner/?fbclid=IwARoXadStBYoQ3KoAMUV_1ijMlHCnDAmCR2hB-oo_fIAiL6vAKIhn_oip2pM.

3. There is some speculation that Bass Reeves inspired the creation of the Lone Ranger.

4. One aspect that has led to some criticism is the fact that we do not see an origin story for Lady Trieu. While we do see the circumstances of how she was conceived, the second part of her origin story is missing. That this is the case for the series' leading Vietnamese character has resulted in some critics questioning the lack of attention paid to the ongoing trauma inflicted on the Vietnamese people by American forces during the Vietnam War. For further discussion, see Viet Thanh Nguyen, "How *Watchmen*'s misunderstanding of Vietnam undercuts its vision of racism," *Washington Post*, December 18, 2019, https://www.washingtonpost.com/outlook/2019/12/18/how-watchmens-misunderstanding-vietnam-undercuts-its-vision-racism/

5. HBO, "Nostalgia (Episodes 4–6)," *The Official Watchmen Podcast*, Podcast Audio, November 25, 2019, https://www.hbo.com/watchmen/watchmen-listen-to-official-podcast

6. HBO, "Nostalgia (Episodes 4–6).

7. HBO, "Nostalgia (Episodes 4–6).

8. Gabriele Schwab, *Haunting Legacies: Violent Histories and Transgenerational Trauma* (New York: Columbia University Press, 2010), 3.

9. HBO, *The Official Watchmen Podcast.*

10. Alan Moore and Dave Gibbons, *Watchmen* (Burbank: DC Comics, 2019), 345.

11. HBO, *The Official Watchmen Podcast.*

12. Raphael Sassaki, "Moore on Jerusalem, Eternalism, Anarchy and Herbie!" *Alan Moore World*, November 18, 2019, https://alanmooreworld.blogspot.com/2019/11/moore-on-jerusalem-eternalism-anarchy.html.

13. Moore had already made this connection between the Klan and superheroes explicit in *Watchmen*, in an article from the right-wing newspaper the *New Frontiersman*: "*Nova Express* makes sneering references to costumed heroes as direct descendants of the Ku Klux

Klan, but might I point out that despite what some may view as their later excesses, the Klan originally came to being because decent people had perfectly reasonable fears." Moore and Gibbons, *Watchmen*, 276.

14. Alison Kinney, "How the Klan Got Its Hood," *The New Republic*, January 8, 2016, https://newrepublic.com/article/127242/klan-got-hood.

15. John Hope Franklin, "*Birth of a Nation*: Propaganda as History," *The Massachusetts Review* 20, no. 3 (Autumn 1979): 431.

16. In Spike Lee's 2018 film *BlacKKKlansman* a scene details the 1915 lynching of Jesse Washington, an act described as being directly inspired by the film.

17. Stephen Weinberger, "*The Birth of a Nation* and the Making of the NAACP," *Journal of American Studies* 45, no. 1 (February 2011): 92.

18. This diversity also extended to the writer's room, as director Nicole Kassell attests: "We knew that we were taking on race and eight out of the 12 writers in the room were not Caucasian." Charles Pulliam-Moore, "*Watchmen* Isn't Being Written by Just White People, Thank Goodness," *Gizmodo*, November 11, 2019, https://io9.gizmodo.com/watchmen-isnt-being-written-by-just-white-people-thank-1839777924.

19. Jonathan W. Gray, "*Watchmen* after the End of History: Race, Redemption, and the End of the World," *ASAP Journal*, February 3, 2020. http://asapjournal.com/watchmen-after-the-end-of-history-race-redemption-and-the-end-of-the-world-jonathan-w-gray/.

20. Gillespie.

21. HBO, *The Official Watchmen Podcast*.

22. Adam Lowenstein, "Allegorizing Hiroshima: Shindo Kaneto's *Onibaba* as Trauma Text," in *Trauma and Cinema: Cross-Cultural Explorations*, ed. E. Ann Kaplan and Ban Wang (Hong Kong: Hong Kong University Press, 2004), 146.

23. James M. Gilmore, "A Eulogy of the Urban Superhero: The Everyday Destruction of Space in the Superhero Film" in *Representing 9/11: Trauma, Ideology, and Nationalism in Literature, Film, and Television*, ed. Paul Petrovic, (Lanham: Rowan & Littlefield, 2015); Tom Pollard, *Hollywood 9/11: Superheroes, Supervillains, and Super Disasters* (New York: Routledge, 2016).

24. Dan A. Hassler-Forest, "From Trauma Victim to Terrorist: Redefining Superheroes in Post 9/11 Hollywood" in *Comics as a Nexus of Cultures: Essays on the Interplay of Media, Disciplines and International Perspectives*, ed. Jochen Ecke and Gideon Haberkorn, (Jefferson, NC: McFarland, 2010), 34.

25. Hassler-Forest, 34.

26. Janet Walker, *Trauma Cinema: Documenting Incest and the Holocaust* (Berkeley: University of California Press, 2005), 19.

27. Clarence Moye, "Director Stephen Williams on Directing Two Outstanding Hours of HBO's *Watchmen*,'" *Awards Daily*, July 28, 2020, https://www.awardsdaily.com/2019/11/26/stephen-williams-watchmen-2019/.

Afterword

ON "UNADAPTABILITY" (OR, REQUIEM FOR A SQUID)

SUZANNE SCOTT

Before consuming a single panel of Alan Moore and Dave Gibbons's *Watchmen*,[1] I knew one thing about it—that it was "unadaptable." This proclamation, like "Han shot first," immediately marked the speaker as a particular genus of media consumer or fan: one who celebrated comics as a distinct art form and held up *Watchmen* as a particularly cerebral mediation of and meditation on that form. It was at its core a case for medium specificity, occasionally undergirded by auteurist understandings of artistic expression and Moore's own oft-cited claim to have crafted something "unfilmable."[2] The scholars featured in *After Midnight*, documenting *Watchmen*'s incarnations across comics, film, and television, tell a different and decidedly more compelling story. Far from being "unadaptable," *Watchmen* is a property that structurally and thematically demands that we reckon with its adaptations, remediations, intertexts, and transmediations. The chapters collected in this volume recognize the significance of *Watchmen*'s origins, but they also vitally celebrate the property's distinct malleability as a site for formal experimentation and social commentary across media platforms.

So why dedicate this afterword to *Watchmen*'s controversial MacGuffin? As this collection's thoughtful ruminations on power, justice, trauma, and nostalgia make clear, there are certainly bigger squid to fry. However, I want to suggest that this tentacled plot point is not merely the prime fodder within ongoing debates around the graphic novel's (un)adaptability, but is the principal site to reconcile the pleasures of medium specificity and transmediality that are central to *Watchmen*'s enduring appeal.

In the graphic novel's climax, a psychic alien squid engineered and deployed by Ozymandias/Adrian Veidt devastates New York in order to create, as the title of the twelfth and final issue of the comic proclaims, "A Stronger Loving World." Thus, as both the comic book and the diegetic

Doomsday Clock strike midnight, Ozymandias rationalizes his actions as a necessary intervention to not only save the world from impending nuclear war, but to actively "help her towards utopia." The accompanying narrative implantation of an alien attack in the cultural consciousness is aided by the same generic conventions that the graphic novel as a whole seeks to challenge and deconstruct, reflecting their enduring power. The science fiction iconography the creature evokes ensures that those who survive the attack will either be "driven mad" or live to propagate the generically powerful narrative of a common otherworldly enemy.

As Ozymandias makes abundantly clear, the squid is totemic. But it has, over time, also become totemic of *Watchmen*'s (un)adaptability. In 2008, news about the alien squid's absence leaked from early test screenings of Zack Snyder's 2009 film adaptation. While adaptation invariably requires difficult editorial choices, Snyder was actively positioned as being up to the supposedly impossible task of adapting the graphic novel in large part because of his reputation as a slavish transcriber of comics source material. Other elements that weren't deemed "essential" to the cinematic retelling, such as the interstitial pirate comic *Tales of the Black Freighter*, were nonetheless adapted into a motion comic and ultimately combined with Snyder's director's cut to create a new "ultimate cut" in 2009, which was touted as "the complete story" on its cover. So whither the squid? Screenwriters David Hayter and Alex Tse simply wrote off the squidless climax as a casualty of cinematic runtime constraints, as "it takes a lot of setup to introduce an interdimensional space squid," and it couldn't just "come out of nowhere."[3]

Set decades after the events of the comic, the HBO *Watchmen* television series did precisely that, dropping a rain of baby squid from the sky without a single line of exposition approximately twenty minutes into the pilot episode. The narrative affordances of serialized television storytelling allowed for this, weaving backstory throughout later episodes and wholly focusing episode 5, "Little Fear of Lightning," on the initial squid attack of the graphic novel and the traumatic aftermath for survivors. Just as the squid originally spilled across gutters and textless pages, formally forcing comic readers to grapple with its scale and carnage and prompting them to move back through the graphic novel to seek clues of its development, HBO's *Watchmen* allowed its squid to sprawl across episodes and weeks.

If Snyder's sidestepping of the giant squid seemed to affirm the limits to *Watchmen*'s adaptability, showrunner Damon Lindelof's approach was emblematic of his claim that the television series sought to "remix" *Watchmen* rather than merely adapt or extend it. Remix is, after all, a citational media practice, often highly dependent on preexisting literacies even as it imagines something new. While the wave of confused tweets and social media posts that accompanied the squid rain of *Watchmen*'s pilot episode suggested that much of the audience was unfamiliar with the source text, the immediate wave of explanatory responses clearly reflects how the on-demand development of fannish literacies can also be medium specific. In 2009, *Watchmen* fans were certainly using digital platforms to debate (and, in some cases, decry) Snyder's decision to replace the squid with a run-of-the-mill nuclear attack. In these debates, however, there was an oft-spoken and far more medium-specific rationale offered for the film adaptation's squid erasure: "If Snyder had kept the original ending, he would almost certainly have gotten unintentional laughs from the audience."[4] Unlike Ozymandias, Snyder could not rely on narrative implantation, speaking to both the limits of adaptation and the industrial demands of tentpole film to appeal to the broadest possible audience.

One significant and rarely remarked upon detail is that Ozymandias draws his design of the squid from multiple artists from within the diegetic world of *Watchmen* working across media forms (painting, music, comics, prose). The transmediated terror draws on the distinct properties of individual media forms to create something larger than the sum of its parts. Most significantly, this plan relies on Ozymandias's "audience" buying his preloaded narrative and not making the connections that audiences in our contemporary media landscape are incredibly adept at making, and that transmedia franchises actively encourage. The squid's presence and/or absence is thus also totemic of contemporary audiences' growing intellectual and infrastructural capacity to perform the sort of metacriticisms and deft textual navigation that originally made *Watchmen* such a singular and significant piece of media.

In a May 2021 interview Snyder noted that, based on his recent experience producing a four-plus-hour cut of *Justice League* for HBO Max, he "might consider" including the giant squid if he ever revisited *Watchmen*.[5] This statement (not to mention the fact that "Snyder Cut" has seemingly become synonymous with "Director's Cut" in the cultural lexicon) is, on one hand, a fitting descendent of Moore's own auteurist proclamations. However, it also suggests that in an era of transmedia franchising and streaming content, we have moved beyond "unadaptability" to a new condition of perpetual revisionism, in which small vocal segments of the audience, coupled with increasingly slippery boundaries of specific media forms within a digital media ecosystem, can produce mutated media objects. Though this collection is pointedly subtitled *Watchmen after Watchmen*, itself a nod to the singularity and significance of the graphic novel, the scholars featured here do not isolate the franchise's past, present, and future. Rather, they collectively engage *Watchmen*'s incarnations as Dr. Manhattan might: invariably interwoven and mutually constitutive, even as they remain attentive to both medium specificity and cultural context.

Watchmen, in all of its instantiations, interrogates how we come to believe what we believe. It is a story about the cost of not interrogating hegemonic narratives, and the individual and societal hurts those narratives can cause. The squid, perhaps, is the most literal embodiment of this, a media effects monstrosity with the ability to directly implant a desired narrative into the cultural consciousness. If the graphic novel's cephalopodic conclusion exemplifies both the destructive power and utopian possibility of bringing people together, then *After Midnight* makes a compelling case for us to move beyond longstanding efforts to narratively implant *Watchmen* as an "unadaptable" object. As the chapters in this collection powerfully suggest, we collectively and culturally need to watch the Watchmen more than ever.

NOTES

1. Alan Moore and Dave Gibbons, *Watchmen* (New York: DC Comics, 1986).
2. Alex Musson and Andrew O'Neil, "The Mustard Interview: Alan Moore," in *Alan Moore: Conversations*, ed. Eric L. Berlatsky (Jackson: University Press of Mississippi, 2012), 194.
3. Alex Billington, "Fascinating Q&A with Watchmen Writers David Hayter and Alex Tse," *FirstShowing.net*, March 18, 2009, https://www.firstshowing.net/2009/fascinating-qa-with-watchmen-screenwriters-david-hayter-and-alex-tse/.
4. Katey Rich, "Great Debate: Does Watchmen Need a Giant Squid?," *Cinemablend*, October 21, 2008, https://www.cinemablend.com/new/Great-Debate-Does-Watchmen-Need-Giant-Squid-10606.html.
5. Mike Ryan, "Zack Snyder on Getting Back to Basics with 'Army of the Dead' after What He Calls 'Torture,'" *Uproxx*, May 14, 2021, https://uproxx.com/movies/zack-snyder-army-of-the-dead-justice-league/.

ABOUT THE CONTRIBUTORS

APRYL ALEXANDER is associate professor in the Graduate School of Professional Psychology at the University of Denver. She received her doctorate in clinical psychology from the Florida Institute of Technology with concentrations in forensic psychology and child and family therapy. Dr. Alexander's research and clinical work focus on violence and victimization, human sexuality, sexual offending, and trauma-informed and culturally informed practice. She is an award-winning researcher, and her work has been published in several leading journals. Dr. Alexander has been interviewed by numerous media outlets, including the *New York Times*, *USA Today*, and *NBC Nightly News*, about her research and advocacy work. Recently, she received the 2019 American Psychological Association's Early Career Award for Outstanding Contributions to Benefit Children, Youth, and Families and the 2019 Michele Alexander Early Career Award for Scholarship and Service and the 2021 Lorraine Williams Greene Award for Social Justice from the Society for the Psychological Study of Social Issues (SPSSI). Dr. Alexander also enjoys bringing psychology to the public through popular media. She is a frequent presenter at Denver Pop Culture Con and has previously contributed to *The Joker Psychology: Evil Clowns and the Women Who Love Them* and *Black Panther Psychology: Hidden Kingdoms.*

ALISIA GRACE CHASE is an associate professor of art and visual culture at SUNY Brockport and the Visual Studies Workshop in Rochester, NY, with a focus on extracinematic culture, contemporary art, time-based media, and comics. Her articles have been included in *Drawing from Life: Memory and Subjectivity in Comic Art*; *The Great American Makeover: Television, History and Nation*; *Virgin Territory: Representing Sexual Inexperience on Film*; and *Difference Reframed: Considering the Legacy of Feminist Art History*; and she regularly contributes to *AFTERIMAGE: The Journal of Media Arts and Cultural Criticism.*

BRIAN FAUCETTE teaches film and English composition courses at a two-year college. His research focuses on the representation of American masculinities in contemporary and classical American film and television. He is the author of *Hawaii Five-O*, which is part of the Wayne State University TV Milestone series. He is the coauthor of the book *Cop Shows: A Critical History of Police Dramas on Television*. His essay on masculinity and the American Western film *3:10 to Yuma* appeared in *The Journal of the West*. He has written essays on masculinity and *Breaking Bad* for the book *Breaking Bad: Critical Essays on the Contexts, Politics, Style, and Reception of the Television Series*, edited by David P. Pierson. His essay on *Doctor Who* branding and the rise of "geek culture" was published in the collection *New Worlds, Terrifying Monsters, Impossible Things: Exploring the Contents and Contexts of "Doctor Who"*. His essay "Light Is Life, Darkness Death: Light and Darkness in *Raw* Deal" was published in the collection *John Alton: Essays on the Cinematographer's Art and Craft*, edited by Leon Lewis.

LAURA E. FELSCHOW is an assistant professor of media studies at SUNY Oneonta. She earned a BFA in film from Syracuse University, MA in media studies with a minor in women's and gender studies from SUNY Buffalo, and PhD in media studies with a portfolio in women's and gender studies from the University of Texas at Austin. Her work has been published in *Journal of Transformative Works and Cultures*, *Media Industries Journal*, *Mediapolis*, and other edited anthologies. Her current research focuses on gender and production in superhero media.

LINDSAY HALLAM is a senior lecturer in film at the University of East London. She is author of the books *Screening the Marquis de Sade: Pleasure, Pain and the Transgressive Body in Film* and the Devil's Advocate edition on *Twin Peaks: Fire Walk with Me*. She is interested in all aspects of horror cinema, having written on topics such as female vampires, torture porn and post-9/11 trauma, mad science films, Italian horror, Australian eco-horror, and the television series *Twin Peaks*.

RUSTY HATCHELL is a PhD candidate in the Department of Radio-Television-Film at the University of Texas at Austin. He currently serves as the lead coordinating editor for *The Velvet Light Trap* and has previously served as a managing editor for *Flow*. His research focuses on contemporary superhero television universes, particularly on the efforts to cultivate narrative continuity as well as industrial production logics that help shape superhero television into its own distinct genre.

DRU JEFFRIES teaches in the Department of English and Film Studies at Wilfrid Laurier University. He is the author of *Comic Book Film Style: Cinema at 24 Panels per Second* (University of Texas Press, 2017) and the editor of *#WWE: Professional Wrestling in the Digital Age* (Indiana University Press, 2019).

HENRY JENKINS is the Provost's Professor of Communication, Journalism, Cinematic Arts and Education at the University of Southern California and the founder and former codirector of the MIT Comparative Media Studies Program. He is the author or editor of 20 books on various aspects of media and popular culture, including *Textual Poachers: Television Fans and Participatory Culture*; *Convergence Culture: Where Old and New Media Collide*; *Spreadable Media: Creating Meaning and Value in a Networked Culture* (with Sam Ford and Joshua Green); *By Any Media Necessary: The New Youth Activism* (with Sangita Shresthova and others); *Popular Culture and the Civic Imagination: Case Studies of Creative Social Change*; and *Comics and Stuff*. He is the cohost of *How Do You Like It So Far?*, a podcast that explores popular culture in a changing world, and has run the *Confessions of an Aca-Fan* blog for more than fifteen years.

JEFFREY SJ KIRCHOFF is the dean of communication, English, and media at Kirkwood Community College. His scholarship on comics and graphic narrative has appeared in *Technoculture*, *International Journal of Comic Art* and *Studies in Comics*, among others. His recent book, *Perspectives on Digital Comics: Theoretical, Critical and Pedagogical Essays*, was published by McFarland in 2019.

CURTIS MAREZ is a professor of ethnic studies at the University of California, San Diego; the former editor of *American Quarterly*, the official journal of the American Studies Association; and the past president of the ASA. A scholar who works at the intersection of cultural studies and ethnic studies, he is the author of three books: *Drug Wars: The Political of Narcotics* (University of Minnesota, 2004); *Farm Worker Futurism: Speculative Technologies of Resistance* (University of Minnesota, 2016); and *University Babylon: Film and Race Politics on Campus* (University of California, 2020). Along with Lisa Duggan, he edits the American Studies Now book series for the University of California Press, and he serves as a member of the UC Press editorial board. He is currently writing a book called *TV in Precarious Places* about streaming TV and racial capitalism.

JAMES DENIS MCGLYNN is a film music scholar and assistant lecturer at the Department of Music, University College Cork. His research explores the rearrangement of pre-existing music in contemporary screen scoring and has appeared in such publications as the *Journal of Popular Music Studies*, *Sonic Scope: New Approaches to Audiovisual Media*, and *RTÉ Brainstorm*. He is currently coediting a special issue of the *Journal of Sound and Music in Games* with Richard Anatone and Andrew S. Powell. Besides his research on screen scoring, James founded the UCC Orchestra and served as the ensemble's conductor for several years. He is also a member of the Irish Gamelan Orchestra, with whom he has performed widely throughout Ireland and in Indonesia.

BRANDY MONK-PAYTON is an assistant professor in the Department of Communication and Media Studies and affiliated faculty in the Department of African and African American Studies at Fordham University. Her research focuses on the theory and history of African American media representation and cultural production across television, film, and digital media. Her work has been published in edited collections such as *Unwatchable* and *From Madea to Media Mogul: Theorizing Tyler Perry* as well as the journals *Film Quarterly*; *Feminist Media Histories*; *Celebrity Studies*, and *Communication, Culture and Critique*. She has also been featured on NPR's *All Things Considered* and *PBS NewsHour*.

CHAMARA MOORE currently works as a visiting assistant professor of English at Dominican University. They received their PhD in English from the University of Notre Dame with minors in gender and screen cultures. Their research reads the Black femme body through Black speculative narratives and practices across literary and visual cultures. Their work has appeared or is forthcoming in *ImageText*, *Meridians*, *Transition*, and *Post45: Contemporaries*.

DREW MORTON is an associate professor of mass communication at Texas A&M University–Texarkana. He is author of *Panel to the Screen: Style, American Film, and Comic Books during the Blockbuster Era*, published by University Press of Mississippi. His publications have appeared in *Animation: An Interdisciplinary Journal*; *Cinema Journal*; *[in]Transition*; *Journal of Graphic Novels and Comics*; and *Studies in Comics*. He is cofounder and coeditor of *[in]Transition*, the award-winning journal devoted to videographic criticism.

MARK C. E. PETERSON is a professor of philosophy and religious studies with the University of Wisconsin Milwaukee. He began his work at the University of Toronto focused primarily on Hegel's natural philosophy and its links to the history of science and technology. These interests evolved to constellate around the larger questions of how humans are related—scientifically, philosophically, and spiritually—to nature. His academic research is currently engaged in a semiotic analysis of the relationship between explanatory and narrative/mythological accounts of nature and a neo-Aristotelian re-examination of environmental ethics.

JAYSON QUEARRY was incubated in a stew of comics and film from an early age, emerging from the soup as a fully cooked manager of a local comic book store. He parlayed that nerdy admixture into a PhD from the School of Film, Media and Theater at Georgia State University. His research interests focus on the intersections between cinema and comics in terms of aesthetics, adaptation, phenomenology, and intertextual narratives, most recently in his dissertation entitled "Universe Diving: Phenomenologically Feeling the 'Universeness' of DC and Marvel Comics."

ZACHARY J. A. RONDINELLI (he/him) is a PhD student in educational studies at Brock University in St. Catharines, ON Canada, as well as a K–12 educator in the Ontario Secondary School system. His primary research interests include comics theory, multimodality, and reading/literacy studies. Rondinelli has been published in *tba: Journal of Art*; *Media and Visual Culture*; *Digital Culture & Education*; and *Canadian Literature: A Quarterly of Criticism and Review*. He is also an active public scholar, having published online scholarship with *The Vault of Culture* and *PopMatters*, as well as printed work in *Sequential: Canadian Independent Comic Book Magazine* and *PanelxPanel*. Most recently, Rondinelli was awarded the 2020 Gilbert Seldes Prize for Public Scholarship in Comics by the Comics Studies Society in recognition of his pandemic-era qualitative social media research project, #WelcomeToSlumberland. This transactional reading project explores individual and collaborative meaning-making practices by engaging with participants in discussion about Winsor McCay's "Little Nemo" comic strips within a digital (social media) landscape. He intends to utilize the data collected from this project in his upcoming dissertation work as a way to harness tensions created at the intersection between comics pedagogy, social media, the public domain, and Platinum Age comics for the purposes of anti-racism and anti-oppression education.

SUZANNE SCOTT is an associate professor of media studies in the Department of Radio-Television-Film at the University of Texas at Austin. She is the author of *Fake Geek Girls: Fandom, Gender, and the Convergence Culture Industry* (NYU Press, 2019), and the co-editor of *The Routledge Companion to Media Fandom* (2018) and *Sartorial Fandom: Fashion, Beauty Culture, and Identity* (University of Michigan Press, forthcoming). Her work on fandom, convergence culture, and transmedia storytelling has been published in *New Media & Society*, *Cinema Journal*, *Critical Studies in Media Communication*, *Feminist Media Histories*, *Transformative Works and Cultures*, and *Participations*.

DAVID STANLEY completed his MA in English at the University of Wisconsin, Milwaukee, where he is currently a PhD student and instructor. His primary research focuses on the function of social media as a radicalization pipeline that increasingly influences real-world politics. Dave's most recent publication is a coauthored article entitled "Fans of Q: The Stakes of Qanon's Functioning as Political Fandom," published in the *Journal for American Behavioral Scientists*.

SARAH PAWLAK STANLEY holds an MA in English from California State Polytechnic University, Pomona, and is currently a PhD candidate at the University of Nevada, Las Vegas. As a visiting assistant professor at Marquette University, Sarah teaches English as well as gender and sexualities studies. Her research focuses on representations of alterity throughout mythology, classic literature, and the modern pop culture through which they are continuously (re)mediated. Rejecting the critical tradition that assumes Stoker's *Dracula* represents his fear of female sexuality, Sarah's current research project centers on reviewing the novel through a sex positivist feminist lens.

TRACY E. MORAN VOZAR joined the Graduate School of Professional Psychology at the University of Denver in 2017 as the director of the Perinatal through Five Mental Health (P–5) Specialty. She also directs the associated Caring for yoU and Baby (CUB) Clinic where she supervises clinical work with caregivers and their young children using individual, dyadic, and group approaches to treatment. Tracy was previously on the faculty at Tulane University in the Department of Psychiatry and Behavioral Science, at the University of Chicago's Department of Psychiatry and Behavioral Neuroscience, and at the Erikson Institute in the Department of Infant Studies. She earned her doctoral degree in clinical psychology from the University of Iowa. Tracy writes and presents on family systems and attachment theories in pop culture, including *Black Panther*, *WandaVision*, Disney princesses, and *Bob's Burgers*. When not working or engaging with pop culture, Tracy is spending time with her family or preparing for the next Mardi Gras.

CHRIS YOGERST is an associate professor of communication in the Department of Arts and Humanities at the University of Wisconsin-Milwaukee. His most recent book, published in 2020 from the University Press of Mississippi, is *Hollywood Hates Hitler! Jew-Baiting, Anti-Nazism, and the Senate Investigation into Warmongering in Motion Pictures*. Chris is also a regular contributor to the *Los Angeles Review of Books*. He has cotaught Superheroes and Mythology with philosopher Mark Peterson for the last few years, which has been one of the most popular courses in UWM's College of General Studies.

INDEX

Page numbers in **bold** indicate illustrations.